Transforming Social Housing

The recent global crisis exposed vulnerabilities of housing markets pointing to the need to build resilience through better policy tools and sustainable provision of social housing. In the context of fiscal austerity, social housing is affected by changing politics, privatization and concentration of urban poverty. *Transforming Social Housing: International Perspectives* explores the differences and similarities in housing policies and practices by focusing on social housing institutions and their ability to influence affordability and quality of housing. The focus is on private and not-for-profit provision in mixed-income developments supported through partnerships and a mix of policy instruments.

The book brings together contributions by leading scholars on key debates affecting social housing in cities around the world. The international perspectives provide an interdisciplinary, robust overview of complex processes of change affecting people, places and homes. It is particularly well suited for students, scholars, policymakers and professionals interested in housing, urban planning and public policy.

The chapters in this book were originally published in various issues of the *Urban Research & Practice* journal.

Sasha Tsenkova is Professor of Planning at the University of Calgary, Canada. She has over 150 publications addressing issues of urban sustainability, community planning and housing policy. Her scholarship is internationally recognised and she has won a number of prestigious awards for international scholars. Her current research focuses on social urbanism and the future of affordable housing in cities.

Transforming Social Housing

International Perspectives

Edited by
Sasha Tsenkova

Routledge
Taylor & Francis Group
LONDON AND NEW YORK

First published 2021
by Routledge
2 Park Square, Milton Park, Abingdon, Oxon OX14 4RN

and by Routledge
52 Vanderbilt Avenue, New York, NY 10017

Routledge is an imprint of the Taylor & Francis Group, an informa business

British Library Cataloguing in Publication Data
A catalogue record for this book is available from the British Library

ISBN 13: 978-0-367-64617-2

Typeset in MinionPro
by Newgen Publishing UK

Publisher's Note
The publisher accepts responsibility for any inconsistencies that may have arisen during the conversion of this book from journal articles to book chapters, namely the inclusion of journal terminology.

Contents

Citation Information

The chapters in this book were originally published in different issues of *Urban Research & Practice*. When citing this material, please use the original volume, issue, and page numbering for each article, as follows:

Chapter 1

Social Housing Transformation: Policy and Institutional Landscapes
Sasha Tsenkova

Chapter 2

Social Rented Housing in the (Dis)United Kingdom: Can Different Social Housing Regime Types Exist within the Same Nation State?
Mark Stephens
Urban Research & Practice, volume 12, issue 1 (2019), pp. 38–60

Chapter 3

Quantifying a century of state intervention in rental housing in Germany
Konstantin A. Kholodilin
Urban Research & Practice, volume 10, issue 3 (2017), pp. 267–328

Chapter 4

The Role of Nonprofits in Meeting the Housing Challenge in the United States
Rachel G. Bratt
Urban Research & Practice, volume 12, issue 1 (2019), pp. 7–37

Chapter 5

The organizational challenges of mixed-income development: privatizing public housing through cross-sector collaboration
Mark L. Joseph, Robert J. Chaskin, Amy T. Khare and Jung-Eun Kim
Urban Research & Practice, volume 12, issue 1 (2019), pp. 61–83

Chapter 6

Non-profit housing, a tool for metropolitan cohesion? The case of the Vienna–Bratislava region

Aurore Meyfroidt
Urban Research & Practice, volume 10, issue 4 (2017), pp. 442–465

Chapter 7

Moving towards age-inclusive public housing in Singapore
Belinda Yuen
Urban Research & Practice, volume 12, issue 1 (2019), pp. 84–98

Chapter 8

Transformative change: energy-efficiency and social housing retrofits in Canadian cities
Sasha Tsenkova
Urban Research & Practice, volume 11, issue 3 (2018), pp. 263–274

Lists of Illustrations

Figures

Chapter 2

Chapter 3

Chapter 4

Chapter 6

Tables

Chapter 7

Chapter 8

Boxes

Chapter 8

Notes on Contributors

Rachel G. Bratt is Professor Emerita, Tufts University and focuses on a range of housing and community development issues, including the role of nonprofit housing organizations. She is the author or co-editor of three books and has written or co-authored dozens of academic and popular articles and book chapters.

Robert J. Chaskin is McCormick Foundation Professor and Deputy Dean for Strategic Initiatives at the University of Chicago School of Social Service Administration, where he holds the UNESCO Chair for Inclusive Urbanism. His most recent book is *Social Exclusion in Cross-National Perspective* (2019).

Mark L. Joseph is Leona Bevis and Marguerite Haynam Associate Professor in Community Development and the Founding Director of the National Initiative on Mixed-Income Communities at the Jack, Joseph and Morton Mandel School of Applied Social Sciences, Case Western Reserve University.

Amy T. Khare is Assistant Research Professor and Research Director of the National Initiative on Mixed-Income Communities, Case Western Reserve University. Amy has 20 years of experience working on housing and community change and is the co-editor of *What Works to Promote Inclusive, Equitable Mixed-Income Communities.*

Konstantin A. Kholodilin is Research Associate at the DIW Berlin (Germany) and Professor at the NRU HSE St. Petersburg (Russia). His research focuses on housing economics, big data and economic history.

Jung-Eun Kim is Expert Adviser at the Division of Social Welfare Policy Coordination, Ministry of Health & Welfare, Republic of Korea. Her research interests include policy coordination for regional equity and development.

Aurore Meyfroidt is Associate Research Fellow at the University of Lyon. She is currently working as a Scientific Secretary of the Observation Platform for Urban Projects and Strategies (POPSU) in France. Her research interests include housing policies and sustainable urban planning in Europe.

Mark Stephens is Ian Mactaggart Chair of Land, Property & Urban Studies at the University of Glasgow in Scotland. He has a long-standing interest in comparative housing research and led the European Commission's Study into Housing and Exclusion.

Sasha Tsenkova is Professor of Planning at the University of Calgary in Canada. She has over 150 publications addressing issues of urban sustainability, community planning and housing policy. Her scholarship is internationally recognised by many awards. Her current research focuses on inclusive urbanism and the future of affordable housing in cities.

Belinda Yuen is Professorial Fellow and Research Director at the Lee Kuan Yew Centre for Innovative Cities, Singapore University of Technology and Design where she directs the Lee Li Ming Programme in Ageing Urbanism. Belinda's research focuses on spatial planning and urban policy analysis for liveable, sustainable and age-friendly cities.

Social Housing Transformation: Policy and Institutional Landscapes

Sasha Tsenkova

The recent global crisis in 2008 exposed vulnerabilities of housing markets, pointing to the need to build resilience through better policy tools and sustainable provision of social housing. In the context of fiscal austerity social housing is on trial, affected by changing politics, privatization and concentration of urban poverty. *Transforming Social Housing: International Perspectives* explores the differences and similarities in housing policies and practices by focusing on social housing institutions and their ability to influence affordability and quality of housing. The book brings together contributions by leading scholars on key debates affecting social housing in cities around the world. The international perspectives provide an interdisciplinary and robust overview of complex processes of change affecting people, places and homes, which is particularly relevant to the transformation of cities in the context of the COVID-19 pandemic. The focus is on private and not-for-profit housing provision in mixed-income developments supported by effective partnerships and a mix of housing policy instruments to create inclusive and healthy cities.

Rethinking Social Housing

The crisis that started in the mortgage markets of the United States in 2007–2008 has had dramatic and sustained impacts on people and housing systems throughout the world. These complex and interlinked crises exposed vulnerabilities of housing markets and low-income households, pointing to the need to build resilience through better policy tools and sustainable provision of social housing. In the context of fiscal austerity and budget cuts in all European and North American countries, the future, purpose and form of social housing are being questioned and re-examined. Social housing is on trial, affected by changing politics, privatization, devolution in responsibilities, shrinking investment by different levels of government, and more importantly by the concentration of urban poverty in some of the public housing estates. Rethinking the role of social housing is of great importance to society and to our cities, where over 80 percent of people live and work, particularly given the rapid growth of urban poverty and vulnerability. Comparative studies indicate a renewed emphasis on the supply of social housing in some European countries and city-wide initiatives to encourage private and not-for-profit provision to minimize 'poverty trap' effects (CECODHAS, 2011; Scanlon *et al.*, 2014). In the post-crisis era, countries with unitary models and a strong social housing legacy have introduced a range of policy instruments and economic stimulus packages to promote supply-side responses in large metropolitan areas.

Housing providers and funding regimes have adjusted to the new environment and some innovative entrepreneurial models have emerged in the Netherlands, Austria and Germany (Bardhan *et al.*, 2012). The emphasis is very much on diversifying social housing suppliers, public/private partnerships and the development of mixed communities in the context of urban regeneration. While there is a growing commitment to social housing in the political rhetoric, few countries, mostly those with unitary systems, have identified new policy instruments to ensure that the investment necessary to meet the need for affordable housing will actually occur (Bardhan *et al.*, 2012; CECODHAS, 2012).

This book explores the differences and similarities in housing policies and practices by focusing on social housing institutions and their ability to influence affordability and quality of housing. First, it demonstrates that housing institutions matter in defining culturally specific processes and housing policy interventions. Second, it broadens the focus of current debates in comparative housing research, emphasizing the importance of policy divergence and institutional transformation in social housing. This is achieved through explicit emphasis on the relationship between housing policies and institutional structures (state, market, civil society) that operate in distinctive ways to influence social housing outcomes (Tsenkova, 2019).

Social Housing Provision Systems

This book on social housing transformation is informed by the convergence-divergence paradigm for comparative housing studies (Kemeny and Lowe, 1998) and advances the notion that systems of social housing provision have become less similar over time with diverging experiences likely to accelerate in the future (Tsenkova, 2009). The core idea of the convergence theory is that similarity of economic and demographic development in different countries will lead to converging housing policies, despite differences in ideology, politics and institutional structures (Burns and Grebler, 1977; Donnison and Ungerson, 1982). Esping-Andersen (1990) made perhaps the most significant attempt to identify patterns of dissimilarity based on distinct welfare state regimes. The approach has been refined through the comparative housing studies of Kemeny (1995) with the development of typologies of 'housing policy regimes'. In the spirit of divergent debates, Ball and Grilli (1997) argued that despite similarities, European countries have distinctive housing systems and there is no evidence of convergence, which was also the case with post-socialist housing systems (Tsenkova, 2009). In countries with unitary systems of social rented housing, the sector operates like a 'social market' in direct competition with other tenures. The institutional arrangements favor non-state ownership by not-for-profit landlords, rents are set below market level but tend to be sensitive to demand and allocation extends access to a more diverse income group. Distortions in pricing are less prevalent, since rental systems not only ensure cost recovery for services, but allow rent setting to be adjusted to a range of property attributes (Kemeny *et al.*, 2005). In western Europe, the Netherlands, Sweden, Denmark, Germany and Austria exemplify the characteristics of unitary systems, while in eastern Europe the Czech Republic and Poland have moved in this direction, given the size of their social housing sector, tenant income mix and emphasis on non-profit social housing providers (Tsenkova, 2014).

In most countries social housing has a residual role and the small sector (less than 5%) operates as a safety net. Due to its limited size, access is reserved for low-income, special needs households, allocation is rationed, rents are heavily subsidized and the administration and management is often handled in a command way by public institutions. All post-socialist countries after a dramatic privatization of public housing in the 1990s fall in this category, as well as Canada, US and Australia. These broad characteristics certainly conceal significant differences in the operation of social housing systems. Stephens in this book argues that despite the fact that in England the social rented sector is close to 20%, it has assumed the characteristics of a 'safety net'. He posits that different social housing regimes can exist within the same nation state. The adoption of austerity measures since 2010 have resulted in England's social housing regime transitioning to an 'ambulance service', while the 'safety net' model is being maintained in Northern Ireland and Wales, and strengthened in Scotland. The housing policy evolution in the (dis) United Kingdom reinforces divergence in the performance of social housing systems and the ability to move to a 'social market' performing a 'wider affordability' role.

It is not surprising that in countries with a small share of social housing, there are limited opportunities for growth. However, recent policy shifts indicate a renewed emphasis on improvements in quality and renovation of existing stock. Tsenkova provides an assessment of the energy-efficiency retrofit programs in Canadian social housing, focusing on program efficiency and effectiveness. In terms of efficiency, the grant programs were highly relevant, timely and successful, generating improvements in two-thirds of the social housing in Toronto, Vancouver and Calgary. The effectiveness of these programs was moderate, with targeted approaches to retrofits, constrained by the lack of sustainability in funding and limited institutional capacity. Similar challenges apply to other countries with a small, financially dependent social housing sector where 'small is not necessarily beautiful' and programs need to operate on a cost recovery principle. Small housing providers face significant challenges in accessing housing finance to meet high investment costs while at the same time maintaining below-market rents and delivering services to vulnerable groups.

These relationships sketched in broad strokes reflect very general aspects of the role of social housing in different countries using two broad housing regime categories. The complexity of institutional arrangements is related to ownership of social housing, which may include rental or ownership (with restrictions on resale) and may be universal or targeted to particular groups. The stock of public housing that was built right after World War II is deteriorating and many countries have moved forward with privatization through redevelopment of mixed-tenure projects or selling of housing units to existing tenants. Social rental housing that is owned and managed by government authorities and/or not-for-profit organizations has become the dominant form of affordable rental housing provided in many jurisdictions but is often under threat of funding cuts (Tsenkova, 2019). Within this general trend of declining stocks, the data also demonstrates that there is wide variation, from a high of 82% in Singapore to a low of 1% in Albania and Montenegro (Tsenkova, 2014). Yuen's chapter on public housing in Singapore signals institutional transformation and design of new policies to adapt the stock to the needs of a rapidly aging population. Public housing is a form of home ownership assistance through subsidized flats built and funded by the Singapore government. Flats in high-density developments are sold on a 99-year lease; resale is in the public market with restrictions for buyers and sellers. While in a few countries in Asia publicly assisted housing is increasing, in most countries the post-crisis period has led to a mix of conservative housing policies applied with a varied degree of efficiency and equity and declining or non-existent investment in new social housing.

Social Housing Institutions: Partnerships

The importance of historic circumstances, politics and institutional structures are critical in defining the parameters for convergence or divergence of social housing, which in turn is manifested in a diversity of institutional arrangements, sector size, rent-setting policies, allocation and, more importantly, differences in the choice of policy instruments (Tsenkova, 2018). The supply of new social housing, in particular, is dependent on the availability of fiscal, financial and regulatory instruments to encourage provision and to deal with the front-end loaded nature of housing costs (Carmona *et al.*, 2003). Different countries have experimented with a range of *fiscal instruments* requiring direct expenditures of the government (grants, subsidies, tax incentives), or indirect, such as depreciation allowances or rent control. A second major stream of subsidies, as the main instrument of housing policy, is applied in all countries through housing vouchers, rent supplements or housing benefits (Scanlon *et al.*, 2014). *Financial instruments* to encourage new supply of social housing relate to the availability of long-term finance and the diversity of mortgage products. In most countries with unitary models, private finance has become dominant and is obtained mainly from banking intermediaries. Borrowing costs from private sector institutions are subsidized in countries with residual social housing systems, borrowing by not-for-profit providers guaranteed and/or complemented by government grants in attempts to leverage private finance (Gherkiere, 2007).

There is a wide range of regulatory policies defining housing standards in the social housing sector and the way social landlords and providers operate through supervision, auditing, and control over allocation procedures. *Regulatory instruments* control operational practices, affecting the physical production, allocation and consumption of housing without imposing restrictions on main institutions and agents in the market (Oxley, 2000). Second, policies in this category include reduction in land costs to promote housing investment in social housing, tenant protection and rent controls. Inclusionary zoning, planning agreements, provision of free public land, and development land taxes have been used to extract some of the 'excess profit' of the landowner and/or provide incentives to developers, particularly in the context of regeneration projects (Tsenkova, 2014).

Two of the chapters in this book illustrate the pathways of German and Austrian housing policies over the past decades, which have resulted in different unitary housing systems. The Austrian policies have resulted in one of the largest and most robust social rental sectors, while Germany has one of the largest private rental sectors with a substantial share operating with a social purpose, under rigorously regulated government contracts. In both countries, the nexus of housing policy and institutions is quite different. Kholodilin demonstrates that the mix of policy instruments in Germany—regulations, subsidies and finance—has mapped out a complex trajectory of change affecting the social rental sector. Housing systems are path dependent and the policy shifts in Germany since World War II have promoted private, market-based institutions that receive supply-side subsidies to provide rental housing to low- and middle-income households. In response to housing shortages, regimes of such regulated rent setting and allocation were initially set for 50 years, while subsequent changes allowed a shorter timeframe. By contrast, in Austria as well as other countries with unitary housing systems, social rental dwellings are owned by not-for-profit organizations, whose social mandate is to provide affordable housing for those in need. Despite the different systems of social renting , both countries over time moved from providing affordable rental housing to large segments of the population to a more targeted system and from an extensive use of bricks-and-mortar subsidies to demand-based housing assistance.

Several chapters in this book explore the institutional context and the myriad of arrangements to finance, provide, allocate and manage social housing through not-for-profit and collaborative partnership models. Pratt's chapter provides an in-depth evaluation of the growing importance of not-for-profit providers in American cities and their strategies to build more social housing. In the context of changing housing policy, the overview centers on policy instruments—fiscal, financial and regulatory—and the lessons learned from several decades to offer useful insights for other countries committed to developing a comprehensive approach. The shift away from direct provision of social housing by public agencies in favor of approaches involving the private and not-for-profit sectors has resulted in a radical departure from past practices in many countries. The chapter by Joseph, Chaskin, Khare and Kim explores forms of new housing supply, including public/private partnerships through privatization of public housing and mixed-income developments. In response to enduring challenges of concentrated urban poverty, the Chicago Housing Authority is partnering with private developers to finance, design, build and manage the new mixed-income developments. These collaborations within the context of the *HOPE VI* and *Choice Neighborhoods* programs generate complex organizational dynamics that would benefit from far greater support to promote effectiveness and accountability.

Meyfroidt's study of not-for-profit housing in the Vienna-Bratislava region points to important spatial manifestations of systems of social housing provision in cities and metropolitan areas. Vienna has one of the most robust systems of not-for-profit housing, which was established in 1918. It has a strong legacy of private, limited-profit housing developers that build and operate social rental housing with significant state and municipal subsidies. There are extensive regulations, but the allocation policies ensure access for a broader population and a social mix. Not-for-profit developers have different legal status, but operate in a hybrid form between market and state. The spatial distribution of social housing, accounting for 60% of the stock, is a critical tool to ensure social mix and social cohesion in Vienna. The organization and institutional strength of the not-for-profit sector is critical for creating adequate housing, fairly distributed among different neighborhoods, and managed efficiently on a cost recovery basis. The study demonstrates asymmetries in the Vienna-Bratislava metropolitan region that are directly attributed to the lack of a comparable social housing system in Slovakia (where social housing accounts for 6% of the stock). This contributes to fragmentation of the cross-border region, sprawling suburbanization and relocation of households to the Austrian side to access affordable housing, while commuting to work in Bratislava.

Concluding Comments

The dominant direction of change in global housing policies is towards less government intervention, a more prominent role for housing markets and the devolution of responsibilities to house the poor and disadvantaged to local governments, civic society and the family. Globalization, the flow of international investment in housing markets, and the overall integration of systems of housing finance have induced some convergence in the institutional mosaic (McNelis, 2016). Social housing is on trial, particularly in the aftermath of the 2008 mortgage crisis and its impacts on housing systems throughout the world. Fiscal austerity and budget cuts have challenged investment in social housing and have forced institutional transformation. City-wide initiatives to encourage private and not-for-profit provision in mixed-income developments seem to be the way forward, regardless of the type of social housing regime—unitary or residual.

One of the greatest challenges in cities today is the shortage of affordable housing affecting over 1.6 billion people. Despite the common challenges facing housing systems in different countries, there are historical and deeply embedded differences in the nature of their housing institutions. There are also significant differences in the political, economic and social drivers affecting housing policy reforms and the transformation of these institutions, which challenge the idea of convergence. Rethinking social housing brings into focus the role and respective contributions of government, private sector and not-for-profit agencies in the provision system. Social housing provision is a dynamic process of interaction between public and private institutions that responds to a mix of policy instruments. Adding another layer of complexity, these interventions in each country can lead to different business strategies for land acquisition and capital mobilization and correspondingly influence important outcomes in terms of output, access, affordability, choice and quality of social housing.

The diversity of national trajectories has significant implications for the ability of housing institutions to adapt to new environments. The ideological shifts in housing policy have marked new relationships between the state, the private sector and civic society. Such rapid institutional transformation is path dependent, but the new institutions are breaking new ground in several ways and finding their own methods of responding to changing economic, social and political imperatives. The main argument in this book is that housing institutions have differential capacities to direct these processes of change, leading to divergent responses in the social housing provision system. The authors explore the myriad of arrangements for financing, providing, allocating and managing social housing through public and non-government models. They review a variety of approaches and pathways that characterize social housing transformation and the evolution of different institutions across the social housing systems. Notwithstanding such path-dependent diversity in different countries and cities, in terms of housing policy, the message is similar. Adequate, good-quality social housing requires sustained housing policy intervention and alignment of policy instruments—fiscal, financial and regulatory—to support the production (supply side) or the consumption (demand side) of housing.

These international perspectives are particularly important today when the world is struggling to respond to the COVID-19 pandemic. The health crisis has exacerbated housing inequalities in cities, illustrating in a compelling way the importance of access to affordable social housing. Now, more than ever, people need a place to call home—a place that provides shelter from economic and social stress; a place to live, work, educate children, care for family members and maintain public safety through social distancing. Governments during recent lockdowns have provided emergency shelter for the homeless, extended mortgage payments, and introduced rent deferrals and other emergency measures to temporarily shelter people from immense housing difficulties and protect the public. The unprecedented challenges to public health in cities have demonstrated the need to consider affordable housing as a critical part of the social infrastructure that requires sustained long-term investment and support to establish a resilient ecosystem of housing providers.

Social inclusiveness in these challenging times should be a key consideration, including recommendations to governments to invest in high-quality affordable housing and diverse neighborhoods. Although people live together, they can be worlds apart socially and economically. Socially inclusive cities promote resilience through efficient growth management, affordable housing, transit-oriented development and public-private partnerships to retain neighborhood vitality and social mix. Such transformations to create safe and inclusive cities require effective collaboration at all levels: government, market institutions and local communities. Important priorities relate to addressing the causes of discrimination and inequality, with a particular focus on the progressive realization of rights to an adequate standard of living for all, including adequate and affordable housing.

Recognizing the fiscal constraints of governments, it is doubtful that we will see a rebound of social housing provision matching the pre-crisis levels or a renewed emphasis on the public sector role. Other models of housing delivery, besides public-private partnerships, need to be introduced such as the multi-sectoral partnerships within and between the public-, private- and not-for-profit sectors supported by the appropriate synergy of policy instruments. Such multi-sectoral partnerships need to be collaborative, have non-hierarchical structures and processes, and shared accountability for outcomes and results.

Acknowledgment

The support of the Social Sciences and Humanities Research Council of Canada is gratefully acknowledged. Additional research on the topic is available at: www.ucalgary.ca/cities/affordable-housing

ORCID

Sasha Tsenkova https://orcid.org/0000-0002-1982-8495

References

Ball, M. and Grilli, M. (1997) Housing Markets and Economic Convergence in the EU. Report for the Royal Institute of Chartered Surveyors and the European Institute. London: South Bank University.

Bardhan, A., Edelstein, R. and Kroll, C. (2012) Global Housing Markets. Crises, Policies and Institutions. Hoboken, NJ: Willey & Sons.

Bums, L. and Grebler, L. (1977) The Housing of Nations: Analysis and Policy in a Comparative Framework. London: Macmillan.

Carmona, M., Carmona, S. and Gallent, N. (2003) Delivering New Homes. Processes, Planners and Providers. London: Routledge.

CECODHAS (2012) Impact of the Crisis and Austerity Measures on the Social Housing Sector. Housing Europe's Observatory Research Briefing, Year 5 / Number 2, February. Brussels: CECODHAS.

Donnison, D. and C. Ungerson (1982) Housing Policy. London: Penguin Books.

Esping-Andersen, G. (1990) The Three Worlds of Welfare Capitalism. Cambridge: Polity Press.

Gherkiere, L. (2007) The Development of Social Housing in the European Union. When General Interest Meets Community Interest. Paris: Dexia Editions, September.

Kemeny, J. (1995) From Public Housing to the Social Market: Rental Policy Strategies in Comparative Perspective. London and New York: Routledge.

Kemeny, J. and Lowe, S. (1998) "Schools of Comparative Housing Research: From Convergence to Divergence". Housing Studies, vol. 13 (2), pp. 161–176.

Kemeny, J., Kersloot, J. and Thalmann, P. (2005) "Non-profit Housing Influencing, Leading and Dominating the Unitary Rental Market: Three Case Studies". Housing Studies, vol. 20 (6), pp. 855–872.

McNelis, S. (2016) "Researching Housing in a Global Context: New Directions in Some Critical Issues". Housing, Theory and Society, vol. 33 (4), pp. 403–423.

Oxley, M. (2000) The Future of Social Housing. Learning from Europe. London: Institute for Public Policy Research.

Scanlon, K., Whitehead, C. and Arrigoitia, M. (eds.) (2014) Social Housing in Europe. Oxford: Wiley-Blackwell.

Tsenkova, S. (2009) Housing Reforms in Post-socialist Europe. Lost in Transition. Heidelberg: Springer-Verlag.

Tsenkova, S. (2014) "The Social Housing Sector in Prague and Warsaw: Trends and Future Prospects". GeoJournal, vol 79 (4), pp. 433–447, doi:10.1007/s10708-014-9535-0

Tsenkova, S. (2018) "Transformative Change: Energy-efficiency and Social Housing Retrofits in Canadian Cities". Urban Research & Practice, vol. 11 (3), pp. 263–274, doi.org/10.1080/17535069.2018.1460028

Tsenkova, S. (2019) "Social Housing on Trial: Institutions + Policy Design". Urban Research and Practice, vol. 12 (1), pp. 1–6, https://doi.org/10.1080/17535069.2019.1566491

Social Rented Housing in the (Dis)United Kingdom: Can Different Social Housing Regime Types Exist within the Same Nation State?

Mark Stephens

Welfare and housing regime literature has treated nation states as being uniform regime types. However, there is growing interest in the possible development of distinct regimes below the level of nation states. This article applies regime theory though a robust analytical framework to the devolution of social housing policy to the Scottish Parliament and Welsh and Northern Ireland Assemblies within the UK. We establish that prior to devolution, the UK's social housing regime was firmly located within a residual model, but one that operated as a 'safety net'. Particularly since the adoption of austerity by the UK Government in 2010 and divergence in political outlook between UK and devolved administrations, England's social housing regime is beginning to morph into an 'ambulance service', whilst the 'safety net' model is being maintained in Northern Ireland and Wales, and strengthened in Scotland. However, with few powers with which to influence the 'wider welfare regime', high levels of poverty mean that the 'boundaries of possibilities' for the devolved administrations to create more than this distinctive regime sub-type – and so to move to a 'social market' performing a 'wider affordability' role – are limited. The theoretical and analytical framework developed in this article is capable of being applied to sub-nation state jurisdictions in other countries, and so enrichen comparative analysis.

1. Introduction

The UK has one of the longest established social rented sectors in Europe (Ravetz 2001). At its peak in the late 1970s, it housed one-third of households. Policy relating to social rented housing (and indeed to housing in general) was conducted through a common Great Britain-wide framework until 1999, with Northern Ireland following similar trends. Since then, policy has been subject to variation between the component nations of the UK as devolved parliaments and assemblies have been established in Scotland, Wales and Northern Ireland. Meanwhile England continues to be governed by the UK ('Westminster') Parliament.

Particularly since the UK Government began a policy of fiscal 'austerity' in 2010, various accounts suggest that social housing policy in the UK is diverging. This article aims to bring new insights into this process by placing it firmly within a theoretical and analytical framework derived from welfare and housing regime literature. This approach is intended to increase our understanding of these developments, and to consider both the potential and limitations of divergence within a nation state. By considering social housing policy within the context of the wider welfare regime, the article also contributes to the growing literature on regionalisation and localisation of welfare regimes (e.g. Johansson and Panican 2016).

Section 2 provides a selective overview of literature on welfare and housing regimes, and on the development of welfare regimes beneath the level of the nation state. Section 3 outlines analytical framework derived from the literature review and outlines four research questions. Section 4 characterises the UK's social housing regime before devolution. Section 5 examines the evolution of devolution within the UK. Section 6 examines developments in social housing policy within this framework. Conclusions are drawn in Section 7.

2. Literature review

Many economists see social or public housing as, at best, a response to inadequately developed or malfunctioning state and market institutions (World Bank 1994). Their view is that anything more than a residual role is likely to be inefficient and crowd out the private market. This approach is reflected in recent interventions by the European Commission in the Netherlands and Sweden, where state guarantees to housing associations and municipal housing companies were seen as representing unfair competition with the private sector unless they catered for those who are unable to access housing through the market (Elsinga and Lund 2013). It also resonates with some housing studies literature in which housing is characterised as being the 'wobbly pillar' of the welfare state (Torgersen 1987), seemingly because, in contrast to other 'pillars' (what Esping-Andersen 1990, identified as 'sectors') such as social security and health, state interventions tend to be exceptional reactions to failures in the market, so market provision remains the norm (Bengtsson 2009).

Historically grounded approaches suggest that the social (and cost) rental sectors that were created in north-west Europe in the twentieth century, by scale alone, came to represent far more than a mere reaction to market malfunctions. Moreover, the litany of criticisms of it as a more extensive well-meaning but 'inefficient and inequitable' intervention (Barr 1987, 367) which 'doesn't "work"' (Green and Malpezzi 2003, 190) sit uneasily alongside the sub-prime catastrophe (Aalbers 2012) brought about by supposedly efficient housing finance mechanisms centred on homeownership (Diamond and Lea 1992).

One of the limitations of narrowly economics-focussed approaches is that they isolate housing systems from wider social and economic institutions. Some housing scholars have adapted Esping-Andersen's (1990) typology of welfare regimes, which still enjoys 'paradigmatic status' in welfare state research (Emmenegger et al. 2015, 3), to housing (e.g. Hoekstra 2003). Others have established frameworks to establish the relationship between housing and the welfare regime. What Stephens and Fitzpatrick et al. (2010) called the 'wider welfare regime' – consisting of the labour market and tax and social security system – produces distinctive patterns of income distribution and poverty (Esping-Andersen and Myles 2009). Where relatively low levels of poverty and income inequality prevail, it is possible to operate social rental sectors as a 'social market': whilst rents are set below market levels, they are nonetheless sensitive to demand and even those tenants in receipt of housing allowances are able to exercise some choice in the trade-off between cost, size and location because they are able to bear some of the marginal cost of housing without being subjected to poverty (Stephens, Burns, and Mackay 2003). Kemeny characterised such housing systems as being 'unitary' and suggested that the social rented sector itself may, in some circumstances, influence, lead or even dominate the rental sector as a whole, and create a viable alternative to homeownership (Kemeny, Kersloot, and Thalmann 2005).

Stephens, Burns, and Mackay (2002, 2003) establish that where high levels of poverty prevail a social market cannot operate without causing great hardship among low income households, but social rented housing can also operate as a safety net, although it nonetheless requires a housing allowance system that prevents housing costs from depressing income levels below social assistance norms. Such a housing 'safety net' can provide an adequate standard of housing and security whilst maintaining a minimum level of disposable income. However, in a safety net system, a social market must give way to one based on administrative allocation: what Kemeny (1995) likened to a 'command economy'. Particularly where the social rented sector is of a small scale, it may be more severely rationed, and may be seen as a form of temporary assistance to be withdrawn when tenants cease to 'need' it. It may assume the characteristic not of a safety net, but of an 'ambulance service' (Stephens 2008).

Welfare and housing regime literature is applied primarily at the level of the nation state. Some literature reflects on the uneven spatial impact of national social programmes within countries (Zweirs and Koster 2015), noting that programmes that might be redistributive at a national level can cause differences between localities to widen. However, the localisation or regionalisation of welfare regimes, which contrasts to the implicit assumption of uniformity at the level of the nation state, has received growing attention. This suggests that policies and programmes developed at below the level of the nation state are challenging 'the principle of interterritorial equivalency' (Lopez-Santana 2015).

The rationale behind this approach lies in the weakening of the authority of the nation state, which marks a structural trend. The ability of national governments to manage their economies nationally has been diminished by globalisation: monetary policy is constrained by the free movement of capital and is now generally the responsibility of independent central banks at a national or even supra-national level in the case of the Euro. Fiscal policy is constrained by more mobile tax bases, notably in the case of multi-national corporations, but also high net worth individuals. The response of increased labour market flexibility has created divisions in the labour force and makes social insurance systems more difficult to operate. Meanwhile, greater diversity in family structures and the demands of ageing populations bring greater complexity to the pattern of needs to which public services are expected to respond. As Johansson and Panican comment,

> Albeit that much social policy remains under the responsibility of national institutions… the mechanisms behind many social risks… and the greater diversity of life courses, risks, needs and preferences arguably require concerted efforts and close dialogue in the arena where people live and act – in local contexts. (Johansson and Panican 2016, 4)

Variation below the level of the nation state often evokes fears that sub-national differences in welfare provision might widen according to the ability of different sub-national jurisdictions to finance them (Lopez-Santana 2015). However, in a climate of fiscal austerity,

> … when a central government retrenches and leaves few protective measures for vulnerable households, this can give incentives for regional authorities to respond by introducing their own policies. (Dol et al. 2016: no pagination)

The extent to which a sub-national jurisdiction can influence policy depends on what legislative, administrative and fiscal powers that it enjoys. A plethora of constitutional arrangements concerning sub-national jurisdictions exist, which may be local, regional or even national and may nest within federal or unitary states.

Housing researchers have also compared housing systems at the level of the nation state, reflecting both the tradition of welfare state research and the development of strong nation-wide subsidised housebuilding programmes that spurred the development of housing studies. It is also notable that researchers turned to the formal impacts of European integration (Kleinman, Matznetter, and Stephens 1998) and of financialisation (Aalbers, 2016) before examining sub-national variations.

As Dol et al. (2016) observe, the limited studies available on Flanders (Winters and Elsinga 2008) and Scotland (Robertson and Serpa 2014; to which we should add Gibb 2015) have developed outside a theoretical framework. Similarly, the recent account of housing policy in the different parts of the UK by McKee et al. provides a useful commentary, but the authors reach the partly tautological conclusion that,

> This re-scaling of public policy-making is fundamentally geographical [sic], and demands a more spatially nuanced understanding of the evolving process of devolution. (McKee, Muir, and Moore 2017, 68)

'Nuance' merely suggests that the subject has become too generalised and differences deserve more attention. Such observations can be unhelpful in a theoretical sense and have been characterised as the 'nuance of the fine-grain' whereby all that is achieved is 'the ever more detailed, merely empirical description of the world.' (Healy 2017, 120). The authors go on to claim that 'there is no such thing as the "UK housing experience" in contemporary housing policy, if indeed there ever was' (ibid.: 69). Yet, without an analytical framework, we can't really say.

Dol et al. (2016) seek to explore the housing policies of three Autonomous Communities in Spain following the economic crisis. They find that all of them shifted the emphasis of subsidised housebuilding towards rental, adopted a variety of schemes to assist distressed mortgagors, gave some substance to the constitutional 'right' to housing through prioritising social housing allocations for homeless and vulnerable households, and experimented with measures ranging from taxation to expropriation to free up unoccupied dwellings for residential use. They conclude that these case studies are consistent with the thesis that when central government retrenches regional authorities are incentivised to respond to protect vulnerable households. However, the authors stop short of considering whether there is evidence of identifiable regional housing regimes or varieties of the national regime.

Housing provides fertile ground for examining whether it is possible for devolved control over housing policy can lead to the creation of distinctive housing regimes or varieties of a common housing regime. It can highlight the importance of social and economic context (because sub-national housing costs vary regionally more than incomes) as well as cultural and political differences. Whilst housing systems are best understood as inter-active wholes, but also to the inertia associated with path dependence:

> [Housing's] physical and social elements of sluggishness... have institutional implications that may serve as obstacles to policy change. (Bengtsson and Ruonavaara 2010, 193)

The UK also provides a useful case study through which to explore the potential for housing regimes to emerge in jurisdictions beneath the level of the nation state. Since 1999, the UK has been transformed from being one of the most centralised states in

Europe to one where substantial powers have been devolved to Scotland, Wales and Northern Ireland. The shared policy heritage provides a benchmark against which to assess change.

3. Theoretical and analytical framework

We construct an analytical framework derived from regime theory to bring new insights into the evolution of housing systems in the UK. Regime theory has provided the most powerful non-structural theoretical framework for comparing (national) housing systems. Structural theories (for example, based around the overwhelming power of economic forces such as globalisation or (linked) ideological hegemonies such as neo-liberalism) imply system convergence regardless of political or institutional frameworks, so preclude divergence. In contrast, regime theories provide an explanatory framework that acknowledges the importance of social and economic institutions that are shaped by potentially divergent cultural and political preferences, and in which public policy plays an important role. They are best interpreted by being historically grounded, particularly where the subject is subject to path dependence, so current policy may not be manifested immediately in system change.

Moreover, regime theory has been adapted successfully to housing, and this is reflected in the body of housing literature that has evolved from the works of Kemeny and Esping-Andersen (see Stephens 2016a for a critical discussion).

The principal methodological innovation in this article is the development of regime theory to sub-state jurisdictions. The framework is, a priori, suitable for re-application in this way because it demands respect for the institutions that have shaped the historic British housing system, the evolving and asymmetric powers that the devolved administrations have enjoyed over a relatively short period, as well as those that they do not.

In contrast to research where the nation state is the unit of analysis, our framework must deal with the evolving and asymmetric pattern of competences, together with path dependency from the British state. Consequently, we have developed set of four hypotheses and linked research questions.

Hypothesis and linked research question 1: Based on the literature review, we can posit that recently created jurisdictions operating at beneath the level of nation state initially inherit a social housing regime from the pre-devolution era. The linked research question is: What kind of social housing regime did the UK have before devolution? The answer provides part of the benchmark against which to analyse change (see Hypothesis 3 below).

Hypothesis and linked research question 2: Devolved administrations' ability to shape the 'wider welfare regime' depends on their ability to influence labour market institutions, taxation and social security. The linked research question is: Are the powers that have been devolved sufficient to alter the wider welfare system? The answer sets the 'boundaries of possibilities' for the social housing regime.

Hypothesis and linked research question 3: Within the 'boundaries of possibilities' presented by the wider welfare regime, devolved administrations require legal competence over the main instruments of social housing policy. They also require the financial resources to support political preferences. Within the powers available, divergence in policy is likely to reflect diversity in politics. The linked research question is: Are the powers that have been devolved sufficient to alter the social housing system?

Hypothesis and linked research question 4: Regimes can shape housing systems through the role of the social rented sector. Subject to the 'boundaries of possibilities' set by the wider welfare regime, the social rented sector may operate as a 'social market' providing a wider affordability function, or as a residual tenure. As a residual system, it may perform the role of a 'safety net' or 'ambulance service'. The linked research question is: To what extent have social housing regimes diverged within the UK as a consequence of devolution? We note that changes in England after 1999 mean that the benchmark against which the devolved administrations are being assessed is a dynamic one (see Hypothesis 1 above).

In summary, we characterise the nature of the social housing regime by employing the frameworks identified in the literature. The social rented sector may operate as a 'social market' (*pace* Kemeny) which plays a 'wider affordability function' (*pace* Stephens); or it may be residual (again *pace* Kemeny), performing the role of either a 'safety net' or an 'ambulance service' (*pace* Stephens). This assessment requires data on the wider welfare system (income distribution/poverty) which sets the 'boundaries of possibilities' for the function of a social rented sector. Within a residual framework, a 'safety net' depends on scale, allocation policies, security of tenure and protection of post-rent incomes through housing allowances. An 'ambulance service' sector is characterised by extreme targeting, its treatment as a temporary form of assistance and lack of protection for residual incomes.

4. The UK's social housing regime before devolution

This section addresses the first research question: What kind of social housing regime did the UK have before devolution? We identify the critical junctures (Table 1) that led to the development of the UK's social housing regime.

Table 1. Critical junctures in UK social housing 1919–1999[1]

Year	Change	Effect
1919–	Dysfunctional private sector	Permanent role of state in provision of social rented housing
1955	End of 'general needs' subsidies; focus on slum clearance	Residualisation
1976	Economic Crisis and IMF loan	End of large-scale social housing building programmes Relative decline in sector
1977 (NI = 1989)	Homeless Persons Act	Residualisation
1979	Change in economic management accelerating de-industrialisation and rising inequality	Residualisation
1980	Right to Buy	Permanent loss of stock Absolute decline in sector Residualisation

4.1. *Wider welfare regime*

The 'wider welfare regime' determines the distribution of incomes before housing costs. During the period (1945 until the mid-1970s) of the 'social democratic consensus', UK governments were committed to the welfare state. Moreover, the economy was growing and near full employment prevailed. Income inequality was relatively low and reached its lowest point in 1977 at 0.24 (Figure 1). Poverty was generally under 15% in the 1960s and also reached its lowest point in 1977 at 11.3%.

However, thereafter the restructuring of the economy and social security system, particularly after the adoption of 'monetarism' in 1979, reversed the trend towards greater income equality. Inequality rose rapidly in the 1980s (Figure 1).

4.2. Scale

The UK has one of the longest established social rented sectors (Ravetz 2001). It dates back to the 1880s, but it was only after the First World War that the central Government provided subsidies to local authorities to provide housing. This was conceived initially to be a temporary intervention until the private market recovered from the war, and shortages were removed (Daunton 1984). However, since the

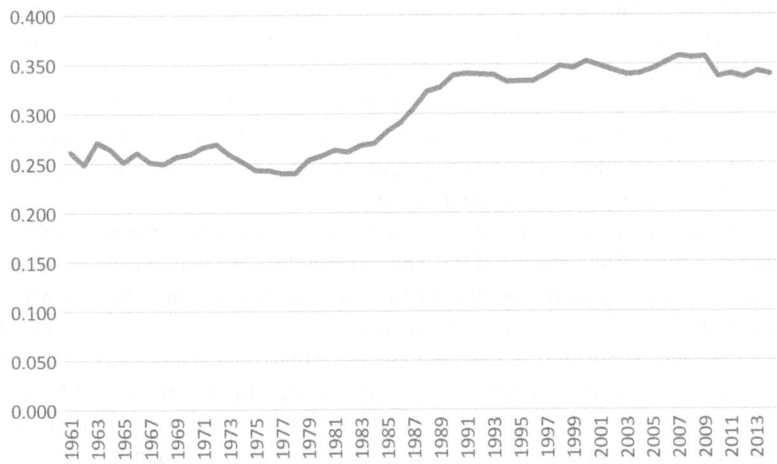

Figure 1. Gini coefficient 1961–2014.
Source: IFS (2016). Note: GB up to 2004; UK after 2004

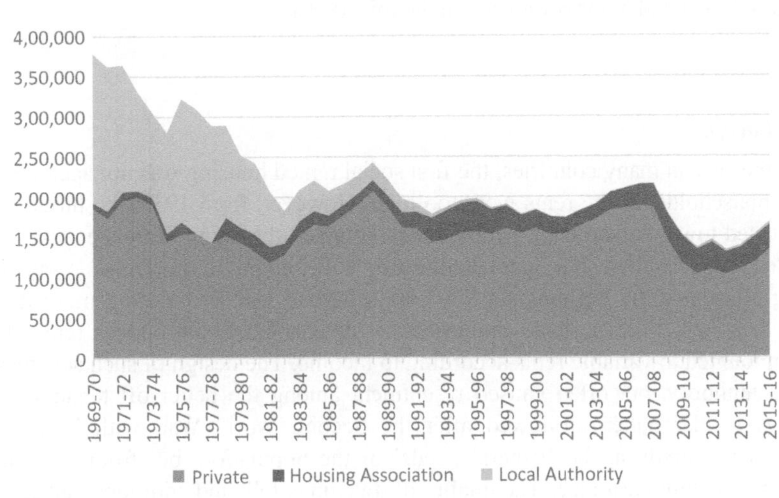

Figure 2. UK House completions by sector (1969/70–2015/16).
Source: DCLG live table 209 (updated 22/11/16)

Table 2. Social rented housing as a percentage of total housing stock.

	1976	1986	1997	2007	2014
England	29.0	26.0	21.9	18.0	17.4
Wales	27.2	24.5	20.3	16.5	16.0
Scotland	54.2	49.3	34.1	24.9	23.4
Northern Ireland	36.8	35.4	26.8	17.0	16.2

Source: Wilcox et al. (2016), Tables 17b, 17d

shortages never were removed the intervention became permanent, so representing the first critical juncture, as the Government became locked into financing (and in the case of local government) owning and managing social rented housing. Substantial council house building took place in the 1930s and again in the 1950s and 1960s. As a consequence, the sector grew to represent one-third of the UK's housing stock in the late 1970s. As Table 2 shows, the sector peaked at higher levels in Scotland and Northern Ireland than in England and Wales.

The era of mass building ended after 1976 as a consequence of the economic crisis that led the Government to seek and receive a loan from the IMF. Thereafter, the social rented housebuilding never recovered (Figure 2), so representing the second critical juncture as the relative size of the sector shrank.

Not only did levels of new build fall, but the stock diminished rapidly as the Thatcher Governments of the 1980s introduced the Right to Buy that enabled tenants to purchase their homes at discounts. An upward pressure on rents also encouraged those tenants who could to buy their homes. The Right to Buy led to the loss of 1.7 million units from the Great Britain social sector between 1980 and 1995 and represents the third critical juncture in the evolution of social housing. Proportionately Right to Buy had a greater impact on the Welsh and Scottish stocks (where 1980–1995 sales represented 34 and 30% of the 1981 stock, respectively) than of the English (25%) (calculated from Wilcox et al. 2016, Tables 17a, 20a, b, c), Moreover, it was the better off tenants living in the more popular dwellings (houses rather than flats) who were most likely to buy their properties, so contributing to the residualisation of the remaining social rented sector. But, as Table 2 shows, the stock of social rented housing was still proportionately larger in Scotland and Northern Ireland in the mid-1990s.

4.3. Allocation

As was the case in many countries, the first social rented housing was not accessible to the poorest households, as the rents were too high. However, from 1930, the thrust of policy was directed towards rehousing people made homeless by slum clearance. This shift was facilitated by subsidies, but local authorities still sought to minimise costs to make housing affordable, by building on low cost suburban land or building more densely in central locations. Further, local authorities were enabled to introduce 'rent rebates' – which amounted to variable rents according to income. The design of such schemes varied by local authority, but often caused resentment among the better off tenants (Finnigan 1984). A similar pattern followed after the Second World War, with local authority housing being firstly at the 'general needs' of the population, but from the mid-1950s once again to slum clearance. The quality of dwellings fell, and additional subsidies were introduced for building high. Individual local authority rent rebate schemes were replaced by a national Housing Benefit system in 1972.

During the period from the 1970s, allocation policies began to become more targeted on people in most (housing) need, representing the fourth critical juncture. From 1977 in Great Britain and 1989 in Northern Ireland, local authorities became obliged by the Homeless Persons Act to provide settled accommodation to unintentionally homeless households in priority need.

4.4. The UK social housing regime

By the 1990s, the UK social rented sector had assumed the characteristic of a 'residual' regime performing a 'safety net' function. A combination of reduction in new build and shrinkage of the stock combined with allocation policies that targeted lets on people in the greatest housing need. Nonetheless, the scale was generally still large enough to play this role. Better off tenants tended to leave the sector through Right to Buy whilst the changing 'wider welfare regime' altered the employment status of social tenants. In 1981, 43% of household heads living in council housing were in full-time employment. By 1991 thus had dropped to one-quarter (Wilcox et al. 2016, Table 34). Among all households, the fall in full-time employment was just four percentage points from 58 to 54%. The sector also housed a proportionately higher share of retired households (ibid.). The safety net model in the UK contrasted with that in the USA where public housing was seen as a form of temporary assistance ('ambulance service') and was on too small a scale to assist significant proportions of the population. Moreover, UK governments remained committed to targeting resources on the poorest and to protecting post-rent incomes through Housing Benefit.

5. Devolution in the UK

In this section, we detail the evolution of devolution within the UK in order to answer the second and third research questions: Are the powers that have been devolved sufficient to alter the wider welfare system? And are they sufficient to alter the social housing system?

As we have seen, 1999 housing legislation in Great Britain developed in the same direction across the country, even if it was sometimes enacted through separate legislation in Scotland, and administered by Scottish and Welsh 'Offices' – departments of the UK Government. Each of the 'critical junctures' identified in the previous section applied across England, Wales, Scotland and Northern Ireland. Moreover, the social security system, and the Housing Benefit system of which it is part, was applied through GB-wide legislation. The situation in Northern Ireland differed somewhat because it had its own ('Stormont') Parliament from its inception in 1921, until its suspension and the introduction of 'direct rule' (by the Westminster Parliament) in 1972 as a result of the 'Troubles'. Although local authority housing was transferred to the Northern Ireland Housing Executive (to prevent discrimination in allocations according to religion), it remained in the public sector and policies evolved in a similar way.

5.1. Scotland

Scotland retained its own legal and education systems after the Act of Union in 1707, and the decentralisation of administrative functions dates back to the establishment of the Scottish Education Department in 1872, and the Scottish Office in 1885. The Parliament established in 1999 following a referendum had both legislative powers and very limited powers over income tax (which have never been used).[2] Legislative powers extend to all areas unless specifically 'reserved' to Westminster in the legislation. Social security and employment law are two of the key areas of domestic policy to be reserved. Further powers have recently been granted under the legislation that followed the UK Government's Calman Commission. However, this was overtaken by the independence referendum in 2014. The Smith Commission that was established in its aftermath led to the Scotland Act that devolves greater powers over income tax and control over specific areas of social security amounting to about 14% of social security spending in Scotland, but these powers are unlikely to be sufficient to make a significant difference to the wider welfare regime. However, the social security powers include the power to vary the 'housing cost element' within Universal Credit (a new means-tested benefit for working age people which combines six separate benefits – including Housing Benefit – into a single benefit; see Stephens, Blenkinsopp, and Gibb 2015).

An important implication of the introduction of the Scottish Rate of Income Tax (SRIT) from 2016 is that the block grant from Westminster will be reduced and that the revenues available to future Scottish Governments will depend to a greater extent on the relative size of the Scottish income tax base, even if the powers to vary tax rates are not used. In 2017, the Scottish Parliament gained the power to set income tax rates and bands for income tax and chose to set the threshold for the payment of the higher rate of income tax lower than in the rest of the UK.

5.2. *Wales*

Wales has enjoyed fewer powers under devolution than Scotland, reflecting in part the loss of distinctive legal system in the sixteenth century, and the country's effective merger with England. However, this is changing. When the Welsh Assembly was established in 1999 following a referendum, it was given powers to pass only secondary legislation in devolved areas. In 2007, the National Assembly for Wales and the Welsh (Assembly) Government were separated, and the Assembly was given limited primary legislative powers through 'Assembly Measures'. Twenty areas of policy are devolved, including housing, planning, health and education. The Assembly's first Housing Act was passed in 2014 and introduces compulsory registration and licensing of private landlords, places a stronger duty on local authorities to prevent homelessness and reforms the Housing Revenue Account subsidy system. Following the UK Government's Silk Commission on Devolution in Wales, the Wales Act 2014 provides for greater income tax raising powers. As in Scotland, the introduction of the Welsh Rate of Income Tax (WRIT) will mean that revenues over time will reflect the performance of the Welsh economy. The UK Government has agreed to place a floor under the relative size of the block grant to Wales for the remainder of the current Parliament (2015–2020), but has made it clear that this is in lieu of the introduction of the WRIT.

5.3. *Northern Ireland*

Northern Ireland was the only one of the devolved nations to have had an elected assembly in the twentieth century. The current Assembly was established following the Good Friday Agreement in 1998, with the first elections held the same year. Full powers were operational from the end of 1999. However, the Assembly was suspended from 2002 to 2007, and it is only since a power-sharing agreement (between the unionist and nationalist parties) was reached that it has been operational for a sustained period of time. At the time of writing, co-operation had broken down, although direct rule had yet to be reintroduced.

The Assembly has full legislative powers ('transferred matters') over a range of 'domestic' policies, including health, education and housing. However, in contrast to Wales and Scotland, the Assembly also has formal legislative power over social security, pensions and child care. This provision dates from the era of the previous Northern Ireland Parliament, when the welfare state was established and the UK Government wished to maintain uniform standards across the UK. Consequently, Northern Ireland's legal control over social security became subject to the 'parity principle' whereby deficits in the Northern Ireland national insurance fund, and payments for social assistance benefits, were made good by Westminster. Whilst legally the Northern Ireland Assembly could choose to diverge from the Great British system, it would have to bear the cost itself.

The Northern Ireland Assembly has limited tax raising powers. It has powers of domestic and non-domestic rates. It gained the power to vary passenger duty on long-haul flights in 2013. It is due to receive power to set rates of Corporation Tax in 2017, to allow it to compete with the Irish Republic's rates that are lower than the UK. However, if the Assembly does cut the tax, any lost revenue will be deducted from the block grant. Capital borrowing powers are set at £200 million per year in 2202 (but may have been increased), with a cumulative maximum of £3 billion. Other borrowing is limited to £250 million for cash flow purposes only.

5.4. Party politics

At the level of the UK, party politics still revolves around the traditional parties of left (Labour) and right (Conservative), although their combined share of the vote has diminished, and in 2010, the first peace-time coalition since 1945 was formed as neither main party had a majority. However, there are long-running differences in political support in the different parts of the UK (Table 3). Scotland and Wales became bastions of the Labour Party, and the long period of Conservative Government from 1979 to 1997 increased support for devolution because during this period Wales and Scotland returned majorities of Labour MPs. However, Scottish politics has undergone dramatic realignment, as the Scottish National Party (SNP) largely replaced the Labour Party as the main party of the

Table 3. Governments and administrations in the UK, Wales, Scotland and Northern Ireland.

	Years	Administrations
UK	1997–2010	Labour majority governments
	2010–2015	Conservative/Liberal Democrat Coalition government
	2015–2017	Conservative majority government
	2017-	Conservative minority government
Wales	1999–	Labour or Labour-led governments
Scotland	1999–2007	Labour/Liberal Democrat Coalition government
	2007–2011	Scottish National Party (SNP) minority government
	2011–2016	SNP majority government
	2016-	SNP minority government
Northern Ireland	1998–2002	Unionist-Nationalist power sharing
	2002–2007	Suspended (direct rule from Westminster)
	2007–2016	Unionist-Nationalist power sharing
	2016-	No agreement

centre left.[3] This reflects Scottish independence having become the principal cleavage in politics since the independence referendum in 2014 (when independence was rejected by 55–45%), at least during the 2014–2017 period. This division is overlaid on the traditional left-right divide with the Conservatives emerging as the main party of the union. Politics in Northern Ireland has long since revolved around the (religion-based) divide between those people who wish to remain part of the UK and those who wish to become part of the Irish Republic. Nonetheless, 'power sharing' means that policy has to evolve on the basis of consensus (or at least agreement).

5.5. Analysis

The devolved administrations all now have legislative competence over key areas of social housing policy, much more limited powers over Housing Benefit. They are largely dependent on the UK government for their budgets, but this is changing as greater powers over income tax are devolved to Scotland and Wales. The devolved administrations have very little control over the 'wider welfare regime' as both employment law and social security are (largely) reserved, so limiting the 'boundaries of possibilities.'

6. Social housing policy after devolution

In this section, we examine housing policies after devolution in order to answer Research Question 4: To what extent have social housing regimes [4] diverged within the UK as a consequence of devolution?

The first decade of devolution saw more continuity than divergence in housing policy between the devolved administrations and the UK, which is attributable in large part to the political similarity between the devolved administrations and the UK Government up to 2010. Thereafter, divergence has become more apparent as in Scotland and Wales centre-left administrations have been governing at the same time as centre right Governments at the UK level have prioritised fiscal 'austerity' and radical reform of public services (Table 3 above).[5]

6.1. The 'wider welfare regime'

It is important to set social housing policy reform within the context of the 'wider welfare regime', which sets the 'boundaries of possibilities' for the type of social housing regime that can be created.

Poverty rates (Figure 3) have generally fallen since 2008, except in Northern Ireland. However, this is partly due to falls in median incomes since the economic crisis began in 2008. Poverty remains lower in England and Scotland (most recently 15% in both) than in Wales (19%) and Northern Ireland (20%). The poverty rates across the UK remain higher than countries such as Austria (12.9%), Denmark (12.2%) and the Netherlands (12.1%) where social markets in housing operate (figures from Eurostat). However, other countries including Sweden (14.5%) and Germany (16.7%) where social markets have operated now have levels of poverty comparable to the UK (ibid.). This may mean that these countries, like the UK, will struggle to operate social markets in housing. Indeed, there is much evidence of the malfunctioning of the Swedish system now (Christophers 2013). In the future and safety net, strategies may need to be developed in countries that have experienced rises in poverty (Stephens 2016b).

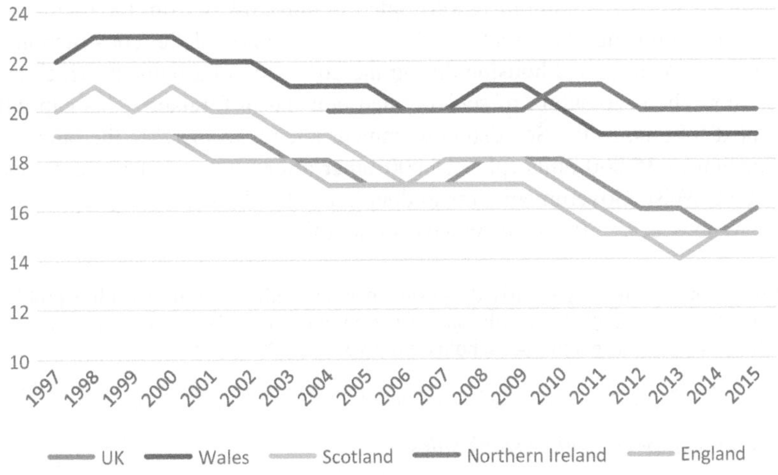

Figure 3. Poverty rates (%) before housing costs in the UK, England, Scotland, Wales and Northern Ireland (1998–2015).
Notes: Poverty = % individuals living in households with equivalised incomes (after tax and social security) below 60% median; 3 year averagesSource: Family Resources Survey

6.2. Scale of the social rented sector

The scale of the social rented sector helps to determine which social housing regime models are possible.

6.2.1. New build

The first area of divergence has been in the provision of new social rented housing, both in terms of scale and its nature.

The UK Coalition Government (2010–15) reduced the capital subsidy for affordable housing in England and shifted subsidy away from 'social' rented housing to what it called 'affordable' rental housing, i.e. housing with rents up to 80% of market rents. During the 5 years to 2015/2016, the completion rate of social rented housing fell from 37,680 units to 6,550, whilst affordable rent housing rose from 1,150 to 16,550 (DCLG, Table 1000). The programme also involved housing associations allowing more than 75,000 units of social housing to be re-let at 'affordable' rents (Wilcox et al. 2016). The new majority Conservative Government elected in 2015 initially continued with the Affordable Homes Programme into the 2015–2018 period, but soon switched unallocated subsidy to promote homeownership. The switch in subsidy to fund 200,000 Starter Homes for ownership is further supported by the requirement of local authorities to promote Starter Homes, and their likely inclusion in the 'affordable' homes category for the purposes of developer contributions. Following the change of premiership in 2016, the Chancellor announced some additional funding for affordable rental building. Even this minor change may be threatened unless the Government provides additional funding for the replacement of dangerous cladding on tower blocks following the Grenfell Tower fire[6] (Wilcox et al. 2017). The enforced reduction in social rents in England by 1% p.a. for 4 years from 2016/2017 is predicted to reduce the output of affordable homes by some 14,000 (OBR 2015).

None of the devolved administrations opted to move away from the traditional model of social rented housing. The Scottish Government supported the construction of some 20,000 units of social rented housing during the 2011–2016 Parliament, which is pro-rata 2.4 times more than the output of social rented housing in England. This gap will widen over the next 5 years, as the Scottish Government intends to increase the output of social rented housing to 35,000 units (plus 15,000 other affordable units) in the 5 years up to 2021, and the Welsh Government aims to double its affordable housing supply to 20,000[7] units (see Wilcox et al. 2017). As Wilcox, et al comment,

> Despite having the most pressurised housing market, with acute affordability problems in some regions… England is the only one of the administrations to shift its investment focus away from the lowest income households. (Wilcox et al. 2016, 70)

6.2.2. Right to Buy and other stock sales

The Right to Buy has been subject to perhaps the widest divergence in housing policy across the nations of the UK since 2010.

For almost all of the last UK Labour Government, the devolved administrations in Scotland and Wales established in 1999 were also led by Labour. During this period, the terms under which Right to Buy could be exercised generally moved in the same direction, with qualification periods rising (at least for new tenants) and maximum discounts tightened. The story was a little more complicated in Scotland where the desire to introduce a 'single' social tenancy for housing association and local authority tenants implied giving them the same rights, including the Right to Buy. However, the Right to Buy for housing association tenants was introduced within the framework of the more restrictive 'modernised' Right to Buy (see Table 4) and was in any case deferred until the last quarter of 2012. Since then, it has had no discernible effect on the sales figures.

Scottish Government *Your right to buy your home. A Guide for Scottish Secure Tenants http://www.gov.scot/Resource/Doc/340579/0112829.pdf*

Since the election of the Coalition in 2010, Right to Buy policy has diverged dramatically. The Scottish Government withdrew RTB from new tenants in 2011 and ended it altogether in 2016. The Welsh Government published a White Paper on the future of Right to Buy in January 2015 (Welsh Government 2015). Following a period of consultation, it announced a further reduction in the maximum discount (by half) and introduced legislation to end the scheme in 2017.

The effect of the lengthening of the qualification period to 5 years and the regionally based maximum discounts caused Right to Buy sales to collapse in England (Figure 4). Under both the Coalition and Conservative governments, Right to Buy policy has moved radically in the opposite direction in an attempt to 'reinvigorate' the scheme in England.

Their policies have restored Right to Buy levels in England to the levels of 2007/08, but not to those seen in the mid-noughties. The increase in maximum discounts and their indexation will be complemented by a reduction in the qualification period to 2 years.

However, the UK's Conservative Government is in the process of extending the Right to Buy to housing association tenants in England. It reached an agreement with the National Housing Federation (which represents the housing associations in England) for a 'voluntary' scheme, which is now subject to a 'large scale regional pilot' (HM Treasury 2016, 27) following legislation allowing the Government to compensate associations for losses arising from the discounts applied to sales. These

Table 4. Right to Buy criteria in England, Scotland, Wales and Northern Ireland.

	England	Scotland	Wales	Northern Ireland
Qualification period	5 years (to be reduced to 2 years under Deregulation Act 2015)	5 years (if tenancy began after 30/9/02 = 'modernised' RTB) 2 years (if tenancy began before 1/10/02 = preserved RTB)	2 years (if tenant before 18/1/05) 5 years (if tenant on or after 18/1/05)	5 years
Discount house	35% plus 1% p.a. up to 70% (raised from 60% in 2014)	20% plus 1% p.a. up to 35% (modernised RTB) 32% plus 1% p.a. up to max 60% (preserved RTB)	32% plus 1% p.a. up to 60%	20% plus 2% p.a. up to 60%
Discount flat	50% plus 2% p.a. up to 70%	20% plus 1% p.a. up to 35% (modernised RTB) 44% plus 2% p.a. up to 70% (preserved RTB)	44% plus 2% p.a. up to 70%	20% plus 2% p.a. up to 60%
Maximum cash discount	£75,000 (since April 2012, now uprated by CPI to £77,900) £100,000 (London since March 2013, uprated by CPI to £103,900) Previously £16,000-£38,000, depending to region	£15,000 (modernised RTB)	£8,000 (June 2015) £16,000 (2003–15) Previously £24,000	£24,000
Housing pressure restrictions	–	Introduced 2002; 2011	Introduced 2011	–
New houses	–	Exempt from scheme if tenancy began from 1/3/11. (New house = built or acquired after 15/6/08)	–	–
Abolition	–	Scheme ended for new tenants after 1/3/11 Scheme ended for all tenants on 31/7/16	Announced June 2015; Bill introduced 2017	–

Source: Parkin (2015) *Comparison of Right to Buy policies in England, Scotland, Wales and Northern Ireland*, House of Commons Briefing Paper Number 07174, 19 August http://researchbriefings.files.parliament.uk/documents/CBP-7174/CBP-7174.pdf

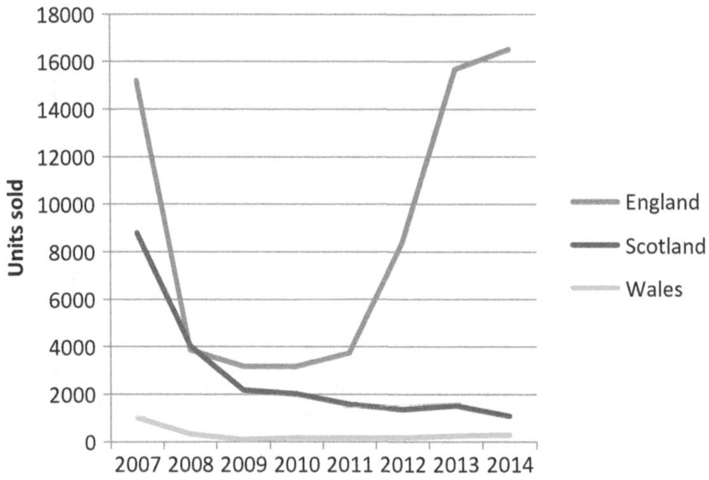

Figure 4. Trends in Right to Buy sales.
Source: Wilcox et al. (2016), Tables 20a, b, c

are supposed to be paid for by forcing local authorities to sell 'higher value' properties when they fall vacant. Whilst such properties are meant to be replaced by other 'affordable' dwellings, these may be 'starter homes' sold at 20% below market value. The UK Government has allocated an additional £250 million to pay for the pilot (HM Treasury 2016, Table 2.1). Although the details of the future scheme have yet to be finalised, the Government has reaffirmed its commitment to finance it through sales of higher value council properties (DCLG 2017b) – a policy that has not been adopted by any of the devolved administrations.

Scotland retains the largest social rented sector (23.4%) in the UK, and this is likely to grow (Table 2). The relative size of the social stock in Wales and Northern Ireland (both 16%) is slightly below that of England (17.4%), but it is likely to fall (more quickly) there than in Wales or Northern Ireland. Scotland's ability to provide a safety net through social renting is likely to increase compared to the rest of the UK. However, England's stock of social rented housing is also decline relative to the rest of the UK, too, leaving Wales and Northern Ireland in an intermediate position.

6.3. Allocations and security of tenure

The UK Government is in the process of changing the terms of the social housing 'offer'. It has abandoned a ('pay to stay') scheme to make local authority tenants on higher incomes to pay a market or near market rents but it 'will work to deliver its commitment to ensure that social housing is occupied by those who need it most through other measures' (HM Treasury 2016, 44).

Nonetheless, the UK Government still intends to introduce another policy to make it obligatory for local authorities to issue fixed term tenancies to new tenants. This follows the reluctance of local authorities to use enabling powers to do so after they were introduced in 2012 (Fitzpatrick and Pawson 2014). Fixed term tenancies may vary from a minimum of two to a maximum of 10 years, although longer tenancies may be issued when dependent children are part of the household. This ends the historic consensus (enforced by law since 1980) that local authority tenancies are for as long as the tenant wishes to stay, so long as they meet the terms of the tenancy. It implies that local authority housing is only a temporary form of assistance, to be withdrawn when it is no longer needed. As the Government Minister argued when introducing the measure,

> ...we believe that continuing to offer social tenancies on a lifetime basis is not an efficient use of scarce social housing. The new clauses will significantly improve landlords' ability to get the best use out of social housing by focusing it on those who need it most for as long as they need it. (quoted by Parkin and Wilson 2016,13)

Fitzpatrick and Watts (2017) suggest that the impact of the policy on the nature of the social rented sector will become apparent over time. They found that many social landlords remain committed to 'homes for life' and that in the short-run there may be little impact on tenancy turnover. However, they also suggest that the policy will induce anxiety among many tenants and impact on their 'ontological security'. Fixed-term tenancies therefore mark another important ideologically driven divergence between England and the devolved administrations. Even if local authorities choose to renew tenancies, it changes the nature of social rented housing, and as such may come to mark a 'critical juncture' which causes the English social housing regime to diverge further from the rest of the UK.

6.4. Homelessness

As noted, a key and distinctive feature of the UK housing system has been what amounts to a legally enforceable right to housing for people who are unintentionally homeless and in 'priority need'. Local authorities are obliged to find settled accommodation for such people, which traditionally meant a secure social tenancy. However, the protection afforded to homeless people has also undergone important divergence.

Since 2012 in Scotland, local authorities' obligations have been extended to all unintentionally homeless people through the abolition of 'priority need'. The most important effect of the change is to extend protection to childless single people and childless couples who are not treated as being vulnerable. The legislation was passed in 2004 with cross-party support, but was phased in to allow local authorities to adapt to the new demands. The measure has been characterised as representing an 'elite consensus' rather than the result of popular pressure (Fitzpatrick and Pawson 2016). It is also possible only because there is greater availability of social rented housing in Scotland.

Wales has also attempted to extend protection for homeless people, but not by abolishing the 'priority need' provisions. Rather the Welsh Government has extended the duty of local authorities to be more active in homelessness prevention, an approach which has been adopted in England under the Homelessness Reduction Act 2017.

However, so far as the 'main duty' of providing secure accommodation is concerned English policy has shifted in the opposite direction. First, local authorities are now permitted to discharge their duties by finding private rented accommodation for eligible homeless households. Whilst this was previously an option if the homeless household agreed, agreement is no longer required. The numbers are so far absolutely small, but have risen quickly and appear to be concentrated in London. Second, local authorities are now permitted to house homeless people outside the local authority area, even if the household has no connections with the host area. Again this very much diminishes the value of the protection previously offered to homeless people and is suggestive of another critical juncture by which the safety net role of the original homelessness legislation is transformed into an ambulance service.

7. Housing costs and poverty

Although Westminster continued to control social security, the devolved administrations have been able to exercise some control over Discretionary Housing Payments, which were introduced to provide temporary assistance to households affected by Housing Benefit cuts. Further, the Scottish Government is being granted limited control over a range of social security benefits in the 2016 Scotland Act, whilst in Northern Ireland, its de *jure* control over social security led to the first significant challenge to the 'parity principle'.

7.1. Discretionary housing payments and the 'bedroom tax'

Discretionary Housing Payments (DHPs) are not devolved to Scotland or Wales, so the schemes operated by Scottish and Welsh local authorities are part of the GB-wide system operated by the Department for Work and Pensions.

However, in Scotland, the 'removal of the spare room subsidy' (RSRS, often called the 'bedroom tax') has been highly controversial and became embroiled in the politics of the 2014 independence referendum. This measure results in social tenants having their Housing Benefit cut if they are 'underoccupying' their accommodation. The measure is seen by many people as being unfair because social landlords have a shortage of smaller flats. The pro-independence campaign was keen to emphasise that Scotland would need to leave the UK in order to escape legislation such as the RSRS. Clearly, it was in the interests of the unionists to demonstrate otherwise. In May 2014, the UK Government moved an Order which devolved the statutory cap on DHPs to Scotland from December 2014 (Scottish Government 2015a). The Scottish Government decided to make £35 million available in 2015/16 to allow local authority to fully mitigate it. This element now dominates the DHP budget in Scotland, as only £13.3 million of the total of £48.3 million is paid for by DWP (Scottish Government 2015b). The Scottish Government intends to use its new powers to alter the housing cost element in Universal Credit mitigate the RSRS in the long run.

In 2013/14, Welsh local authorities received £7.1 million from DWP to operate the DHP. The cost of the RSRS in Wales is estimated at £23 million a year, and the Welsh Government has not sought to mitigate it fully. Instead, it has made more modest sums (£1.3 million) available from its Homelessness Prevention fund. This is to be used to 'address the root problems behind people's circumstances in order to achieve long lasting change' (Welsh Government 2014).

The post-2010 benefit cuts were controversial in Northern Ireland and their implementation was delayed, resulting in 'fines' amounting to £100 million a year for 2 years (Hazell 2015). Eventually the legislation was passed in 2015, but this has meant that the idea of 'parity of timing' at least has been breached (ibid.). DHP are available only for private tenants, but they will be extended to social tenants as a short-term measure to allow tenants affected by the RSRS time to downsize.

7.2. Future restrictions on housing benefit

The UK Government is intending to introduce restrictions on the eligible rent for financial assistance for social tenants in receipt of Housing Benefit and Universal Credit (which is gradually being introduced in place of six separate social assistance benefits including

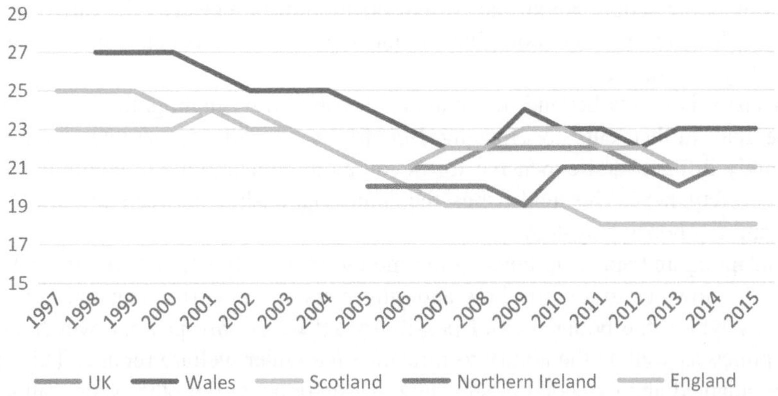

Figure 5. Poverty after housing costs in the UK, England, Scotland, Wales and Northern Ireland (1997–2015).
Notes: Poverty = % individuals living in households with incomes after tax and social security and housing costs below 60% of the national median; 3 year averagesSource: Family Resources Survey

HB). Since the 1990s, private tenants' HB was limited to the median market rent in their housing market area. In 2011, it was limited to the 30th percentile of rents. Additionally, single people aged under 25 were subject to a Shared Room Rent based on shared accommodation, and this was raised to 35 in 2012. From 2019, the UK Government intends to phase in these limitations to social tenants.

Again these and other measures[8] represent a reduction in the housing safety net. The Scottish Government has the powers to mitigate some of these changes, but this will become increasingly costly, as the money would need to come from its own budget and limited tax base.[9] The importance of housing costs to the poverty rate is clearly shown in Figure 5. Whilst much of the difference between Scotland and England reflects differences in market conditions, the role of social rented housing and Housing Benefit plays a role, too. But the important point is that there are limits to the ability of devolved administrations to shape their own social housing regimes.

8. Conclusions

The UK is in the process of divergence away from a single social housing regime, reflecting growing divergence in party politics in the context of fiscal austerity. Divergence is partly attributable to English radicalism which has set the country on course to shift social rented housing away from a safety net and towards an ambulance service model. However, the devolved administrations have also acted at least to retain the safety net model in Wales and Northern Ireland, whilst in Scotland, there is an effort to strengthen it through the extension of homeless people's rights to housing, the abolition of Right to Buy, the mitigation of the 'bedroom tax' and the commitment to an enhanced social housebuilding programme.

Nonetheless, there are clear limits to divergence. The key constraint is that the UK still operates a single 'wider welfare regime'. Labour market institutions and social security still largely operate as a UK system, with the result that the devolved administrations could not develop a social market model of social rented housing whilst the 'wider welfare regime' continues to produce high levels of income inequality and poverty.

There is therefore scope, within the current devolution frameworks for varieties of social housing regime sub-type, but not of social housing regime – a conclusion that nonetheless takes us beyond 'nuance'.

Our analysis points beyond the limits of devolution by highlighting its fragility. It is possible that further cuts to Housing Benefit by the UK Government will make it increasingly difficult and expensive for devolved administrations to continue to provide effective safety nets. This underlines the inter-relationship between the wider welfare regime and the housing system.

By adapting and applying housing regime theory to sub-nation state jurisdictions, our framework allows us to identify how and why housing systems are changing in a meaningful way within the boundaries of possibility set by de *jure* powers over housing and related policy as well as the ability to influence the wider welfare regime. This approach could be adapted and extended to sub-state jurisdictions within other states, although the underlying distinctive political cultures that drive divergence may be more pronounced in a plurinational state[10] such as the UK, rather than (say) a federal system with a more homogenous political culture.

Disclosure statement

No potential conflict of interest was reported by the author.

Notes

1. The provision for the transfer of local authority housing to housing associations from 1988 marks a further critical juncture in UK housing policy. It was pursued by the devolved administrations in Wales and Scotland (notably in Glasgow where almost £1 billion of housing debt was written off by the UK Treasury). See Stephens (2013) for an account of such transfers. Whilst this marks an important de *jure* change in ownership and governance, it has not affected the role of social rented housing within the framework of this article. This interpretation is supported by the decision of the Office of National Statistics to reclassify housing associations as public sector non-financial organisations in England in 2015 and the rest of the UK in 2016.
2. Until very recently, the devolved administrations remain almost entirely funded by a block grant from the UK grant, which is allocated according to a population-based ('Barnett') formula. Within the formula, it is changed in spending in England that drive changes to the grant to the devolved administrations.
3. The SNP describes itself as being a 'social democratic' party and its nationalism as 'civic' in nature, i.e. citizenship is derived from residence rather than place of birth or ethnicity. Hence, the Scottish Government argued for EU nationals resident in Scotland to be entitled to vote in the EU referendum in 2016, and subsequently to be given residency rights post-Brexit.
4. The most significant difference elsewhere in the housing system relates to the reforms to the private rented sector being introduced in Scotland. Greatly increased security of tenure will apply to new tenancies from the end of 2017, and provision has been made for second generation rent controls in pressurised markets. In the rest of the UK, the sector will remain within the framework of insecure tenancies established on new tenancies in 1989.
5. A further complication arises from the changes that have occurred following the replacement of David Cameron with Theresa May as Prime Minister following the EU referendum in 2016. May's government has either not implemented or rowed back from some of the far-reaching policies contained in the 2016 Housing and Planning Act, which was conceived under Cameron's premiership. Moreover, something of a change in emphasis was indicated by a White Paper (DCLG 2017a), although further uncertainty has arisen since the Conservatives unexpectedly lost their overall majority in the June 2017 election, the energies of the

government directed towards negotiating Brexit whilst the ministry responsible for housing is having to focus on the aftermath of the Grenfell Tower fire.

6. On 14 June 2017, a fire in Grenfell Tower, a local authority tower block in London, killed at least 80 residents. The spread of the fire has been attributed to recently fitted cladding, which has been found on many tower blocks throughout England. No such cladding was found in tower blocks in Scotland where different building regulations and enforcement mechanisms apply.
7. The Welsh Government is coy about how many of these will be social rented. The total includes 6,000 units provided under Help to Buy (Welsh Government 2016).
8. A 'benefit cap', limiting the overall amount working age households could receive in social security benefits was introduced in 2013, mainly affecting people living in very high cost areas such as London and those with large numbers of children. In 2017, the cap was lowered, with the effect that proportionately more households outside London – including in the devolved administrations – are now affected (Wilcox et al. 2017).
9. So far mitigation of Housing Benefit cuts has been met from within the existing budget, suggesting that expenditure priorities have been changed in favour of housing support. The Scottish Government has the option to increase income tax rates, but it has so far been reluctant to do so, so this will be a significant test.
10. The view that the UK is in effect a plurinational state has gained support since the 2014 referendum on Scottish independence. See (McHarg 2014).

References

Aalbers, M., ed. 2012. *Subrpime Cities: The Political Economy of Mortgage Markets*. Oxford: Wiley-Blackwell.

Aalbers, M. 2016. *Financialization of Housing: A Political Economy Approach*. London: Routledge.

Barr, N. 1987. *The Economics of the Welfare State*. London: Weidenfeld and Nicolson.

Bengtsson, B. 2009. "Political Science as the Missing Link Inn Housing Studies." *Housing, Theory and Society* 26 (1): 10–25. doi:10.1080/14036090802704106.

Bengtsson, B., and H. Ruonavaara. 2010. "Introduction to the Special Issue: Path Dependence in Housing." *Housing, Theory and Society* 27 (3): 193–203. doi:10.1080/14036090903326411.

Christophers, B. 2013. "A Monstrous Hybrid: The Political Economy of Housing in Early Twenty-First Century Sweden." *New Political Economy* 18 (6): 885–911. doi:10.1080/13563467.2012.753521.

Daunton, M. 1984. "Introduction." In *Councillors and Tenants: Local Authority Housing in English Cities*, edited by M. J. Daunton, 1919–1939. Leicester: Leicester University Press.

DCLG. 2017a. *Fixing Our Broken Housing Market, Cm 9352*. London: DCLG.

DCLG. 2017b. *Department for Communities and Local Government Response to the Communities and Local Government Committee's Report into Housing Associations and the Right to Buy*, Cm 9416. London: DCLG.

Diamond, D., and M. Lea. 1992. "Housing Finance in Developed Countries: An International Comparison of Efficiency." *Journal of Housing Research* 3 (1):1-271.

Dol, K., E. C. Mazo, N. L. Llop, J. Hoekstra, G. C. Fuentes, and A. E. Etxarri. 2016. "Regionalization of Housing Policies? An Exploratory Study of Andalusia, Catalonia and the Basque Country." *Journal of Housing and the Built Environment*. doi:10.1007/s10901-9528-z.

Elsinga, M., and L. Lund. 2013. "The Effect of EU Legislation on Rental Systems in Sweden and the Netherlands." *Housing Studies* 28 (7): 960–970. doi:10.1080/02673037.2013.803044.

Emmenegger, P., J. Kvist, P. Marx, and K. Petersen. 2015. "Three Worlds of Welfare Capitalism: The Making of a Classic." *Journal of European Social Policy* 25 (1): 3–13. doi:10.1177/0958928714556966.

Esping-Andersen, G. 1990. *The Three Worlds of Welfare Capitalism*. Cambridge: Polity Press.

Esping-Andersen, G., and J. Myles. 2009. "Economic Inequality and the Welfare State." In *The Oxford Handbook of Economic Inequality*, edited by W. Salverda, B. Nolan, and T. M. Smeeding, 639–664. Oxford: Oxford University Press.

Finnigan, R. 1984. "Council Housing in Leeds: Social Policy and Urban Change." In *Councillors and Tenants: Local Authority Housing in English Cities*, edited by M. J. Daunton, 1919–1939. Leicester: Leicester University Press.

Fitzpatrick, S., and B. Watts. 2017. "Competing Visions: Security of Tenure and the Welfarisation of English Social Housing." *Housing Studies*. doi:10.1080/02673037.2017.1291916.

Fitzpatrick, S., and H. Pawson. 2014. "Ending Security of Tenure for Social Renters: Transitioning to "Ambulance Service" Social Housing." *Housing Studies* 29 (5): 597–615. doi:10.1080/02673037.2013.803043.

Fitzpatrick, S, and H. Pawson. 2016. "Fifty Years Since Cathy come Home : Critical Reflections On The Uk Homelessness Safety Net." *International Journal Of Housing Policy* 16 (4): 543–555. doi: 10.1080/14616718.2016.1230962.

Gibb, K. 2015. "Housing Policy in Scotland since Devolution: Divergence, Crisis, Integration and Opportunity." *Journal of Poverty and Social Justice* 23 (1): 29–42. doi:10.1332/175982715X14229585605431.

Green, R. K., and S. Malpezzi. 2003. *US Housing Markets and Housing Policy*. Washington, DC: Urban Institute Press.

Hazell, R. 2015. *Devolution and the Future of the Union*. London: UCL. https://www.ucl.ac.uk/constitution-unit/publications/tabs/unit-publications/163.pdf/.

Healy, K. 2017. "Fuck Nuance." *Sociological Theory* 35 (2): 118–127. doi:10.1177/0735275117709046.

HM Treasury. 2016. *Autumn Statement 2016*, Cm 932. London: HM Treasury.

Hoekstra, J. 2003. "Housing and the Welfare State in the Netherlands: An Application of Esping-Andersen's Typology." *Housing, Theory and Society* 20 (2): 58–71. doi:10.1080/14036090310000634.

Institute of Fiscal Studies. 2016. *Incomes in the UK*. London: IFS.

Johansson, H., and A. Panican. 2016. "A Move Towards the Local? the Relevance of A Local Welfare System Approach." In *Combating Poverty in Local Welfare Systems: Active Inclusion Strategies in European Cities*, edited by H. Johansson and A. Panican, 1–28. London: Macmillan.

Kemeny, J. 1995. *From Public Housing to the Social Market: Rental Policy Strategies in Comparative Perspective*. London: Routledge.

Kemeny, J., J. Kersloot, and P. Thalmann. 2005. "Non-Profit Housing Influencing, Leading and Dominating the Unitary Rental Market: Three Case Studies." *Housing Studies* 20 (6): 855–872. doi:10.1080/02673030500290985.

Kleinman, M., W. Matznetter, and M. Stephens, eds. 1998. *European Integration and Housing Policy*. London: Routledge.

Lopez-Santana, M. 2015. *The New Governance of Welfare States in the United States and Europe: Between Decentralization and Centralization in the Activation Era*. Albany : State University of New York Press.

McHarg, A. 2014. What Does the Union Need to Do to Survive? UK Constitutional Law Association blog, 24 September https://ukconstitutionallaw.org/2014/09/26/aileen-mcharg-what-does-the-union-need-to-do-to-survive/.

McKee, K., J. Muir, and T. Moore. 2017. "Housing Policy In The Uk: The Importance Of Spatial Nuance." *Housing Studies* 32 (1): 60–72. doi: 10.1080/02673037.2016.1181722.

Office of Budgetary Responsibility. 2015. *Economic and Fiscal Outlook*, Cm 9088. London: Office of Budgetary Responsibility.

Parkin, E (2015) Comparison of Right to Buy policies in England, Scotland, Wales and Northern Ireland, House of Commons Briefing Paper Number 07174, London: House of Commons, August

Parkin, E., and W. Wilson. 2016. "Social housing: The end of 'lifetime' tenancies in England?" House of Commons Library Briefing Paper No. 07173, May http://researchbriefings.files.parliament.uk/documents/CBP-7173/CBP-7173.pdf.

Ravetz, A. 2001. *Council Housing and Culture*. London: Routledge.

Robertson, D., and R. Serpa. 2014. "Social Housing in Scotland." In *Social Housing in Europe*, edited by K. Scanlon, C. Whitehead, and M. F. Arrigoitia, 43–59. Chichester: Wiley Blackwell.

Scottish Government. 2015a. Welfare Reform (Further Provision) (Scotland) Act 2012 – Annual Report 2015. http://www.gov.scot/Resource/0048/00480461.pdf.

Scottish Government. 2015b. Discretionary Housing Payments in Scotland as at 30 September 2015. http://www.gov.scot/Resource/0048/00489627.pdf.
Stephens, M. 2016a. "Using Esping-Andersen and Kemeny's Welfare and Housing Regimes in Comparative Housing Research." *Critical Housing Analysis* 3 (1): 19–29. doi:10.13060/23362839.2016.3.1.250.
Stephens, M. 2016b. *Housing Regimes 20 Years After Kemeny.* Edinburgh: Urban Institute.
Stephens, M., S. Fitzpatrick, M. Elsinga, G. van Steen, and Y. Chzhen. 2010. *Study on Housing Exclusion: Welfare Policies, Housing Provision & Labour Markets*. Brussels: European Commission.
Stephens, M., J. Blenkinsopp, and K. Gibb. 2015. *The Devolution of Housing Benefit and Social Security: Rebalancing Housing Subsidies in Scotland.* Edinburgh: Shelter Scotland.
Stephens, M. 2013. "Social Housing in the United Kingdom." In *The Future of Public Housing: Ongoing Trends in the East and the West*, edited by J. Chen, M. Stephens, and Y. Man, 199–213. Heidelberg: Springer.
Stephens, M., N. Burns, and L. Mackay. 2002. *Social Market or Safety Net? British Social Rented Housing in a European Context.* Bristol: Policy Press.
Stephens, M., N. Burns, and L. Mackay. 2003. "The Limits of Housing Reform." *Urban Studies* 40 (4): 767–789. doi:10.1080/0042098032000065290.
Stephens, M. 2008. "The Role of the Social Rented Sector." In *The Future of Social Housing*, edited by S. Fitzpatrick and M. Stephens, 27–38. London: Shelter.
Torgersen, U. 1987. "Housing: The Wobbly Pillar under the Welfare State." *Scandinavian Housing and Planning Research* 4 (10). doi:10.1080/02815737.1987.10801428.
Welsh Government. 2014. *Evaluation of Additional Discretionary Housing Payments Funding Provided by the Welsh Government to Local Authorities in Wales for 2013/14*, 3. http://gov.wales/docs/desh/publications/140919-discretionary-housing-payments-funding-en.pdf.
Welsh Government. 2015. The Future of the Right to Buy and Right to Acquire. A White Paper for Social, January Housing. http://gov.wales/docs/desh/consultation/150603-right-to-buy-consultation-summary-of-resposes-en.pdf.
Welsh Government. 2016. Taking Wales Forward 2016-21. http://gov.wales/docs/strategies/160920-taking-wales-forward-en.pdf.
Wilcox, S., J. Perry, M. Stephens, and P. Williams. 2016. *UK Housing Review 2016.* Coventry: Chartered Institute of Housing.
Wilcox, S., J. Perry, M. Stephens, and P. Williams. 2017. *UK Housing Review Briefing*. Coventry: Chartered Institute of Housing.
Winters, S., and M. Elsinga. 2008. "The Future of Flemish Social Housing." *Journal of Housing and the Built Environment* 23 (3): 215–230. doi:10.1007/s10901-008-9113-1.
World Bank. 1994. *Housing: Enabling Markets to Work.* Washington, DC: World Bank.
Zweirs, M., and F. Koster. 2015. "The Local Structure of the Welfare State: Uneven Effects of Social Spending on Poverty within Countries." *Urban Studies* 52 (1): 87–102. doi:10.1177/0042098014523688.

Quantifying a century of state intervention in rental housing in Germany

Konstantin A. Kholodilin

The paper aims at measuring the general state intervention in rental housing market in Germany from 1913 through 2015. Four policy classes are considered: Incentives for social housing, tenant protection, housing rationing, and rent controls. Based on a legislation analysis, for each class an index measuring the degree of regulation is constructed. The indices reflect dramatic increases in regulations during and after the World Wars. The 2010s are characterized by a surge in all classes of regulations related to the growing housing scarcity in large cities due to interregional migration leading to a geographical mismatch between housing supply and demand.

1. Introduction

The economic and social role of the housing market is difficult to overestimate. Housing satisfies one of the basic needs – the need for shelter. It is the most important component of household expenditure and wealth. For example, in Germany, according to German Federal Statistical Office (Destatis), housing expenditure – rental payments, housing repair, and heating – makes up one-third of the total expenses of private households, whereas the housing wealth (6.3 trillion euros at the end of 2012) accounts for more than a half of the wealth of private households (about 12.3 trillion euros), see SVR (2013).

For more than a century, governments have been actively intervening in the functioning of the rental housing market. In many industrialized countries, the state applies a wide battery of policy tools – including tenant protection, rationing of housing, rent controls, and provision of social housing – in order to manipulate housing markets. The general purpose is to provide affordable rental dwellings to tenants, especially those with low incomes. The regulations affect supply of, demand for, and price of housing. However, often the regulations have unintended consequences. For example, the objective of rent controls is to keep the existing rental dwellings affordable. At the same time, restricting rents can make rental housing unprofitable and lead investors to concentrate more on owner-occupied dwellings, thus decreasing the supply of rental units. It can also cause a deterioration in the quality of rental dwellings, because landlords may try to increase their profitability by reducing maintenance costs. This would result in a decrease in demand for rental housing, since it would be stigmatized by society and considered to be housing for the poor. Furthermore, housing regulation affects many other aspects, such as ethnic segregation (Andersen et al. 2016), gentrification (Andersson and Magnusson Turnerc 2014), income distribution (Heylen 2013), and integration of immigrants (Nguyen 2015), to name a few.

Thus, a change in any of these regulations is a highly political issue[1] that is closely scrutinized by the entire population, especially in countries or municipalities with large share of tenants. Therefore, it is important to provide evidence supporting an answer to the question of whether and to what extent these policies facilitate attaining the desired outcomes and lead to unintended ones.

However, before this can be done, housing market regulations need to be quantified. Therefore, the aim of this paper is to construct an index measuring the degree of the general state intervention in the German rental housing market. This is a paramount task, given an extreme variety and complexity of the legislation. Nevertheless, even a crude measure of regulations can prove useful in the econometric analysis of the housing markets.

The remainder of the paper is structured as follows. Next section overviews the existing literature on regulation indices, with a special focus on policies concerning real estate markets. Section 3 outlines the regulation index methodology used in this study. Section 4 describes in more detail the construction of the indices for the four regulation classes considered in this study (tenant protection, rationing of housing, rent controls, and social housing) and of a composite index. The evolution of each regulation class between 1913 and 2015 is examined. Special attention is paid to the developments of 2013–2015, since they point to a substantial tightening of the rental housing market controls in Germany. Finally, Section 5 concludes.

2. Literature review

The literature on measuring formal regulations has quite a long history. It uses several approaches.

2.1. Survey approach

The historically first approach is based on surveys. Noam (1983) constructs an index of building codes strictness for more than 1100 American localities that is a sum of the restriction costs of 14 major code provisions for builders. A similar approach is applied by Gyourko, Saiz, and Summers (2008), who conduct a nationwide survey of local land use regulations in 2649 US municipalities. Rental controls are quantified using survey approach in Malpezzi and Ball (1993). They undertake what is possibly the most ambiguous project by summarizing rent controls regulations in 51 countries. Andrews, Sánchez, and Johansson (2011) also construct a rental market regulations index using survey data. It comprised five indicators (control of rent levels, control of rent increases, ease of tenant eviction, tenure security, and deposit requirements) and based on replies to the 2009 organisation for economic co-operation and development housing questionnaire. The index covers private rental market and social housing in 23 countries. It varies between 0 and 6, increasing in degree of control. It can be used to carry out cross-country comparisons, but lacks a time dimension. The disadvantage of the survey indices is that they provide just a snapshot, not a time series representing changing regulation.

2.2. Regulation counting approach

Another approach is represented by the counting measures of regulation, as exemplified by Nicoletti, Scarpetta, and Boylaud (2000) and Alesina et al. (2005). These are weighted sums of binary indicators, taking a value of 1, when a corresponding type of regulation exists, and 0, otherwise.

2.3. Numeric target approach

El-Shagi, Michelsen, and Rosenschon (2014) suggest an approach to measuring regulation intensity concerning the energy efficiency of housing. In their case, the regulation is measured by a single numeric variable, namely the upper bound of energy consumption of new housing. This approach has, thus, a very limited application field but can be used as a complement to the regulation computing approach.

2.4. Mixed approach

Cuerpo et al. (2014) develop their rental market regulation index using 7 subindicators: rental level control; rental increases control; procedural formalism; deposit requirements for tenants; justified reasons for tenant eviction; eviction notification requirements; and average duration of a representative contract. Their analysis covers 27 European Union member states and is based both on country-specific legal acts and reports of different specialized organizations. The index is computed using principal components analysis. Similar to the survey approach, it produces a cross section but not a panel–data indicator.

2.5. Page counting approach

Dawson and Seater (2013) take a different approach in that they compute their index of the federal regulation in the USA as the number of pages in the Code of Federal Regulations. They hope that their measure at least partially captures the complexity of regulation. Dawson and Seater (2013) claim also that their measure is more precise and covers a much longer period than the alternative measures. However, a more complex regulation does not necessarily mean that it is more stringent or more liberal. A more detailed law can imply more exceptions that reduce its sphere of application and, thus, the state intervention into economy.

3. Methodology

3.1. Policy classes and elementary regulations

Our approach is similar to that of Nicoletti, Scarpetta, and Boylaud (2000) in that we decompose the regulation body into individual policy classes. Although the battery of the tools applied within the framework of the housing market policy is very extensive and complex, we concentrate on four major classes of regulations:

(1) *Social housing*: Fostering measures and restrictions concerning construction and exploitation of social housing.
(2) *Protection of tenants from eviction*: Regulations restricting the possibilities to evict tenants by the landlords.

(3) *Rationing of housing*: Regulations aimed at preservation and redistribution of the scare housing.
(4) *Rent controls*: Regulations imposing upper bounds on rents or their growth rates.

Due to the limitation of space, several other important regulations are not considered here, namely: state control over the quality of housing; tax treatment of the income of landlords/homeowners and residential property; housing allowances to the low-income tenants; subsidies to homeowners; and transition regulations designed to guarantee a smooth transformation of East German housing market in the early 1990s. Their quantification is left for future research.

The focus is not always on whole Germany: between 1945 and 1990, only the state intervention in West Germany is considered. The missing regulation for the highly regulated rental market in East Germany should lead to too low index entries if a nationwide index was to be constructed for that period. Thus, the paper is confined to the rental market interventions under a market economy; considering a centrally planned economy, as it existed in the German Democratic Republic, goes beyond the scope of the paper.

Moreover, the issue of law enforcement is not tackled here. This is an important issue, given the budget limitations of the executive and judicial powers that sometimes preclude the effective enforcement of the legal acts. However, due to its complexity, the analysis of this issue is also left to be the subject of future research.

Furthermore, primarily central government intervention is considered. In Germany, rental market is regulated largely by the legal acts issued by the central authorities. Nevertheless, federal states have a wide latitude in implementing these regulations at the local level. They can also issue laws and ordinances that extend federal acts. However, tracing the development of regional regulations falls outside the scope of this paper as it is too time and space consuming, due to a large number of regions and changes in administrative borders following World War II (WWII), it is left for a future research.

The idea behind the regulation index is to examine over an extended period of time all federal laws and ordinances related to housing policy and to extract all individual rules belonging to the aforementioned regulation classes. The composite regulation index is obtained by aggregating the individual, or elementary, rules. This can be done using the following algorithm:

(1) For each class of regulation, a set of relevant elementary regulations has to be identified. An elementary regulation is such a rule that can take either binary values (1, if it exists; or 0, otherwise) or numeric values (e.g., tax rate or amount of assigned monetary means).
(2) For each elementary regulation j of class i, an index is created:
   - either a dummy variable:

$$I_{ijt} = \begin{cases} 1 & \textit{if regulation } j \textit{ is in force in period } t \\ 0 & \textit{otherwise} \end{cases}, \tag{1}$$

where j is an elementary regulation and t is the time index.

   - or a numeric variable: $N_{ijt} \in \mathrm{IR}$. Further, the variable is transformed into an index as follows:

$$I_{ijt} = \frac{N_{ijt}}{\max(N_{ijt})}. \tag{2}$$

(3) The elementary regulation indices are aggregated for each class of regulation i by averaging them:

$$\mathrm{HRI}_{it} = \frac{w_{it}}{J}\sum_{j=1}^{J} I_{ijt}, \tag{3}$$

where w_{it} is an index of application sphere of regulations of class i in period t. It varies between 0 and 1, where 0 corresponds to none dwellings subject to regulations, while 1 means that all dwellings are under regulation. Thus, it decreases as more dwellings are excepted from regulations: for example, newly built or large ones.

(4) Based on individual indices, a composite regulation index can be constructed as a simple average[2]:

$$\mathrm{HRI}_t = \frac{1}{I}\sum_{i=1}^{I} \mathrm{HRI}_{it}. \tag{4}$$

Strictly speaking, the last step is not necessary. In the econometric analysis, both composite and individual regulation indices can be applied. The index varies between 0 (completely free market) and 1 (totally regulated market). For example, before World War I (WWI), when government intervention was virtually inexistent, the index should be 0. After and during wars, when rationing of housing, tenant protection, and rent controls are introduced, the values of both individual indices and composite should increase pointing to an intensified state intervention. In the postwar period, an additional impetus to the intervention is given by an active social housing policy, which is aimed to substitute for insufficient private building activity. As a result, the corresponding subindex and composite index should rise. Deregulation should lead to decreasing index values, for less strict rationing and rent controls as well as less generous state support to the social housing lead to lower values of the corresponding individual indices and, consequently, of the composite index.

3.2. Sphere of application of regulations

The sphere of application of housing market regulations varies: It was extended when housing market became tight and was gradually relaxed when the economic and political situation changed.

First, from the very beginning, the tenant protection and rent controls were limited to the so-called old housing, that is, dwellings built before 1 July 1918, see Tables 3 through 7. Similarly, in 1950, a process of relaxing housing market regulations was initiated. In particular, the new dwellings built after 20 June 1948 without state aid were exempted from tenant protection, housing rationing, and rent controls; see Tables 3–7. Therefore, new construction naturally led to a narrowing of the application sphere of these regulations. Thus, the latter can be approximated by the share of the newly built housing. Given that the data on housing stock are gathered through censuses and microcensuses that take place irregularly, the missing observations are imputed using a linear interpolation.

Therefore, between 1922 and 1937 for tenant protection and between 1922 and 1936 for rent controls, the sphere of application can be computed as:

$$w_t = \alpha_{AB}^{1918}\alpha_{other}, \tag{5}$$

where α_{AB}^{1918} is the share of housing built before 1 July 1918; and α_{other} is a share of housing *not freed* from regulations due to other exceptions (e.g., exemptions for large, expensive, or vacant dwellings). The latter are difficult to quantify precisely, for the corresponding statistical data are not available.

Between 1950 and 1960, the sphere of application can be defined as follows:

$$w_t = \alpha_{AB}^{1948} \alpha_{other}, \tag{6}$$

where α_{AB}^{1948} is the share of housing built before 20 June 1948.

The importance of introducing the old-housing correction can be illustrated by the following figures: In 1936, when the first liberalization wave was over, the share of old housing was just below 79%, while in 1965, it was just 56% of the total housing stock. Thus, very quickly the regulated sector shrank simply due to the new construction. Even if further deregulation measures were not taken, the house market restrictions would dwindle.

Second, in 1960, the liberalization process was intensified, see Table 3. Its progress was linked to an indicator of housing market tightness[3]:

$$\mathrm{TI}_t = 100 \times \left(\frac{N_t^{HH} - 0.5 N_t^{HH_1}}{N_t^{HU}} - 1 \right), \tag{7}$$

where N_t^{HH} is the number of households; $N_t^{HH_1}$ is the number of one-person households; and N_t^{HU} is the number of dwellings. The numerator represents the effective number of households (*Wohnparteien*). Only one half of singles are taken into account, because singles are theoretically more likely to be sharing dwellings with somebody else. If the housing market tightness indicator was less than 3%, the regulations (housing rationing, tenant protection, and rent controls) could be abandoned. It was the government of each federal state of West Germany that, based on the indicator, selected which districts (*Kreise*) were freed from regulations.

We approximate this process by the corresponding district-specific indicators (*rechnerisches Wohnungsdefizit in den Kreisen*) that were published in the statistical yearbooks between 1961 and 1965. The market tightness indicator shows wide regional variation. For example, in 1958, it varied between 0% (rural district Pirmasens in Rhineland-Palatinate and eight rural districts in Baden-Württemberg) and 42.9% (city of Marburg in Hesse). Lower Saxony was the federal states with largest housing shortage, while Baden-Württemberg had the least tight markets.

Thus, the sphere of application of tenant protection from eviction after 1960 can be expressed as:

$$w_t = \alpha_{AB}^{1948} \frac{\sum_{k=1}^{K} \omega_k \mathbb{I}\left(\mathrm{TI}_{tk}\right)}{\sum_{k=1}^{K} \omega_k}, \tag{8}$$

where ω_k is the share of district k in the national housing stock, according to the census of buildings conducted in 1961,[4] and $\mathbb{I}\left(TI_{tk}\right)$ is an indicator variable defined as

$$\mathbb{I}\left(\mathrm{TI}_{tk}\right) = \begin{cases} 1 & \textit{if } \mathrm{TI}_{tk} \geq 3 \\ 0 & \textit{otherwise} \end{cases}. \tag{9}$$

Thus, w_t represents the approximate share of the part of housing stock that is still subject to regulations.

4. Housing regulations

A systematic analysis of German housing regulations can be found in Blumenroth (1975), Führer (1995), Kerner (1996), and especially in Kofner (1997, 1999, 2004). However, none attempt to quantify the regulations. To fill this gap, in this section, the indices for four regulation classes (social housing, tenant protection, rationing of housing, and rent controls) are developed and combined to a composite index of housing market regulations. In addition, since these studies were completed, important new regulations were implemented, which are accounted for in this paper.

Below the regulation classes are presented in their historical order.

4.1. Social housing policy

The social housing policy is dictated by the concern that not everybody can have access to an appropriate housing at reasonable rent. Therefore, the main purpose of this policy is providing the housing to socially weak persons. Typically, these are poor, and also families with many children, disabled, and refugees.

The relevant legal federal level acts concerning social housing policy are listed in Table 1. The legislation is summarized by the following main categories:

(1) *Subject*: Persons that benefit from the policy encouraging housing construction.
(2) *Object*: Types of housing that are promoted by the social housing policy.
(3) *Fostering*: Construction incentives.
(4) *Restrictions*: Constraints imposed on the exploitation of social housing by the investors/landlords.
(5) *Plan*: Quantitative housing construction plans, when applicable.
(6) *Expenditure*: Amount of expenses on social housing assigned by the federal government.
(7) *Guarantees*: Amount of credit guarantees assumed by the federal government.

Based on the changes in categories 3, 4, 6, and 7 individual regulation indices are constructed. For categories 3 and 4, binary variables are introduced (see Section 4.1.1), while categories 6 and 7 result in numeric variables (see Section 4.1.2).

4.1.1. Fostering construction

The following incentives fostering construction are possible:

- Provision of state aid in form of housing construction loans with low or no interest and subsidies;
- Provision of credit guarantees by the government;
- Reduction of taxes (in particular, of land tax) and fees;
- Provision of building land through sale at reasonable (reduced) price or lease (*Beschaffung von Bauland*) – in certain cases, the land is expropriated – and land development (*Baulanderschließ ung*);
- Provision of premia for building society savers (*Wohnungsbauprämien*);

Table 1. Legislation on social housing.

Date	Law title	Summary	Source
10 June 1914	G, betreffend Bürgschaften des Reichs zur Förderung des Baues von Kleinwohnungen für Reichs- und Militärbedienstete	**Subject**: workers and low-income civil servants of German Reich, military staff. **Object**: small dwellings. **Incentives**: loan guarantees for up to 25 million M starting from fiscal year 1915.	RGBl, 219
24 August 1918	G zur Abänderung des § 1 Abs. 1 des G, betreffend Bürgschaften des Reichs zur Förderung des Baues von Kleinwohnungen für Reichs- und Militärbedienstete	**Subject**: workers and low-income civil servants of German Reich, military staff, war-disabled, and widows of those who perished in the war. **Object**: small dwellings. **Incentives**: loan guarantees for up to 25 million M starting from fiscal year 1915.	RGBl, 1091
31 October 1918	Bestimmungen des Bundesrats für die Gewährung von Baukostenzuschüssen aus Reichsmitteln	**Incentives**: subsidies to builders in order to cover their construction costs. **Validity period**: during war and some transition period thereafter. **Sharing**: 50% Reich, 50% federal states and municipalities. **Sphere of application**: areas with urgent need for small and middle (*Klein- und Mittelwohnungen*) dwellings for urban and rural population. **Obligations**: for at least 10 years (1) rent set in accordance with municipality; (2) prohibition to use land plot for different purposes than housing; and (3) preference to large families, families of war participants, war-disabled, and war victims.	ZBl, 1160
09 December 1919	VO zur Behebung der dringendsten Wohnungsnot	**Subject**: no explicit definition. **Object**: small and medium dwellings (*Klein- und Mittelwohnungen*). **Incentives**: (1) provision of land, also through expropriation; (2) exemption from some prescriptions; and (3) local authorities must provide access to their supply networks and drainage systems and reasonable conditions.	RGBl, 1968
10 January 1920	Bestimmungen des Reichsrats über die Gewährung von Darlehen aus Reichsmitteln zur Schaffung neuer Wohnungen	**Aim**: to combat housing shortage and foster settlements (*Siedlungswesen*). **Incentives**: loans (*Reichsdarlehen*). **Sharing**: municipalities must contribute at least $\frac{1}{3}$ of loans provided by Reich. **Rent**: for newly constructed dwellings using state loans, rents are set by municipality. Each 5 years, municipality can review situation at local rental housing market and, when necessary, update rents. **Obligations**: during the 20 years after loan receipt, (1) prohibition to use land plot for purposes other than housing; (2) provision of housing to the predefined number of persons and preference for large families, families of war participants, war-disabled, and war victims; (3) prohibition to enlarge buildings on the land plot; and (4) buyer must take over all obligations related to the loan.	ZBl, 56

(*Continued*)

Table 1. (Continued)

Date	Law title	Summary	Source
12 February 1921	G, betreffend die vorläufige Förderung des Wohnungsbaues	**Incentives**: Federal states must spend at least 30 Marks per capita on housing construction.	RGBl, 175
26 March 1926	G über die Bereitstellung von Kredit zur Förderung des Kleinwohnungsbaues	**Expenditure**: To encourage the granting of bridging loans for first mortgages for small apartments, the Ministry of Labor is empowered to grant loans to federal states with a 12 months maturity. The amount of loans is 200 million RM.	RGBl, 179
07 March 1928	G über die Bereitstellung von Kredit zur Förderung des Kleinwohnungsbaues (BaukreditG 1928)	**Guarantees**: In financial year 1928, Ministry of Finance assumes guarantees of up to 200 million RM for the credits to *Deutsche Bau- und Bodenbank AG*, which should provide bridging loans for the small housing construction.	RGBl, 53
26 March 1929	G über die Bereitstellung von Kredit zur Förderung des Kleinwohnungsbaues (BaukreditG 1929)	**Guarantees**: Between 1 April 1929 and 31 March 1932, Ministry of Finance assumes guarantees of up to 250 million RM for the credits to *Deutsche Bau- und Bodenbank AG*.	RGBl, 81
26 July 1930	G über die Bereitstellung von Kredit zur Förderung des Kleinwohnungsbaues (BaukreditG 1930)	**Guarantees**: Between 1 April 1929 and 31 March 1936, Ministry of Finance assumes guarantees of up to 300 million RM for the credits to *Deutsche Bau- und Bodenbank AG*.	RGBl, 419
10 January 1931	Reichsgrundsätze für den Kleinwohnungsbau	**Subject**: no explicit definition, but special mention of families with many children and severely disabled. **Object**: small rental (*Kleinwohnungen*) and owner housing construction. Upper size and equipment standards for the state-aided housing are set. **Incentives**: loans and interest subsidies. **Restrictions**: economically viable (*wirtschaftlich tragbar*), but upper bounded rents.	RGBl, 9
26 October 1933	DVO über die Steuerbefreiung für neu errichtete Kleinwohnungen und Eigenheime	**Subject**: no explicit definition. **Object**: small rental and owner housing construction. Upper size standards for the state-aided housing are set. **Incentives**: lower taxation (land tax, *Grundsteuer*).	RGBl, 773
04 February 1936	G zur Übernahme von Reichsbürgschaften für den Kleinwohnungsbau	**Guarantees**: the maximum Reich's guarantee amount cannot exceed 250 million RM.	RGBl, 56
15 July 1936	VO über den Höchstbetrag für Reichsbürgschaften für den Kleinwohnungsbau	**Guarantees**: the maximum Reich's guarantee amount is raised to 400 million RM.	RGBl, 578
24 March 1937	2. VO über den Höchstbetrag für Reichsbürgschaften für den Kleinwohnungsbau	**Guarantees**: the maximum Reich's guarantee amount is raised to 500 million RM.	RGBl, 446

(Continued)

Table 1. (Continued)

Date	Law title	Summary	Source
04 October 1937	3. VO über den Höchstbetrag für Reichsbürgschaften für den Kleinwohnungsbau	**Guarantees**: the maximum Reich's guarantee amount is raised to 700 million RM.	RGBl, 1131
15 December 1938	4. VO über den Höchstbetrag für Reichsbürgschaften für den Kleinwohnungsbau	**Guarantees**: the maximum Reich's guarantee amount is raised to 900 million RM.	RGBl, 2011
15 November 1940	Erlaß zur Vorbereitung des deutschen Wohnungsbaues nach dem Kriege	**Subject**: families with many children. **Object**: rental and owner housing construction. First time the notion of 'social housing' (*sozialer Wohnungsbau*) is mentioned. **Restriction**: rent/housing cost for owners must stay in a 'healthy relationship' to the income of the housing recipients. **Plan**: in the first postwar year, 300,000 new dwellings are to be constructed. Size and equipment standards for the postwar social housing are set. **Incentives**: not specified.	RGBl, 1495
20 December 1940	VO über den Höchstbetrag für Reichsbürgschaften auf dem Gebiete des Wohnungswesens, Siedlungswesens und Städtebaues	**Guarantees**: the maximum Reich's guarantee amount cannot exceed 1225 million RM.	RGBl, 1649
24 April 1950	1. WohnungsbauG	**Subject**: wide circles of population, especially employees. **Object**: rental and owner housing construction. Upper bounds for size and lower bounds for equipment of dwellings are set. **Incentives**: (1) state aid (low-interest or interest-free loans or subsidies); (2) credit guarantees; (3) lower taxation (land tax); (4) sale of land at reasonable prices or lease; and (5) exemption from housing rationing. **Plan**: within 6 years 1.8 million social dwellings are to be constructed. **Guarantees**: the Bund assumes guarantees up to 100 million DM. **Restrictions**: (1) upper bounds for rents taking into account housing characteristics (size of region, equipment, location); and (2) state-aided social housing is only for eligible persons.	BGBl, 83
25 August 1953	G zur Änderung und Ergänzung des 1. WohnungsbauG	**Plan**: between 1951 and 1956, 2 million social dwellings are to be constructed. **Guarantees**: the Bund assumes guarantees up to 100 million DM. **Expenditure**: in financial years 1953 through 1956, federal authorities assign 500 million DM in federal budget for social housing.	BGBl, 1037

(Continued)

Table 1. (Continued)

Date	Law title	Summary	Source
27 June 1956	2. WohnungsbauG (Wohnungsbau- und FamilienheimG)	**Subject**: wide circles of population, especially low-income households (specific upper bounds). **Object**: rental and owner housing construction. Upper bounds for size and lower bounds for equipment of dwellings are set. **Incentives**: (1) state aid (low-interest or interest-free loans or subsidies); (2) credit guarantees; (3) lower taxation and fees (land tax); (4) sale of land at reasonable prices or lease; (5) exemption from housing rationing; (6) exemption from rent controls; (7) provision of premia for building society savers; (8) lower accident insurance premia; and (9) lower payment in case of early repayment of state-provided loans. **Plan**: between 1957 and 1962, 1.8 million social dwellings are to be constructed. **Guarantees**: the Bund assumes guarantees up to 500 million DM. **Expenditure**: in financial year 1957, federal authorities assign 700 million DM in federal budget for social housing. Each consecutive year this amount is to be reduced by 70 million DM. **Restrictions**: (1) rent should cover current expenses (*Kostenmiete*); and (2) state-aided social housing is only for eligible persons.	BGBl, 523
24 August 1965	G zur verstärkten Eigentumsbildung im Wohnungsbau und zur Sicherung der Zweckbestimmung von Sozialwohnungen (WoBauÄndG 1965)	**Expenditure**: From financial year 1965, federal authorities assign 210 million DM in federal budget for social housing. **Restrictions**: (1) rent should cover current expenses; (2) state-aided social housing is only for eligible persons (*Wohnberechtigte*); and (3) misuse and transformation (*Zweckentfremdung und bauliche Veränderung*) of social housing require permission.	BGBl, 945
21 December 1967	G zur Verwirklichung der mehrjährigen Finanzplanung des Bundes, II. Teil FinanzänderungsG 1967	**Expenditure**: From financial year 1968, federal authorities assign 150 million DM in federal budget for social housing.	BGBl, 1259
17 December 1967	G zur Durchführung des langfristigen Wohnungsbauprogramms	**Expenditure**: From financial year 1971, federal authorities assign 150 million DM in federal budget for social housing.	BGBl, 1993

(*Continued*)

Table 1. (Continued)

Date	Law title	Summary	Source
1 September 1976	Wohnungsbau- und FamilienheimG – II. WoBauG	**Subject**: wide circles of population, especially low-income households (specific upper bounds). **Object**: rental and owner housing construction. Upper bounds for size and lower bounds for equipment of dwellings are set. **Incentives**: (1) state aid; (2) credit guarantees; (3) lower taxation and fees; (4) sale of land at reasonable prices or lease; (5) exemption from housing rationing (not applicable anymore); (6) exemption from rent controls; (7) provision of premia for building society savers; (8) lower accident insurance premia; (9) lower payment in case of early repayment of state-provided loans; (10) provision of housing allowances; and (11) provision of subsidies and loans for expenses (*Aufwendungen*). **Guarantees**: exact amount no longer specified. **Restrictions**: (1) rent should cover current expenses; and (2) state-aided social housing is only for eligible persons.	BGBl, 2673
20 February 1980	WohnungsbauänderungsG 1980 – WoBauÄndG 1980	**Subject**: upgrading upper bounds for income of social housing recipients.	BGBl, 159
11 July 1985	Wohnungsbau- und FamilienheimG – II. WoBauG	**Subject**: wide circles of population, especially low-income households (specific upper bounds). **Object**: rental and owner housing construction. Upper bounds for size of dwellings are set. **Incentives**: (1) state aid; (2) credit guarantees; (3) lower taxation and fees; (4) sale of land at reasonable prices or lease; (5) exemption from rent controls; (6) provision of premia for building society savers; (7) lower accident insurance premia; (8) lower payment in case of early repayment of state-provided loans; (9) provision of housing allowances; and (10) provision of subsidies and loans for expenses. **Restrictions**: (1) rent should cover current expenses and (2) state-aided social housing is only for eligible persons.	BGBl, 1284
14 August 1990	Wohnungsbau- und FamilienheimG – II. WoBauG	**Subject**: wide circles of population, especially low-income households (specific upper bounds). **Object**: rental and owner housing construction. Upper bounds for size of dwellings are set. **Incentives**: (1) state aid; (2) credit guarantees; (3) lower taxation and fees; (4) sale of land at reasonable prices or lease; (5) exemption from rent controls; (6) provision of premia for building society savers; (7) lower accident insurance premia; (8) lower payment in case of early repayment of state-provided loans; (9) provision of housing allowances; and (10) provision of subsidies and loans for expenses. **Restrictions**: (1) rent should cover current expenses; and (2) state-aided social housing is only for eligible persons.	BGBl, 1730

(*Continued*)

Table 1. (Continued)

Date	Law title	Summary	Source
19 August 1994	Wohnungsbau- und FamilienheimG – II. WoBauG	**Subject**: upgrading upper bounds for income of social housing recipients.	BGBl, 2137
13 September 2001	G zur Reform des Wohnungsbaurechtes	**Subject**: low-income households (specific upper bounds). **Object**: rental and owner housing construction and modernization. Size of dwellings should be reasonable. **Incentives**: (1) state aid (loans and subsidies); (2) credit guarantees; and (3) sale of cheaper land. **Expenditure**: From financial year 2002, federal authorities provide federal states 230 million euro yearly for social housing. **Restrictions**: (1) Rent should cover current expenses. Rent increases after modernization are allowed; and (2) state-aided social housing is only for eligible persons.	BGBl, 2376
29 December 2003	HaushaltsbegleitG 2004 (HBeglG 2004)	**Expenditure**: in financial year 2004, the annual amount of financial help is 110 million euro, from financial year 2005 on, annual amount is 202.4 million euro.	BGBl, 3076
05 September 2006	Föderalismusreform-BegleitG	**Expenditure**: federal funds are no longer assigned for social housing. However, between 1 January 2007 and 31 December 2013, federal states can use 518.2 million euro from the federal budget.	BGBl, 2098
15 July 2013	G zur Errichtung eines Sondervermögens 'Aufbauhilfe' und zur Änderung weiterer G (AufbauhilfeG)	**Expenditure**: between 1 January 2014 and 31 December 2019, federal states can use 518.2 million euro from the federal budget.	BGBl, 2401
20 October 2015	AsylverfahrensbeschleuningungsG	**Expenditure**: between 1 January 2016 and 31 December 2019, federal states can use 1018.2 million euro from the federal budget.	BGBl, 1722

Notes: (1) 'G' denotes 'Gesetz' (primary law); (2) 'VO' denotes 'Verordnung' (secondary law or ordinance); (3) 'DVO' denotes 'Durchführungsverordnung' (implementing ordinance); (4) 'RGBl' stands for 'Reichsgesetzblatt' (Law Gazette of German Reich); (5) 'ZBl' stands for 'Zentralblatt für das Deutsche Reich' (Central Gazette of German Reich); (6) 'BGBl' stands for 'Bundesgesetzblatt' (Law Gazette of Federal Republic Germany); and (7) In column 'Date', the dates format DD-MM-YYYY is used.

- Reduction of accident insurance premia;
- Reduction of payment in case of early repayment of state-provided loans;
- Provision of housing allowances for tenants and home owners;
- Provision of subsidies and loans for housing expenses (*Aufwendungen*);
- Exemption from housing rationing;
- Exemption from rent controls; and
- Exemption from certain prescriptions regarding construction and land use.

Thus, incentives take the form of direct help from the government (loans, subsidies, guarantees), reduction of payments in favor of the state (taxes and fees), or exemption from certain rules imposed by the government (housing rationing, rent controls, land use rules).

Each incentive is represented as a binary variable. The fostering index is computed as a sum of all these binary variables, see upper panel of Figure 1.

4.1.2. Real federal-planned expenditure and guarantees

Between 1914 and 2006, federal laws and ordinances specifying the amount of the federal budget that could be spent on fostering the housing construction either in form of

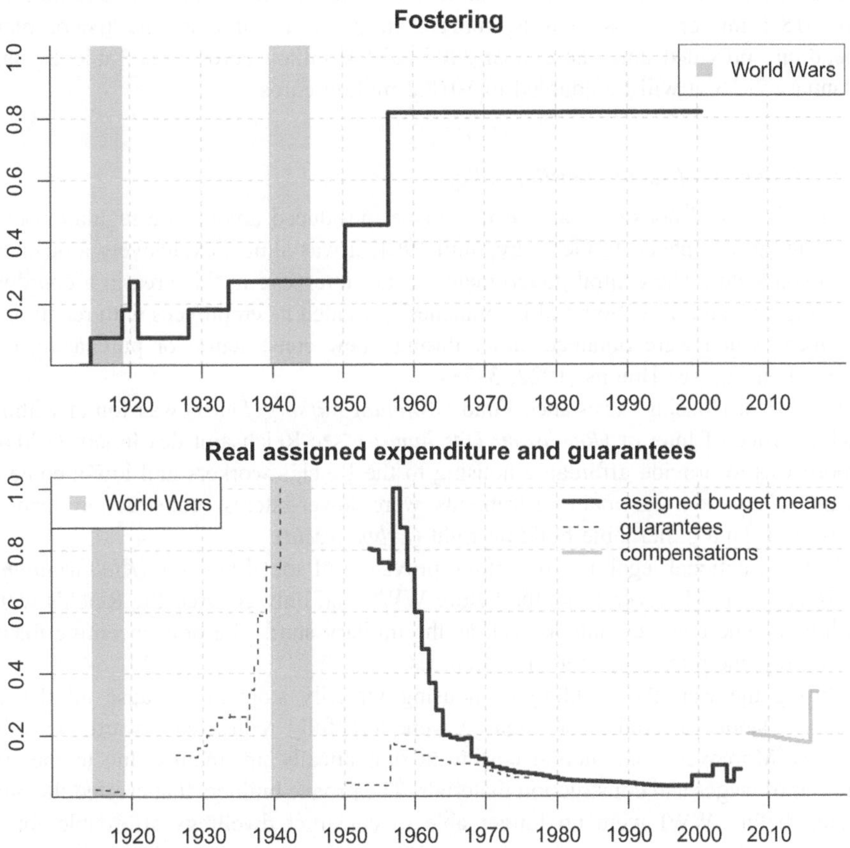

Figure 1. Indices of social housing policy, 1913–2015.

guarantees (*Bürgschaften*) or in form of direct financing (*Finanzierung*) were enacted. Federal states were obliged to complement central government aid with their own means. Often, they provided much more than required (e.g., Schmidthuysen 1928, 168).

Each time the amount of state aid was denominated in the currency that was in circulation in that period: Mark until 1918, Reichsmark between 1926 and 1948, Deutsche Mark between 1949 and 2001, and Euro thereafter. In order to create a comparable index of real-planned federal expenditure on housing construction, the nominal amounts are to be deflated by a corresponding construction cost. As such, we use the so-called recovery value (including the sales tax) of the housing buildings constructed in 1913/1914 (*Wiederherstellungswerte für 1913/1914 erstellte Wohngebäude einschließlich Umsatzsteuer*). It reflects the changes in construction cost over time.[5] The two big advantages of the deflator are that (1) it covers a long period of time between 1913 and 2014 with small interruptions in 1922–1923 (Hyperinflation) and 1948 (currency reform) and (2) it is expressed in the corresponding currency. The indices of real-planned federal expenditure and guarantees are obtained by dividing the nominal indices by the deflator and shown in the lower panel of Figure 1. The index of real guarantees is available from 1926 to 1976, while that of real-assigned means starts in 1953 and ends in 2005. The former attains its peak in 1940; the latter in 1953. Afterwards, both rapidly decline. Since 2007, formally, the central government does not cofinance social housing. However, it participates in its financing by providing compensation means (*Finanzierung beendeter Finanzhilfen*) on the interim basis to the federal states. In 2007, the compensation means were 518.2 million euros, that is, more than twice as large as the federal-planned expenditure provided until the end of 2005 (202.4 million euros), see Table 1. Starting in January 2016, it will be doubled to 1018.2 million euros.

4.1.3. *Evolution of social housing policy*

Historically, social housing was the first to be introduced among the regulation classes considered in this paper. In Germany, until 1901, it was almost exclusively a business of the federal states. The central government did not intervene in this area in a coordinated and comprehensive way. Some of its branches[6] provided its employees with rental or staff dwellings, which were obtained either through new construction or purchasing of the existing housing, see Brauns (1922, 3378).

In 1901, a Housing Assistance Fund (*Wohnungsfürsorgefonds*) was found within the Reich's Office of Interior (*Reichsamt Des Innern*), see Reichsamt des Innern (1904). Its purpose was to provide affordable housing to the Reich's workers and low-income civil servants (*Beamten*). Its main instruments were lower-interest construction loans and provision of land at heritable building right (*Erbbaurecht*).

The first national legal act concerning provision of social housing (*Kleinwohnungen*) was issued in 1914, several months before WWI, and only covered the Reich's workers and low-income civil servants as well as the military staff. The only incentive fostering housing was the provision of loan guarantees.

During the war, the building of housing virtually stopped, because all the spare resources (labor, materials, and money) were forcefully redirected toward the military purposes. Moreover, construction cost went dramatically up, mainly due to the strong increases of wages and construction materials. The private builders that erected the bulk of housing before WWI were no longer able to construct dwellings affordable for low-income households. Therefore, in August 1918, even before the end of the war, the central government extended its social housing policy to war disabled and widows of those who

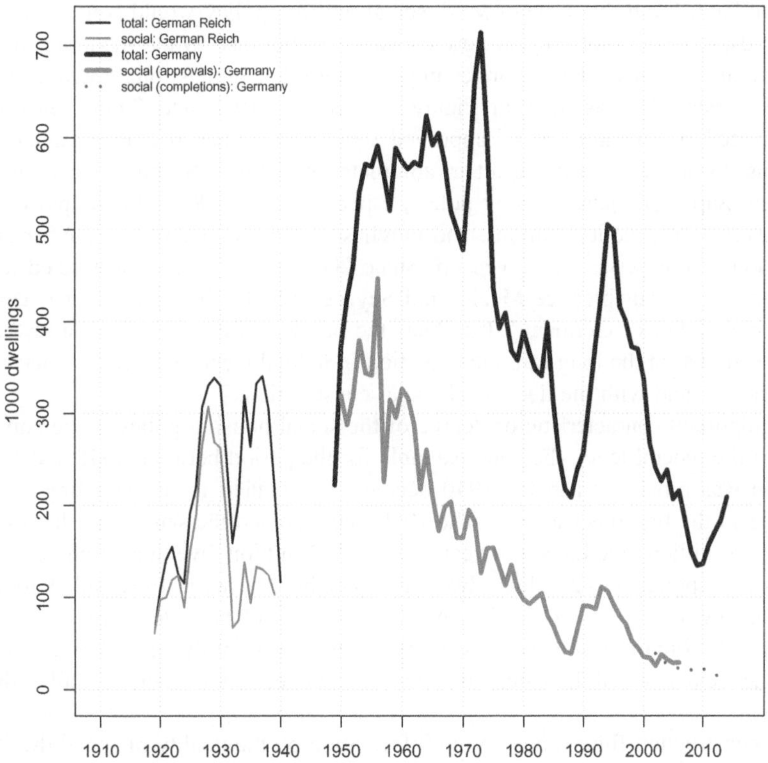

Figure 2. Social housing construction, 1913–2015.
Sources: (1) social housing construction 1919–1939 – Witt (1979), p. 403; (2) social housing construction 1950–2006 – Destatis.

perished in the war. Thus, for the first time, the German Government took the responsibility to provide housing beyond those in its employment.

In the first half of 1920s, due to hyperinflation, high reparation payments, and, last but not least, due to other housing market regulations, housing construction was extremely slow to recover, see Figure 2. Initially, the state aid took form of construction subsidies, state loans, and credit guarantees. The aid was provided by the central government, federal states, and municipalities. In some cases, federal laws determined the sharing of aid between the national and regional levels. Often, federal states by far exceeded the amount of help prescribed by federal laws, see Schmidthuysen (1928, 168). Since 1933, tax reductions were added as stimulus. In 1950, the provision of land at reasonable prices by the local authorities and exemption from housing rationing were introduced. In 1956, the list of incentives was substantially extended to include, in addition to the above-mentioned forms of help, the following ones: provision of premia for the savers of building societies; reduction of accident insurance premia; reduction of payment in case of early repayment of state-provided loans; and exemption from rent controls. By 1976, the exemption from rationing was no longer necessary, since this policy was reduced to a minimum. It was replaced by provision of state subsidies, covering in part the current expenditure of landlords, so that they would be able to keep low rents for social housing. In 2001, the social housing policy underwent a large reduction. Most of the incentives were canceled, leaving only four: (1) cheap loans; (2) subsidies; (3) credit guarantees; and

(4) cheap land. From that time onward, social housing policy would concentrate on poor households, extended not only to new construction but also to the modernization of the existing housing stock. These changes in policy correlate quite strongly with actual social housing construction, as seen in Figure 2. Between 1950 and 2006, construction is approximated by the number of approved dwellings. It has two disadvantages. First, approvals do not necessarily result in completed dwellings. Second, it does not reflect the entire output of social housing policy, especially after 2001. This output consists of new constructions, modernizations, and purchases of existing dwellings. After 2006, the publication of this series was given up. Since 2002, a new series constructed jointly by federal states is available; see Mezler and Seyfried (2010). In Figure 2, it is denoted as 'social (completions): Germany'. It reflects the number of completed social dwellings. It can be seen that, in the long run, the reduction in federal means devoted to social housing goes hand in hand with the decline of social construction.

An important characteristic of degree of the social housing policy is the construction plans. At the federal level, they are available for the period between 1940 and 1962. The first plan was proclaimed in the 1940 decree.[7] It provided for constructing 0.3 million dwellings in the first postwar year. The 1950 plan adopted the same goal: It was planned to build 1.8 million dwellings in 6 years, that is, 0.3 million dwellings each year. In 1953, the plan was upgraded to 2 million dwellings to be built between 1951 and 1956. In 1956, it was downgraded: Between 1957 and 1962, it was planned to construct 1.8 million dwellings. As Figure 2 shows, these targets were successfully met. Between 1950 and 1962, the actual social housing construction attained on average 323,000 dwellings annually.

The construction figures convey no information on the quality of social dwellings. In fact, between 1920 and 1985, the legally prescribed living standards in social housing (size and equipment) underwent major changes, as Table 2 shows. Stressed by the Great Depression, the authorities considered the social housing as dwellings for the poor that should be inexpensive in construction. Therefore, their size should be kept small and all 'unnecessary' facilities (such as individual bathrooms within dwellings) avoided. After WWII, social housing was seen as a solution for wide circles of population, not just the poor. Therefore, Germany adopted relatively high standards of social housing.

4.2. Protection from eviction

In Germany, like in many other war participating states,[8] tenant protection was introduced at the outbreak of WWI. As early as 1914, days after fighting started, a moratorium on litigation against active military personnel was imposed. Introduced initially as an interim measure, it turned out to be the most resilient one. In Germany, it remains in place, even in 2016.

The German federal regulations concerning the protection of tenants from eviction are presented in Table 3. The three main categories of this policy are:

- *Automatic prolongation of rental contracts* concluded for some definite period after their expiry.
- *Reasons to evict tenants*. Based on international comparisons, the following eviction reasons allowed by law are identified:
    - Tenant does not pay rent;
    - Tenant is unduly utilizing or misusing his dwelling in such a way as to endanger the dwelling or the whole building;

Table 2. Evolution of social housing standards.

Date	Size	Equipment
31 October 1918		Dwellings that, according to their size, alignment, number of rooms, height, and equipment (*Größ e, Anordnung, Raumzahl, Raumhöhe und Ausstattung*), meet typical for the location needs of low- and middle-income people, especially those of large families
01 October 1920	Living area: 70 m^2, in dwellings for families with children 80 m^2	Dwellings that, according to their size, alignment, number of rooms, height, and equipment, do not exceed necessary requirements
10 January 1931	Living area: 32–45 m^2, in dwellings for families with children 60 m^2	**Maximum equipment**: the equipment must facilitate the economical and simple housekeeping and avoid unnecessary expenses. The central community facilities (heating, hot water, provision, bath, laundry) are only allowed if they do not increase the charges to tenants. In order to reduce the cost and rent, providing dwellings with individual bathrooms must be given up. Otherwise, the equipment should correspond to the local habits. Laundries, cellars, and lofts (*Bodenräume*) are to be limited to the necessary extent
20 March 1931	Maximum useful living area is 90 m^2, including living and bedrooms as well as kitchen. Secondary rooms (*Nebenräume*) must be within locally typical standards	
26 October 1933	Useful area: (1) for rental social housing, it must not exceed 75 m^2; (2) for owner occupied housing, it must not exceed 150 m^2	
15 October 1940	Between 62 m^2 (3-room dwellings) and 86 m^2 (5-room dwellings)	Within 5 years following the war: (1) 80% of new dwellings will have a large kitchen and three bedrooms + shower room with separate WC + balcony; (2) 10% will have one room more and 10% one room less; (3) in all cases, there must be a dining room and a storeroom
24 May 1950	(1) for dwellings fostered through lower taxes: living area of 80 m^2 or 120 m^2 for large families; and (2) for dwellings built with state aid, the living area should be between 32 and 65 m^2. It can be smaller in dwellings for singles or larger in dwellings for big families	

(*Continued*)

Table 2. (Continued)

Date	Size	Equipment
27 June 1956	(1) family homes (*Familienheim*) with a single dwelling for owner – 120 m^2; (2) family homes with two dwellings – 160 m^2; (3) owner-occupied dwellings in condominiums – 120 m^2; (4) other dwellings – 85 m^2	**Minimum equipment**: cooking space, modern sanitary facilities inside the dwelling, fitted bathroom or furnished shower and sink, sufficient storage room, connection for oven, electric burners connection in all rooms, adequate storage or corresponding spare room, shared laundry room, and storage room for strollers and bicycles
24 August 1965	(1) family homes with a single dwelling – 130 m^2; (2) family homes with two dwellings – 180 m^2; (3) owner-occupied dwellings in condominiums – 120 m^2; and (4) other dwellings – 90 m^2	**Minimum equipment**: cooking space, modern sanitary facilities inside the dwelling, fitted bathroom or furnished shower and sink, sufficient storage room, connection for oven, electric burners connection in all rooms, adequate storage or corresponding spare room, shared laundry room, and storage room for strollers and bicycles
11 July 1985	(1) family homes with a single dwelling – 130 m^2; (2) family homes with two dwellings – 200 m^2; (3) owner-occupied dwellings in condominiums – 120 m^2; and (4) other dwellings – 90 m^2	**Minimum equipment**: No prescriptions for minimum equipment anymore
13 September 2001	The size of dwellings built with state aid should correspond to their purpose	

Note: In column 'Date', the dates format DD-MM-YYYY is used.

Table 3. Legislation on protection of tenants from eviction.

Date	Law title	Summary	Source
04 August 1914	G, betreffend den Schutz der infolge des Krieges an Wahrnehmung ihrer Rechte behinderten Personen	**Beneficiaries**: army members and military prisoners. Lawsuits against beneficiaries of the law are stopped. The limitation ends after the war is over.	RGBl, 328
15 December 1914	Bekanntmachung, betreffend Einigungsämter	Disputes between tenants and landlords, mortgage debtors and creditors are to be settled by arbitration councils (*Mieteinigungsamt*).	RGBl, 511
07 October 1915	Bekanntmachung über das Kündigungsschutz der Hintergebliebenen von Kriegsteilnehmern	**Beneficiaries**: family members of fallen war participants. They can terminate rental contracts on a statutory deadline. The termination cannot be opposed if continuation of rental contract would lead to a disproportionate detriment for the widow and heirs.	RGBl, 642
26 July 1917	Bekanntmachung zum Schutze der Mieter	Arbitration councils can decide upon a validity of rental contract termination by landlord and eventually order its prolongation. Their decisions are made at 'reasonable discretion' (*nach billigem Ermessen*), without any possibility of appeal. Arbitration councils consist in equal proportion of landlord and tenant representatives. **Expiry date**: the determination of expiry date is left by the Reich Chancellor.	RGBl, 659
23 September 1918	Bekanntmachung zum Schutze der Mieter	Arbitration councils can (1) decide upon a validity of rental contract termination by landlord and eventually order its prolongation for up to 1 year and (2) prolongate a non-terminated contract for up to 1 year. In areas with especially acute housing shortage, federal state authorities can order that (1) arbitration councils can prohibit contract termination, if its aim is to raise rent; and (2) contracts are prolongated for an indefinite time, if landlords terminated contracts without having informed the arbitration council. Arbitration council decisions are made at 'reasonable discretion', without any possibility of appeal. Arbitration councils consist in equal proportion of landlord and tenant representatives. **Expiry date**: the determination of expiry date is left by the Reich Chancellor.	RGBl, 1140

(*Continued*)

Table 3. (Continued)

Date	Law title	Summary	Source
01 June 1923	G über Mieterschutz und Mieteinigungsämter	Rental contact can be terminated on complaint from the landlord by a court judgment. **Termination reasons**: (1) if tenant is causing serious problems for either the landlord or other tenants (landlord can be required to compensate moving costs); (2) if tenant is unduly utilizing or misusing his dwelling in such a way as to endanger it or the whole building (landlord can be required to compensate moving costs); (3) if tenant, without landlord's permission, allows a third party to use his dwelling (landlord can be required to compensate moving costs); (4) if tenant had not paid rent for an excessive period of time; or (5) if landlord urgently needs the rented out dwelling and their refusal would constitute a serious injustice for the landlord. **Sphere of application**: (1) applicable also to subletting and (2) not applicable to housing constructed after 1 July 1918. **Expiry date**: The law expires at 1 July 1926.	RGBl, 353
30 June 1926	G über Mieterschutz und Mieteinigungsämter	Rental contact can be terminated on complaint from the landlord by a court judgment. **Termination reasons**: (1) if tenant is causing serious problems for either the landlord or other tenants (landlord can be required to compensate moving costs); (2) if tenant is unduly utilizing or misusing his dwelling in such a way as to endanger it or the whole building (landlord can be required to compensate moving costs); (3) if tenant, without landlord's permission, allows a third party to use his dwelling (landlord can be required to compensate moving costs); (4) if tenant had not paid rent for an excessive period of time; or (5) if landlord urgently needs the rented out dwelling and their refusal would constitute a serious injustice for the landlord. **Sphere of application**: (1) applicable also to subletting of housing; (2) not applicable to housing constructed after 1 July 1918; and (3) not applicable to dwelling obtained by dividing large vacant dwellings (5+ rooms). **Expiry date**: The law expires effective 1 July 1927.	RGBl, 347

(Continued)

Table 3. (Continued)

Date	Law title	Summary	Source
30 June 1927	G zur Verlängerung der Geltungsdauer des MieterschutzG und des ReichsmietenG	**Expiry date**: G über Mieterschutz und Mieteinigungsämter is prolongated through 31 December 1927.	RGBl, 131
24 December 1927	G zur Verlängerung des MieterschutzG und des ReichsmietenG	**Expiry date**: G über Mieterschutz und Mieteinigungsämter is prolongated through 28 February 1928.	RGBl, 513
17 February 1928	G über Mieterschutz und Mieteinigungsämter	Rental contact can be terminated on complaint from the landlord by a court judgment. **Termination reasons**: (1) if tenant is causing serious problems for either the landlord or other tenants (landlord can be required to compensate moving costs); (2) if tenant is unduly utilizing or misusing his dwelling in such a way as to endanger it or the whole building (landlord can be required to compensate moving costs); (3) if tenant, without landlord's permission, allows a third party to use his dwelling (landlord can be required to compensate moving costs); (4) if tenant had not paid rent for an excessive period of time; or (5) if landlord urgently needs the rented out dwelling and their refusal would constitute a serious injustice for the landlord. **Sphere of application**: (1) applicable also to subletting of housing; (2) not applicable to housing constructed after 1 July 1918; and (3) not applicable to dwelling obtained by dividing large vacant dwellings (5+ rooms). **Expiry date**: the law expires at 31 March 1930.	RGBl, 25
08 March 1930	G zur Verlängerung der Geltungsdauer des MieterschutzG	**Expiry date**: G über Mieterschutz und Mieteinigungsämter is prolongated through 30 June 1931.	RGBl, 32
02 December 1930	VO des Reichspräsidenten zur Sicherung von Wirtschaft und Finanzen	**Sphere of application**: not applicable to dwellings becoming vacant.	RGBl, 517
08 December 1931	4. VO zur Sicherung von Wirtschaft und Finanzen und zum Schutze des inneren Friedens	**Sphere of application**: not applicable to expensive dwellings (annual peacetime (*Jahresfriedensmiete*) rent not exceeding from 450 RM in small settlements (*Ortsklasse D*) to 1600 RM in Berlin). Arbitration councils make decisions without landlord and tenant representatives.	RGBl, 700

(*Continued*)

Table 3. (Continued)

Date	Law title	Summary	Source
27 April 1933	G über Mieterschutz und Mieteinigungsämter	Rental contact can be terminated on complaint from the landlord by a court judgment. **Termination reasons**: (1) if tenant is causing serious problems for either the landlord or other tenants (landlord can be required to compensate moving costs); (2) if tenant is unduly utilizing or misusing his dwelling in such a way as to endanger it or the whole building (landlord can be required to compensate moving costs); (3) if tenant, without landlord's permission, allows a third party to use his dwelling (landlord can be required to compensate moving costs); (4) if tenant had not paid rent for an excessive period of time; or (5) if landlord urgently needs the rented out dwelling and their refusal would constitute a serious injustice for the landlord (landlord may terminate, if he needs the dwelling for himself, provided that he owns the house for at least 3 years and does not occupy any dwelling in it). **Sphere of application**: (1) not applicable to subletting; (2) not applicable to housing constructed after 1 July 1918; (3) not applicable to dwellings obtained by dividing large vacant dwellings (5+ rooms); (4) not applicable to expensive dwellings (annual peacetime rent not exceeding from 450 RM in small settlements to 1600 RM in Berlin); and (5) not applicable to new contracts for vacant dwellings concluded after 31 March 1931. **Expiry date**: no expiry date anymore.	RGBl, 235
18 April 1936	G zur Änderung des Reichsmietengesetzes und des Mieterschutzgesetzes	**Sphere of application**: again applicable to vacant dwellings.	RGBl, 371

(*Continued*)

Table 3. (Continued)

Date	Law title	Summary	Source
04 December 1937	1. VO zur Ausführung der VO über Kündigungsschutz für Miet- und Pachträume	**Sphere of application**: (1) again applicable to housing constructed after 1 July 1918, but not applicable to housing built after 30 November 1937; (2) again applicable to dwellings obtained by dividing large vacant dwellings (5+ rooms); (3) tenant protection extended to newly built housing (*Neubauten oder durch Um- oder Einbauten neugeschaffene Räume, die nach dem 1. Juli 1918 bezugsfertig geworden sind*); and (4) applicable from 1 December 1937 for old housing that was completed before 1 July 1918 (*Altbauten*), if annual peacetime rent is below 1200 RM in large cities (*Ortsklasse A*), or, in Berlin, 1600 RM.	RGBl, 1325
31August 1938	2. VO zur Ausführung der VO über Kündigungsschutz für Miet- und Pachträume	**Sphere of application**: (1) not applicable to homesteads (*Kleinsiedlerstellen*); and (2) not applicable to some small cases involving non-profit housing cooperatives (gemeinnützige Wohnungsunternehmen in der Rechtsform der eingetragenen Genossenschft).	RGBl, 1070
30 April 1939	G über Mietverhältnisse mit Juden	**Sphere of application**: not applicable when tenants are Jewish, while landlords are not.	RGBl, 864
05 September 1939	3. VO zur Ausführung der VO über Kündigungsschutz für Miet- und Pachträume	**Sphere of application**: applicable in virtually all cases. **Termination reasons**: landlord may no longer terminate the rental contract, except if he needs the dwelling for himself, provided that he owns the house for at least 3 years and does not occupy any dwelling in it.	RGBl, 1670
14 August 1940	5. VO zur Ausführung der VO über Kündigungsschutz für Miet- und Pachträume	Tenant needs a permission from arbitration council to carry out a housing swap, that is, transfer of his dwelling to a third party (*Wohnungstausch*). **Termination reasons**: landlord may again terminate the rental contract, if he needs the dwelling for himself for military important purposes, provided that he owns the house for at least 3 years and does not occupy any dwelling in it.	RGBl, 1104
10 September 1942	VO zur Änderung und Ergänzung des G über Mietverhältnisse mit Juden	**Sphere of application**: (1) not applicable when tenants are Jewish, while landlords are not and (2) in Berlin, Munich, and Vienna, not applicable when tenants are Jewish, regardless of landlord's ethnicity.	RGBl, 1235

(*Continued*)

Table 3. (Continued)

Date	Law title	Summary	Source
15 December 1942	MieterschutzG	Rental contact can be terminated on complaint from the landlord by a court judgment. **Termination reasons**: (1) if tenant is causing serious problems for either the landlord or other tenants (landlord can be required to compensate moving costs); (2) if tenant is unduly utilizing or misusing his dwelling in such a way as to endanger it or the whole building (landlord can be required to compensate moving costs); (3) if tenant, without landlord's permission, allows a third party to use his dwelling (landlord can be required to compensate moving costs); (4) if tenant had not paid rent for an excessive period of time; or (5) if landlord urgently needs the rented out dwelling and their refusal would constitute a serious injustice for the landlord (landlord may terminate, if he needs the dwelling for himself for military important purposes, provided that he owns the house for at least 3 years and does not occupy any dwelling in it). **Sphere of application**: not applicable for subletting, if subtenant equipped his room with furniture and fixtures (*Einrichtungsgegenstände*). Tenant needs a permission from arbitration council to carry out a housing swap. The functions of arbitration councils are performed by local courts.	RGBl, 712
24 April 1950	1. WohnungsbauG	**Sphere of application**: not applicable to dwellings built after 31 December 1949 using tax reductions or without state help.	BGBl, 83
27 November 1951	VO über Ausnahmen vom Mieterschutz	**Sphere of application**: (1) not applicable to dwellings built between 20 June 1948 and 31 December 1949, without state loans or subsidies and (2) not applicable to rental commercial property.	BGBl, 926
31 March 1953	WohnraumberwirtschaftungsG	**Termination reasons**: (1) landlord needs the housing for his own purposes and the housing authority certifies that it will assign him the dwelling in question when it becomes vacant; (2) landlord plans to demolish the house damaged during the war and to build a new one; or (3) landlord of a temporary housing decides to rebuild it.	BGBl, 97

(*Continued*)

Table 3. (Continued)

Date	Law title	Summary	Source
23 June 1960	G über den Abbau der Wohnungszwangswirtschaft	**Termination reasons**: if renting prevents landlord from justified economic use of the land plot. **Sphere of application**: (1) not applicable to large dwellings (5+ rooms including kitchen in areas with 100,000 inhabitants; 6+ rooms with kitchen in areas with 100,000+ inhabitants; in houses with at most two dwellings, one of which being owner occupied); (2) not applicable to housing cooperatives; and (3) not applicable in all regions, where the ratio of households (one-person households are treated as a half household) to dwellings is greater than or equal to 1.03. The tenant protection in those areas should be eliminated no later than 31 December 1965. **Expiry date**: MieterschutzG expires effective 31 December 1965.	BGBl, 389
24 August 1965	G zur Änderung des Schluß termins für den Abbau der Wohnungszwangswirtschaft und für weitere Maßnahmen auf dem Gebiete des Mietpreisrechts	**Expiry date**: MieterschutzG expires effective 31 December 1967.	BGBl, 969
25 November 1971	G über den Kündigungsschutz für Mietverhältnisse über Wohnraum	**Termination reasons**: (1) tenant substantially violated his contractual obligations; (2) landlord needs the dwelling for himself or his relatives (in case of converting rental dwelling to owner one, this right can be executed only 3 years after purchase); or (3) renting prevents landlord from justified economic use of the land plot. **Sphere of application**: not applicable to housing rented for temporary use (*vorübergehender Gebrauch*) and (2) not applicable to housing equipped by landlord with furniture and fixtures and not let for a permanent use by a family.	BGBl, 1839

(*Continued*)

Table 3. (Continued)

Date	Law title	Summary	Source
18 December 1974	2. G über den Kündigungsschutz für Mietverhältnisse über Wohnraum	**Termination reasons**: (1) tenant substantially violated his contractual obligations; (2) landlord needs the dwelling for himself or his relatives (in case of converting rental dwelling to owner one, this right can be executed only 3 years after purchase); or (3) renting prevents landlord from justified economic use of the land plot. **Sphere of application**: not applicable to housing rented for temporary use; (2) not applicable to housing equipped by landlord with furniture and fixtures and not let for a permanent use by a family; and (3) not applicable to houses with at most two dwellings, one of which being owner occupied.	BGBl, 3603
17 May 1990	G zur Erleichterung des Wohnungsbaus im Planungs- und Baurecht sowie zur Änderung mietrechtlicher Vorschriften (Wohnungsbau-Erleichterungsgesetz – WoBauErlG)	**Termination reasons**: (1) tenant substantially violated his contractual obligations; (2) landlord needs the dwelling for himself or his relatives (in case of converting rental dwelling to owner one, this right can be executed only 3 years after purchase); or (3) renting prevents landlord from justified economic use of the land plot. **Sphere of application**: not applicable to housing rented for temporary use; (2) not applicable to housing equipped by landlord with furniture and fixtures and not let for a permanent use by a family; (3) not applicable to houses with at most two dwellings, one of which being owner occupied; and (4) not applicable to houses with three dwellings, where the landlord lives, when at least one dwelling was completed through upgrading (*Ausbau*) or extension (*Erweiterung*) between 31 May 1990 and 1 June 1995.	BGBl, 926
20 July 1990	G zur Verbesserung der Rechtsstellung des Mieters bei Begründung von Wohnungseigentum an vermieteten Wohnungen	**Termination reasons**: landlord needs the dwelling for himself or his relatives. In case of converting a rental dwelling to owner one, this right can be executed only 5 years after purchase. **Sphere of application**: in areas where sufficient supply of rental dwellings under reasonable conditions is particularly endangered.	BGBl, 1456

(*Continued*)

Table 3. (Continued)

Date	Law title	Summary	Source
22 April 1993	G zur Erleichterung von Investitionen und der Ausweisung und Bereitstellung von Wohnbauland (Investitionserleichterungs- und WohnbaulandG)	**Termination reasons**: landlord needs the dwelling for himself or his relatives. In case of converting a rental dwelling to the owner one, this right can be executed only up to 10 years after purchase. However, eviction will not take place, if it would represent an unjustified hardship for the tenant, unless he is provided by landlord with a reasonable dwelling (*angemessener Ersatzwohnraum*) under acceptable conditions. **Sphere of application**: in areas, where sufficient supply of rental dwellings under reasonable conditions is particularly endangered.	BGBl, 466
25 June 2001	G zur Neugliederung, Vereinfachung und Reform des Mietrechts (MietrechtsreformG)	**Termination reasons**: (1) tenant substantially violated his contractual obligations; (2) landlord needs the dwelling for himself or his relatives (in case of converting rental dwelling to owner one, this right can be executed only 3 years after conversion, in areas with insufficient supply of housing at reasonable conditions, this period is extended to 10 years); or (3) renting prevents landlord from justified economic use of the land plot. **Sphere of application**: not applicable to houses with at most two dwellings, one of which is owner occupied.	BGBl, 1149

Notes: (1) 'G' denotes 'Gesetz' (primary law); (2) 'VO' denotes 'Verordnung' (secondary law, or ordinance); (3) 'RGBl' stands for 'Reichsgesetzblatt' (Law Gazette of German Reich); (4) 'BGBl' stands for 'Bundesgesetzblatt' (Law Gazette of Federal Republic Germany); and (5) In column 'Date', the dates format DD-MM-YYYY is used.

  - Tenant modifies dwelling without landlord's permission/damages building;
  - Tenant sublets his dwelling without landlord's permission;
  - Tenant substantially violated his contractual obligations;
  - Tenant uses dwelling differently than agreed in the contract (converts dwelling to business premises);
  - Tenant transfers his dwelling to somebody else;
  - Tenant's business carried out in his dwelling is immoral or dangerous for the house;
  - Dwelling remains unoccupied more than 6 months during the year;
  - Tenant occupies two or more dwellings in the same settlement;
  - Tenant has a similar dwelling at his disposal;
  - Tenant charges excessive rent to subtenant;
  - Tenant causes serious problems for either the landlord or other tenants;
  - Tenant declines to recognize an officially permitted rent increase;
  - Majority of tenants request that the tenant be expelled from the house;
  - Landlord needs the dwelling for himself or his relatives;
  - Landlord plans to demolish the house in order to build a new one;
  - Landlord of temporary housing decides to rebuild it;
  - Landlord decides to build a new house even if the old one is not wreck;
  - Renting prevents landlord from justified economic use of the land plot;
  - Land plot is expropriated by the state; and
  - House is declared wreck;
- *Transfer of rental dwelling to tenant's relatives*:
  - After tenant's death and
  - During the lifetime of the tenant.

The index of the tenant protection policy is displayed in Figure 3. It shows three long waves of protection from eviction: (1) 1914–1933: (2) 1936–1965; (3) 1970 – present. In the first two cases, the increase in the intervention degree was dictated by catastrophic housing conditions caused by world wars. In the early 1970s, it was the coalition of social democrats and liberals that reintroduced regulations concerning the tenant eviction.[9] Apparently, this re-intensification of regulations made tenant protection an inevitable component of German social market economy.

4.3. Rationing of housing

Housing rationing policies played an important role in Germany throughout most of the twentieth century. This can be explained by the unprecedented scale of housing stock destructions and refugee inflow that Germany experienced in the course of two world wars. The policies can be grouped into the following six categories:

- *Registration of housing* implying the obligation of landlords to inform the local authorities about vacant dwellings in their buildings.
- *Preservation of housing* meaning that the demolishing of housing was prohibited; as was the conversion of dwellings to nonhousing uses (e.g., as offices or holiday apartments) or merging several dwellings into one.
- *Creation of housing* implies, unlike the new housing construction, the expansion of the existing housing through its reconstruction or reconversion from nonhousing uses. Paradoxically, it can be fostered by exempting the owners from some of the

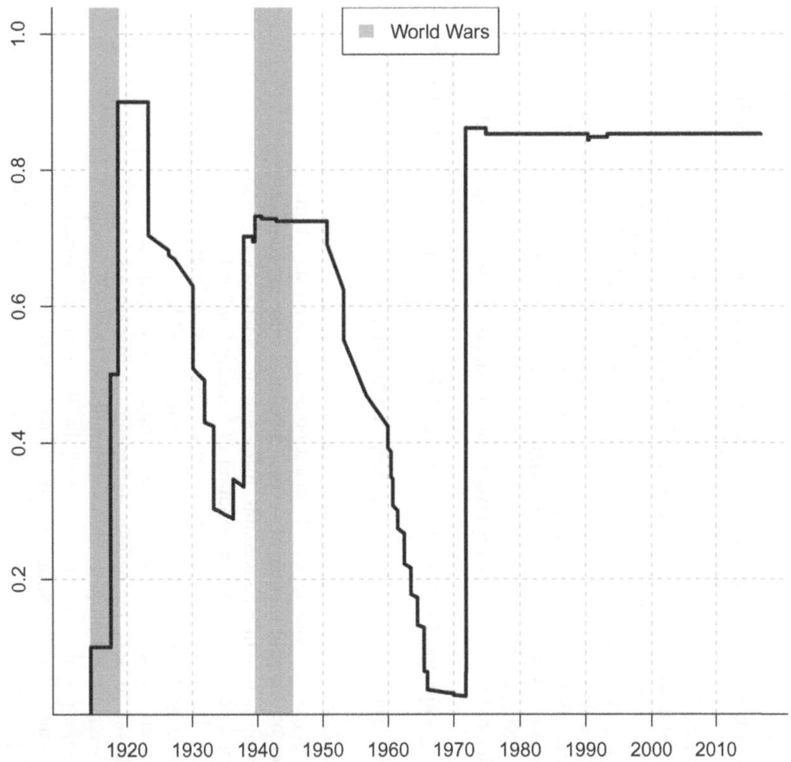

Figure 3. The index of tenant protection regulations, 1913–2015.

urban planning and construction standards. It can be carried out relatively quickly and does not require large investments.

- *Redistribution of housing* means a forceful assignment of tenants to the vacant or sometimes even underutilized housing. In the former case, the landlord is forced to accept tenant for vacant dwelling, while in the latter case, it is the principal tenant who must share his dwelling with subtenants assigned by the state to vacant rooms. The assignment of new tenants is often subject to certain ranking as a function of their needs (disabled, families with many children, refugees) or merits (military order bearers or participants of resistance to the Nazi regime).
- *Restrictions of freedom of movement*, which signifies hindering the immigration to and easing the outmigration from the areas with especially acute housing shortage.
- *Introduction of social conservation areas* (*soziale Erhaltungsgebiete*) implies a protection of a balanced social composition of population in particular urban areas. These policies are of a relatively recent origin. In Germany, they were introduced in 1976 and are popularly known as *Milieuschutz*.[10]

Table 4 lists German federal legal acts concerning the rationing of housing. Many of the laws trace general lines of regulation, while the details are to be determined at the level of federal states or even municipalities. Given a large number of regions in Germany, we confine ourselves as a rule to considering the federal legislation. However, since 1971, the subnational regulations are also taken into account.

Table 4. Legislation on rationing of housing.

Date	Law title	Summary	Source
23 September 1918	Bekanntmachung über Maß nahmen gegen Wohnungsmangel	Introduction of housing rationing in areas with acute housing shortage: (1) registration of vacant housing; (2) preservation (demolition and conversion of housing to other uses are prohibited); and (3) redistribution of housing (authorities can force landlords to lodge tenants or confiscate dwellings). **Expiry date**: the determination of expiry date is left by the Reich Chancellor.	RGBl, 1143
11 May 1920	G über Maß nahmen gegen Wohnungsmangel	Confirmation of the provisions of the 1918 Act and restriction of freedom of movement. **Expiry date**: the law expires on 30 September 1921.	RGBl, 949
11 July 1921	G, betreffend Verlängerung der Geltungsdauer des G über Maß nahmen gegen Wohnungsmangel	**Expiry date**: the 1920 Act is prolongated through 31 March 1922.	RGBl, 933
20 March 1922	G über Verlängerung der Geltungsdauer des WohnungsmangelG und der SammelheizungsVO	**Expiry date**: the 1920 Act is prolongated through 30 June 1922.	RGBl, 279
26 March 1923	G über Verlängerung der Geltungsdauer des WohnungsmangelG	**Expiry date**: the 1920 Act is prolongated through 30 June 1923.	RGBl, 217
28 July 1923	WohnungsmangelG	Introduction of housing rationing in areas with acute housing shortage: (1) registration of vacant housing; (2) preservation (demolition and merger of several dwellings into one require permission, while conversion of housing to other uses is prohibited); and (3) redistribution of housing (authorities can force landlords to lodge tenants or confiscate dwellings; displaced Germans and families with many children are to be preferred when provided with housing). Federal states are allowed to issue regulations restricting the freedom of movement and property rights of landlords. Dwelling swaps require permission. Newly created dwellings are not subject to rationing. **Expiry date**: no expiry date determined.	RGBl, 754
02 December 1930	VO des Reichspräsidenten zur Sicherung von Wirtschaft und Finanzen	**Expiry date**: elimination of housing rationing from 1 April 1934.	RGBl, 517

(*Continued*)

Table 4. (Continued)

Date	Law title	Summary	Source
08 December 1931	4. VO des Reichspräsidenten zur Sicherung von Wirtschaft und Finanzen und zum Schütze des inneren Friedens	**Sphere of application**: (1) not applicable to expensive dwellings (annual peacetime (*Jahresfriedensmiete*) rent not exceeding from 300 RM in small settlements (*Ortsklasse C und D*) to 800 RM in Berlin); (2) not applicable to dwellings of non-profit housing companies (*gemeinnützige Wohnungsunternehmen*); and (3) not applicable to company-owned (*Betrieb*) housing used to lodge employees. **Expiry date**: WohnungsmangelG expires effective 1 April 1933.	RGBl, 699
20 April 1939	Verordnung zur Erleichterung der Wohnungsbeschaffung für kinderreiche Familien	Registration of vacant dwellings and their provision to families with many children.	RGBl, 815
29 July 1941	VO über das Verbot der Umwandlung von Wohnungen in Räume anderer Art	Made conversion of housing to other uses subject to obtaining permission from the local authorities. It extended to the settlements with 10,000 and more inhabitants.	RGBl, 451
14 August 1942	VO über das Verbot der Zweckentfremdung von Wohnungen	Converting housing to other uses (offices, factories, warehouses) prohibited. It applies also to State and NSDAP bodies. **Expiry date**: The act expires on 31 December 1945.	RGBl, 545
27 February 1943	VO zur Wohnraumlenkung	Registration of housing. Creation of housing through reconstruction and expansion of existing buildings. Reconvertion of misused housing. Assignment of registered housing to the privileged persons. Hindering inmigration to and fostering outmigration from the territories with an acute housing shortage.	RGBl, 127
21 June 1943	VO zur Wohnraumversorgung der luftkriegsbetroffenen Bevölkerung	Registration of housing and its provision in the first place to those affected by bombing. Definition of underused dwellings. Expansion of existing dwellings. Utilization of misused dwellings.	RGBl, 355
08 March 1946	KontrollratsG Nr. 18 WohnungsG	Very similar to VO zur Wohnraumlenkung. Most difference concern the list of privileged persons.	

(*Continued*)

Table 4. (Continued)

Date	Law title	Summary	Source
24 April 1950	1. WohnungsbauG	**Sphere of application**: dwellings constructed after 31 December 1949 using tax reductions or without state help is freed from the rationing.	BGBl, 83
15 June 1950	G Nr. A – 9 der Alliierten Hohen Kommission	Restoration of the freedom of movement in West Germany.	ABl, 414
31 March 1953	WohnraumberwirtschaftungsG	**Regulations**: (1) registration of housing; (2) redistribution of vacant housing; (3) prohibition of housing misuse; and (4) conservation, creation, and improvement of housing. **Sphere of application**: (1) not applicable to dwellings built without any state aid and with tax reductions and (2) not applicable to dwellings built between 21 June 1948, and 31 December 1949, without state loans or subsidies.	BGBl, 97
3 June 1960	G über den Abbau der Wohnungszwangswirtschaft	**Regulations**: (1) registration of housing; (2) redistribution of vacant housing; (3) prohibition of housing misuse; and (4) conservation, creation, and improvement of housing. **Sphere of application**: (1) rationing is eliminated in all regions, where the ratio of households (one-person households are treated as a half household) to dwellings <1.03; (2) not applicable in large dwellings (5+ rooms including kitchen in communities with <100,000 inhabitants; 6+ rooms in communities with 100,000+ inhabitants); (3) not applicable in expensive dwellings (if in areas with population [0, 20,000) monthly rent exceeds 25–40 DM depending on number of rooms; in areas with population (20,000, 100,000) monthly rent exceeds 32.5–50 DM; in areas with population 100,000+ monthly rent exceeds 45–70 DM); (4) not applicable to dwellings in houses with no more than two dwellings, one being owner occupied; and (5) not applicable to dwellings in housing cooperatives. **Expiry date**: the rationing should be eliminated no later than 31 December 1965.	BGBl, 389

(*Continued*)

Table 4. (Continued)

Date	Law title	Summary	Source
24 August 1965	G zur Änderung des Schluß termins für den Abbau der Wohnungszwangswirtschaft und für weitere Maß nahmen auf dem Gebiete des Mietpreisrechts	**Expiry date**: postponement of the elimination of rationing through 31 December 1967.	BGBl, 969
04 November 1971	G zur Verbesserung des Mietrechts und zur Begrenzung des Mietanstiegs sowie zur Regelung von Ingenieur- und Architektenleistungen	Federal states are entitled to issue secondary legislation on the misuse of housing.	BGBl, 1745
18 August 1976	G zur Änderung des BundesbauG	Introduction of § 39 h '*Erhaltung baulicher Anlagen*'. The community can identify the social conservation areas, where the permission to demolish, reconstruct, or modify the building structure can be denied in order to preserve the social composition of the population of those territories, if it is necessary due to city planing reasons.	BGBl, 2221
08 December 1986	G über das BauGbuch	Introduction of § 172 '*Erhaltung baulicher Anlagen und der Eigenart von Gebieten*'. In social conservation areas, the demolition, reconstruction, and change in the use of dwellings require permission.	BGBl, 2191
18 August 1998	G zur Änderung des BauGbuchs und zur Neuregelung des Rechts der Raumordnung (Bau- und RaumordnungsG 1998 – BauROG)	In social conservation areas, the demolition, reconstruction (if above contemporary standards), change in the use of dwellings, and conversion of rental housing in condominiums require permission.	BGBl, 2081

Notes: (1) 'G' denotes 'Gesetz' (primary law); (2) 'VO' denotes 'Verordnung' (secondary law, or ordinance); (3) 'RGBl' stands for 'Reichsgesetzblatt' (Law Gazette of German Reich); (4) 'BGBl' stands for 'Bundesgesetzblatt' (Law Gazette of Federal Republic Germany); (5) 'ABl' stands for 'Amtsblatt der Alliierten Hohen Kommission' (Law Gazette of Allied High Commission); and (6) In column 'Date', the dates format DD-MM-YYYY is used.

4.3.1. Prohibition of housing misuse

In 1971, the authority to prohibit the misuse of housing (*Zweckentfremdungsverbot von Wohnraum*) was delegated to federal states. They obtained the right to issue secondary legislation acts (ordinances or *Rechtsverordnungen*) to determine the regions – typically entire cities or rural districts – with insufficient provision of affordable housing and prohibit the misuse of housing, see Table 5. While in some federal states, like Bavaria and Schleswig-Holstein, the state-level ordinances contain exact lists of the corresponding areas, other states, like Baden-Württemberg and Hesse, delegate the right to introduce prohibitions to the municipalities themselves. Since 2006, under the framework of the federalism reform, federal states, or Bundesländer, are entitled to enact their own laws (*Gesetz*) prohibiting housing misuse.[11] Between 1971 and 2015, the regulations at the subnational level underwent several major changes. Starting in the early 1970s, many federal states of West Germany took advantage of these regulations. In the first half of the 1990s, after reunification, East German federal states followed their example. However, by the beginning of the 2000s, experiencing excess housing supply, the regulations were given up in most states. Nevertheless, since the late 2000s, when housing rents and prices started to rise again, the interdiction to use dwellings for nonhousing purposes has been reintroduced in many federal states (e.g., Baden-Württemberg, Berlin, North Rhine-Westfalia). Therefore, for the 1971–2015 period, an index of housing misuse prohibition is constructed based on the regulations adopted by individual federal states. For each state, a regulation dummy variable is created. The national index is a weighted average of these dummies, where the weights are the respective shares of the federal states in German housing stock as of 2013. The resulting index is displayed in the upper panel of Figure 4. The weights vary a lot: between 1.2% of national housing stock for Saarland and 15.0% for Bavaria. The black vertical line shows the timing of the federal law that introduced the prohibition of housing misuse.

4.3.2. Social conservation areas

The policy of conserving social composition of urban areas is motivated by the fear of gentrification. The policy makers are afraid that due to improvements in the quality standards of housing in certain neighborhoods, rents will rise. Hence, lower-income inhabitants will eventually be forced to move out from their usual environment (*Milieu*), only to be replaced with higher-income inhabitants. As a result, the social structure of those neighborhoods will undergo dramatic changes. In the long run, this is expected to lead to a segregation by income level and possibly by ethnicity, given that both are often correlated. Moreover, the intra-city migrations can lead to geographical shifts in demand for social infrastructure, thus, raising the monetary cost of the process.

These policies are of a relatively recent origin. In Germany, they were introduced in 1976 and are popularly known as *Milieuschutz*. Their general purpose is to prevent social transformation through conservation of the housing stock. They are also assumed to address the issue of a shortage of cheap rental dwellings by preventing their transition to upper-end market segments. This goal can be achieved using a variety of regulations.

The first group of these regulations overlaps with that of prohibiting the misuse of housing. In particular, both prohibit demolition (*Abriss* or *Rückbau*, since 1976) and conversion of dwellings to nonhousing purposes (*Nutzungsänderung*, since 1986).

The second group of regulations concentrates on reconstruction of housing (*Änderung der baulichen Anlagen*, since 1976). The notion of reconstruction implies

Table 5. Regional legislation on prohibition of housing misuse.

Bundesland	Law title	Action	Date
Baden-Württemberg	7. VO der Landesregierung über das Verbot der Zweckentfremdung von Wohnraum	Introduction	11 December 2001
Baden-Württemberg	Not prolongated	Removal	31 December 2006
Baden-Württemberg	G über das Verbot der Zweckentfremdung von Wohnraum	Introduction	19 December 2013
Bavaria	1. VO über das Verbot der Zweckentfremdung von Wohnraum	Introduction	01 January 1972
Bavaria	2. VO über das Verbot der Zweckentfremdung von Wohnraum	Introduction	27 March 1972
Bavaria	VO	Introduction	05 December 1989
Bavaria	VO über das Verbot der Zweckentfremdung von Wohnraum	Introduction	28 July 1992
Bavaria	2. VO zur Änderung der VO über das Verbot der Zweckentfremdung von Wohnraum	Introduction	22 July 1997
Bavaria	G über das Verbot der Zweckentfremdung von Wohnraum	Introduction	01 January 2009
Bavaria	G zur Änderung des ZwEWG	Prolongation	22 March 2013
Berlin	VO über das Verbot der Zweckentfremdung von Wohnraum	Introduction	09 February 1973
Berlin	WoZwEntfrV	Introduction	18 December 1984
Berlin	G zur Beseitigung der Zweckentfremdung von Wohnraum	Introduction	08 March 1990
Berlin	1. G zur Rechtsvereinfachung und Entbürokratisierung	Removal	17 December 2003
Berlin	G über das Verbot der Zweckentfremdung von Wohnraum	Introduction	29 November 2013
Berlin	VO über das Verbot der Zweckentfremdung von Wohnraum	Introduction	04 March 2014
Brandenburg	Zweckentfremdungsverbot-VO	Introduction	10 February 1993
Brandenburg	G	Introduction	22 December 1997
Brandenburg	2. VO über das Verbot der Zweckentfremdung von Wohnraum	Introduction	11 March 1998
Brandenburg	VO zur Aufhebung landesrechtlicher Vorschriften auf dem Gebiet des Wohnungs- und Mietrechts	Removal	28 December 2000
Bremen	VO über das Verbot der Zweckentfremdung von Wohnraum	Introduction	24 September 1979
Bremen	Aufhebung von ZweVO	Removal	31 December 1998
Hamburg	VO über das Verbot der Zweckentfremdung von Wohnraum	Introduction	07 December 1971
Hamburg	G über den Schutz und die Erhaltung von Wohnraum	Introduction	08 March 1982
Hesse	1. Hessische VO über das Verbot der Zweckentfremdung von Wohnraum	Introduction	25 January 1972
Hesse	WoZwEntfrVO	Introduction	10 January 1991
Hesse	VO zur Aufhebung des Verbots der Zweckentfremdung von Wohnraum	Removal	27 May 2004

(*Continued*)

Table 5. (Continued)

Bundesland	Law title	Action	Date
Mecklenburg-Vorpommern	G zur Ãœbertragung der Aufgaben nach Artikel 6 des G zur Verbesserung des Mietrechts und zur Begrenzung des Mietanstiegs sowie zur Regelung von Ingenieur- und Architektenleistungen	Introduction	25 June 1996
Mecklenburg-Vorpommern	Aufhebung der ZweVO	Removal	29 May 2004
Lower Saxony	VO über das Verbot der Zweckentfremdung von Wohnraum	Introduction	20 March 1991
Lower Saxony	not prolongated	Removal	01 January 2004
North Rhine-Westphalia	G zur Erhaltung und Pflege von Wohnraum für das Land Nordrhein-Westfalen	Introduction	06 November 1984
North Rhine-Westphalia	Verbot der Zweckentfremdung von Wohnraum	Introduction	12 June 2001
North Rhine-Westphalia	Verbot der Zweckentfremdung von Wohnraum	Introduction	27 September 2001
North Rhine-Westphalia	Aufhebung der ZweVO	Removal	01 January 2007
North Rhine-Westphalia	WohnungsaufsichtsG	Introduction	10 April 2014
Rhineland-Palatinate	LandesVO über das Verbot der Zweckentfremdung	Introduction	29 June 1993
Rhineland-Palatinate	LandesVO	Introduction	02 July 1996
Rhineland-Palatinate	not prolongated	Removal	31 July 1999
Saxony	VO über das Verbot der Zweckentfremdung von Wohnraum	Introduction	12 December 1996
Saxony	not prolongated	Removal	31 December 1998
Saxony-Anhalt	LandesVO zur Änderung der LandesVO über das Verbot der Zweckentfremdung von Wohnraum	Introduction	15 March 1993
Saxony-Anhalt	VO über das Verbot der Zweckentfremdung von Wohnraum	Introduction	17 January 1996
Saxony-Anhalt	VO zur Aufhebung der VO über das Verbot der Zweckentfremdung von Wohnraum	Removal	01 June 1999
Schleswig-Holstein	LandesVO über das Verbot der Zweckentfremdung von Wohnraum	Introduction	14 March 1990
Schleswig-Holstein	VO	Prolongation	14 October 1994
Schleswig-Holstein	not prolongated	Removal	31 December 1999
Thuringia	Thüringer VO über die Genehmigungspflicht der Zweckentfremdung von Wohnraum	Introduction	11 May 1992

Notes: (1) 'G' denotes 'Gesetz' (primary law); (2) 'VO' denotes 'Verordnung' (secondary law, or ordinance); (3) In column 'Date', the dates format DD-MM-YYYY is used.

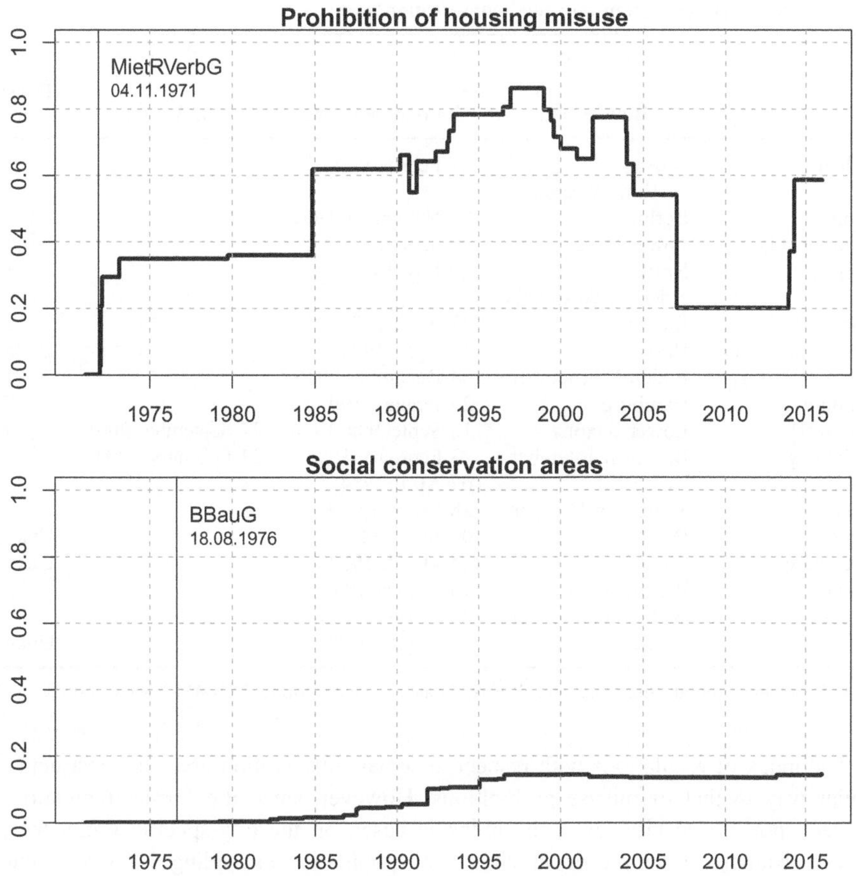

Figure 4. Indices of Bundesland-specific prohibitions of housing misuse and of city-specific regulations of social conservation areas, 1971–2015.

both, merger of dwellings and modernization. Initially, any modernization could be subject to prohibition in social conservation areas. Since 1998, only modernization above some average contemporary housing standards requires permission. Whereas modernizations that upgrade housing to the average level can be tolerated, those exceeding this level are treated as threatening the social composition of the neighborhood. Nationally, there is not a general valid list of such modernizations. Therefore, the local average standard can be used as a benchmark, where local can mean both federal state and the neighborhood. Alternatively, minimum housing construction standards (*bauordnungsrechtliche Mindestanforderung*) can be used as a threshold (see Geβner 2008, 30). In fact, each local authority compiles its own list. Examples of such modernizations include adding an elevator, construction of a second balcony or terrace, and installation of a floor heating or chimney.[12]

The third group of regulations intends to prevent the conversion of rental dwellings into the owner occupied ones and of rental houses into condominiums (*Gründung von Sondereigentum*, since 1998). This group was the latest to be imposed.

Unlike prohibitions of housing misuse, the regulation on social conservation areas covers relatively small neighborhoods rather than entire cities.

Table 6. Regional legislation on social conservation areas.

City	Bundesland	Introduction date	Removal date	Number of protected areas
Aachen	North Rhine-Westphalia	28 February 1993		1
Berlin	Berlin	07 November 1991		22
Braunschweig	Lower Saxony	20 September		1
Cologne	North Rhine-Westphalia	20 July 1996		1
Erlangen	Bavaria	07 April 1989		1
Frankfurt am Main	Hesse	17 April 1990		Unknown
Freiburg (Breisgau)	Baden-Württemberg	04 December 2015		1
Hamburg	Hamburg	23 January 1995		7
Hannover	Lower Saxony	18 September 1986	27 September 2001	4
Heidelberg	Baden-Württemberg	23 February 1996	22 February 2004	1
Kassel	Hesse	07 April 1984		2
Lübeck	Schleswig-Holstein	28 February 1979		2
Munich	Bavaria	01 July 1987		Unknown
Nuremberg	Bavaria	24 March 1982		Unknown
Potsdam	Brandenburg	10 August 1992		3
Stuttgart	Baden-Württemberg	28 February 2013		Unknown
Wiesbaden	Hesse	15 August 1987		Unknown

Notes: In columns 'Introduction date' and 'Removal date', the dates format DD-MM-YYYY is used.

The index of regulations with respect to social conservation areas is constructed in a similar way to that of misuse prohibitions. However, since the former regulations are decided upon at the city level, the index is based on the city-specific ordinances, see Table 6. Namely, a sample of 71 cities with population exceeding 100,000 is chosen. These include more than 32% of the total housing stock of Germany and about 30% of population. The corresponding official body in each city was contacted to request information about social conservation areas. If at least one such an area is available, a binary variable is created for the respective city, taking the value of 1 from the period when the regulation came in force onward. The nationwide index is computed based on the city-specific binary variables as a weighted average. The weights correspond to the share of the respective city in the total German housing stock as of 2011. Thus, the resulting index rather represents the lower bound of regulations, since it is based on a subsample of German urban settlements. However, it can be safely assumed that social conservation areas are unlikely to exist in smaller towns. The index is depicted in the lower panel of Figure 4. Between 1971 and 2015, there were 17 cities with social conservation areas. The average size of these cities (over 690,729 persons) is much larger than that of all 71 cities in the sample (343,340 persons). To the best of our knowledge, as of 2016, only two cities – Hannover and Heidelberg – have rescinded social conservation regulations.

4.3.3. Evolution of housing rationing

The index of housing rationing regulations is largely based on the federal legal acts. Each of the six groups has an equal weight. For each group, a dummy variable is constructed. The overall index of housing rationing is the sum of the corresponding dummy variables

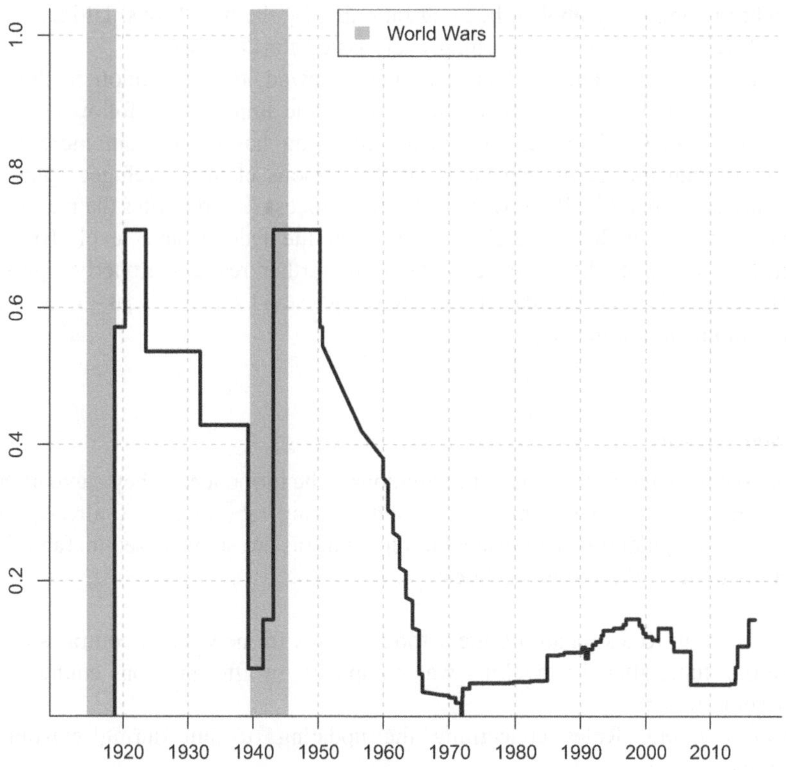

Figure 5. The index of housing rationing regulations, 1913–2015.

and is scaled so to vary between 0 (no state intervention) and 10 (maximum state intervention). The index is shown in Figure 5. In addition, the figure highlights the world wars (shaded areas), which are strongly linked to the introduction or reactivation of housing rationing.

It should be noted that rationing of housing contains not only very weak forms (e.g., registration, where landlords have to inform about vacant dwellings) but also the forceful redistribution of housing. Therefore, it should be said that the index controls rather for the share of dwellings affected than not for the intensity of regulation.

The first German housing rationing act was issued during WWI on 23 September 1918. It was a cornerstone for the state intervention into the property rights of landlords. It contained the first four elements of housing rationing, namely: registration, preservation, creation, and redistribution of housing. In 1920, the possibility of restricting the freedom of movement was also provided for.

The rationing of housing was gradually abolished through 1934. Thus, it took 16 years to dismantle the corresponding regulations. Nevertheless, the period without state intervention was very short. The outbreak of WWII led to reintroduction of the rationing of housing, as seen in Figure 5.

The housing shortage after WWII was huge. Due to the regulations imposed before war, market forces were switched off. Hence, the government was obliged to keep a firm grip on the existing housing stock. It was only in 1960 that a federal law was promulgated that sought to completely abolish housing rationing by the mid-1960s. Ultimately, it was only in 1967; thus, the second rationing cycle lasted for 28 years.

Only a few years later, in 1971, the state renewed its intervention in the housing market. Its magnitude was well below that during and immediately following the world wars. Since 2010, the intensity of housing rationing has been again increasing. The growth of foreign migration, especially of the persons claiming refugee status, which dramatically accelerated in 2015, will bolster this process. Shortly after the massive influx of refugees started in 2015, legislative efforts at the federal state level (Bremen and Hamburg) were triggered.[13] The objective is to further restrain property rights of the landlords, so that the state can easier allocate refugees and socially weak German citizens to the becoming scarce housing.

4.4. Rent controls

Rent controls were the fourth class of regulations to be introduced. They came after WWI, when social housing, tenants' protection, and housing rationing were already in place. German federal regulations with respect to rent controls are summarized in Table 7. These are quantified along the following lines:

- *Rent setting*: Rules regarding the setting of rents for new rental contracts (either for the first time, after the dwelling was completed, or after previous contract finished by some reason).
- *Rent updating*: Rules concerning the updating of rent during existing rental contracts.
- *Sphere of application*: Segments of the market that are free from regulations (e.g., large, expensive, newly constructed dwellings, or housing in certain regions).
- *Expiry date*: Date, at which regulations are planned to be abolished. In many cases, shortly before this date, these are prolongated.

For rent setting and updating, binary variables are constructed. The index of rent controls is computed using Equation (3), with sphere of application as a time-varying weight, w_{it}.

4.4.1. Capping limit and rental brake

For two recent regulations – the capping limit (*Kappungsgrenze*) and the rental brake (*Mietpreisbremse*) – instead of using simple nationwide binary variables, weighted averages of region-specific dummy variables are used. The latter are defined for the lowest administrative level, that is, municipalities (*Gemeinden*).

The capping limit was first introduced in 1982, see Table 7. It represents a cap on updating the rent within an existing contract. Initially, it was allowed to raise rent at most by 30% within 3 years, which corresponds to 9.1% annually. In 1993, the limit was lowered to 20% within 3 years (6.3% in a year). Finally, in 2013, the federal states were empowered to determine areas, where a sufficient supply of rental dwellings under reasonable conditions is particularly endangered (*wenn die ausreichende Versorgung der Bevölkerung mit Mietwohnungen zu angemessenen Bedingungen in einer Gemeinde oder einem Teil einer Gemeinde besonders gefährdet ist*) and where the capping limit could be further lowered to 15% rent increase within 3 years (4.8% annually). Thus, it generated a possibility for region-specific capping limits. Since then, 11 out of 16 German federal

Table 7. Legislation on rent controls.

Date	Law title	Summary	Source
24 March 1922	ReichsmietenG	**Rent setting**: (1) existing contracts: rent fixed at peacetime level (*Friedensmiete*) on 1 July 1914; (2) new contracts: rent fixed on 1 July 1914 level of comparable rents (*ortsüblicher Mietzins*), which are observed for dwellings in the same area, with the same type and location; and (3) contracts for housing completed between 1 July 1914 and 30 June 1918: peacetime rent updated by change in construction cost. Basis rent (*Grundmiete*): interest + operating cost (*Betriebskosten*: taxes, public charges, insurance fees, administrative costs, etc.) + maintenance cost. **Sphere of application**: not applicable to new housing, that is, dwellings obtained after 1 July 1918 through new construction (*Neubauten*), reconstruction (*Umbauten*), and fixture (*Einbauten*).	RGBl, 273
10 July 1926	G zur Änderung des ReichsmietenG	**Rent updating**: in case of modernization (*bauliche Veränderungen*) increasing the practical value of housing (*Gebrauchswert*), tenants can be charged a higher rent (*Zusatzmiete*) to cover reasonable interest and repayment of principal.	RGBl, 403
11 March 1927	VO über Festsetzung einer Mindesthöhe der gesetzlichen Miete	**Rent updating**: From 1 April 1927, legal rent (*gesetzliche Miete*) is 110% of peacetime rent; from 1 October 1927, it is 120% of peacetime rent.	RGBl, 72
30 June 1927	G zur Verlängerung des MieterschutzG und des ReichsmietenG	**Expiry date**: ReichsmietenG is prolongated through 31 December 1927.	RGBl, 131
24 December 1927	G zur Verlängerung des MieterschutzG und des ReichsmietenG	**Expiry date**: ReichsmietenG is prolongated through 28 February 1928.	RGBl, 513
20 February 1928	ReichsmietenG	**Rent setting**: (1) existing contracts: rent fixed as a percentage of peacetime rent; (2) new contracts: rent fixed at 1 July 1914 level of comparable rents, which are observed for dwellings in the same area, with the same type and location; and (3) contracts for housing completed between 1 July 1914 and 30 June 1918: peacetime rent updated by change in construction cost. Rent should cover interest for borrowed and own capital + operating cost + maintenance cost. **Rent updating**: in case of modernization increasing the practical value of housing, tenants can be charged a higher rent to cover reasonable interest and repayment of principal. **Sphere of application**: (1) not applicable to housing completed after 1 July 1918; (2) not applicable to dwellings obtained by dividing large vacant dwellings (5+ rooms); (3) not applicable to dwellings obtained from vacant commercial properties; (4) not applicable to state-owned housing; (5) not applicable to dwellings of nonprofit housing companies providing cheap housing to poor people; and (6) not applicable to large dwellings (at least six rooms without kitchen, storeroom, and maid's chamber with at least 100 m^2 living space) becoming vacant after 31 March 1928, if contract duration >2 years. **Expiry date**: 31 March 1930.	RGBl, 38

(*Continued*)

Table 7. (Continued)

Date	Law title	Summary	Source
08 March 1930	G zur Verlängerung der Geltungsdauer des ReichsmietenG	**Expiry date**: ReichsmietenG is prolongated through 30 June 1931.	RGBl, 32
02 December 1930	VO des Reichspräsidenten zur Sicherung von Wirtschaft und Finanzen	**Sphere of application**: not applicable to dwellings of nonprofit housing companies (*gemeinnützige Wohnungsunternehmen*). **Expiry date**: ReichsmietenG is prolongated through 1 April 1936.	RGBl, 517
08 December 1931	4. VO des Reichspräsidenten zur Sicherung von Wirtschaft und Finanzen und zum Schütze des inneren Friedens	**Rent setting**: (1) old housing: from 1 January 1932, on, legal rent is decreased by 10% of peacetime rent and (2) new housing (built after 1 July 1918): from 1 January 1932, on, rent decreases proportionally to the officially prescribed interest rate decrease. **Sphere of application**: (1) not applicable to housing completed after 1 July 1918, also through division (*Teilung*) and conversion from commercial property; (2) not applicable to subletting; (3) not applicable to expensive dwellings (annual peacetime (*Jahresfriedensmiete*) rent not exceeding from 450 RM in small settlements (*Ortsklasse D*) to 1600 RM in Berlin); and (4) not applicable to rental commercial properties. **Expiry date**: ReichsmietenG is prolongated through 1 April 1933.	RGBl, 699
18 April 1936	G zur Änderung des ReichsmietenG und des MieterschutzG	**Rent setting**: (1) existing contracts: rent fixed as a percentage of peacetime rent; (2) new contracts: rent fixed on 1 July 1914, level of comparable rents, which are observed for dwellings in the same area, with the same type and location; and (3) contracts for housing completed between 1 July 1914, and 30 June 1918: peacetime rent updated by change in construction cost. Rent should cover interest for borrowed and own capital + operating cost + maintenance cost. **Rent updating**: in case of modernization increasing the practical value of housing, tenants can be charged a higher rent to cover reasonable interest and repayment of principal. **Sphere of application**: (1) not applicable to housing completed after 1 July 1918; (2) not applicable to dwellings obtained through division and conversion from commercial property after 1 July 1918; (3) not applicable to state-owned dwellings; (4) not applicable to dwellings of nonprofit housing companies; (5) not applicable to rental commercial properties; (6) not applicable to subletting; (7) not applicable to dwellings that are temporary let for special purposes; and (8) not applicable to dwellings where landlord is employer and tenant is employee. **Expiry date**: no expiry date anymore.	RGBl, 371

(Continued)

Table 7. (Continued)

Date	Law title	Summary	Source
26 November 1936	VO über das Verbot von Preiserhöhungen	**Rent updating**: (1) rent increases are forbidden. Higher than the legal rent cannot be negotiated. If the rent on 18 October 1936 was higher than the legal rent, it will be set back to the legal level when new rental contract is concluded; (2) new contracts: rent fixed on 18 October 1936 level; (3) modernization cost can be charged to tenants; and (4) increases in legal or contractual burdens imposed on landlord and occurring after 18 October 1936, can be charged to tenants. **Sphere of application**: unchanged compared to ReichsmietenG of 1936.	RGBl, 955
24 April 1950	1. WohnungsbauG	**Rent setting**: (1) for dwellings built after 31 December 1949, using tax reductions, at most a rent covering costs can be set (*Kostenmiete*) and (2) for dwellings built after 31 December 1949 without state help, rent can be set without limitations (*Marktmiete*). **Sphere of application**: not applicable to dwellings built after 31 December 1949 using tax reductions or without state help.	BGBl, 83
29 November 1951	VO PR Nr. 71/51 über Maß nahmen auf dem Gebiete des Mietpreisrechts	**Rent setting**: (1) for dwellings built up to 17 October 1936, the rent cannot be lower than the rent that existed at that time (reference date rent or *Stichtagsmiete*); (2) for dwellings built between 18 October 1936 and 8 September 1945, without state aid (loans or subsidies), the rent is determined by actual construction cost, but at most 110% of comparable construction cost as of 17 October 1936; (3) for dwellings built between 9 May 1945 and 20 July 1948 without state aid, the rent is set at 110% of rent for comparable housing as of 17 October 1936; (4) for dwellings built between 20 June 1948 and 31 December 1949, without state aid, the rent is determined by profitability calculation (*Ertragsberechnung*) accounting for construction and exploitation costs, but at most 150% of rent for comparable newly built dwellings as of 17 October 1936; (5) for dwellings built after 31 December 1949, with tax reductions, the reference date is set; and (6) for dwellings built after 31 December 1949 with state aid, the reference date is set. **Rent updating**: for dwellings built up to 17 October 1936, if the rent is lower than typical local rent (*ortsübliche Miete*) for dwellings of the same type, location, and equipment, then the price setting authorities can allow its updating to the customary local level. **Sphere of application**: not applicable to dwellings built between 20 June 1948 and 31 December 1949 without state aid.	BGBl, 920

(*Continued*)

Table 7. (Continued)

Date	Law title	Summary	Source
27 July 1955	G über Maß nahmen auf dem Gebiete des Mietpreisrechts (1. BundesmietenG)	**Rent updating**: (1) existing contracts: for dwellings built before 20 June 1948, the rent may be raised by 10%. Additionally, it can be raised by up to 15% depending on their equipment (e.g., bath, water heating, cellar, and central heating); (2) new contracts: for dwellings built before 20 June 1948, the newly negotiated rent may be raised to up to 133.33% of the rent allowed by price setting legislation (*preisrechtlich zulässige Miete*); (3) for dwellings built between 20 June 1948 and 31 December 1949, with state aid, the rent may be raised to cover current expenses (*laufende Aufwendungen, Kostenmiete*); and (4) for dwellings freed from rent controls, rent increases are limited from above by a reasonably raised rent (cost covering rent). **Sphere of application**: not applicable to dwellings built between 20 June 1948 and 31 December 1949, without state aid.	BGBl, 458
27 June 1956	2. WohnungsbauG (Wohnungsbau- und FamilienheimG)	**Rent setting**: (1) for dwellings built with state aid, the rent can be set to cover current expenses; (2) for dwellings built with tax reductions, the rent may be set freely but not exceed the level covering current expenses; and (3) for dwellings built without state aid, the rent can be set freely.	BGBl, 523
23 June 1960	G über den Abbau der Wohnungszwangswirtschaft	**Rent updating**: (1) existing contracts: for dwellings built before 20 June 1948, the rent may be raised by 15%. Additionally, it can be raised up to certain amount that depends on the size of settlement, number of rooms, and equipment of dwelling (bath and central heating); (2) for dwellings built between 20 June 1948 and 31 December 1949, with state aid, the rent may be raised to cover current expenses; and (3) for dwellings built between 20 June 1948 and 31 December 1949, with tax reductions, the rent may be set freely but not exceed the level covering current expenses. **Sphere of application**: fixed rents should be liberalized between 1 July 1963 and 1 January 1966. **Expiry date**: The law expires effective 31 December 1965.	BGBl, 389
25 July 1963	VO über die angemessen erhöhte Miete nach der Mietpreisgabe	**Rent updating**: (1) for dwellings built through 20 June 1948, rents are gradually freed, but upper bounds on their reasonable (*angemessener*) increases are set depending on settlement size, year of construction, and equipment of dwelling (in areas with 20,000 inhabitants, highest rents are 0.75–1.65 DM/m^2; in areas with (20,000, 100,000) inhabitants, 0.85–1.80 DM/m^2; in areas with 100,000+ inhabitants, 0.90–2.00 DM/m^2) and (2) for dwellings built after 20 June 1948, with state aid, the reasonable rent is cost covering.	BGBl, 532

(*Continued*)

Table 7. (Continued)

Date	Law title	Summary	Source
24 August 1965	G zur Änderung des Schluß termins für den Abbau der Wohnungszwangswirtschaft und für weitere Maßnahmen auf dem Gebiete des Mietpreisrechts	**Rent updating**: (1) for dwellings built through 20 June 1948, rents are gradually freed, but upper bounds on their reasonable increases are set depending on settlement size, year of construction, and equipment of dwelling (in areas with 20,000 inhabitants, highest rents are 0.75–1.65 DM/m^2; in areas with (20,000, 100,000) inhabitants, 0.85–1.80 DM/m^2; in areas with 100,000+ inhabitants, 0.90–2.00 DM/m^2); (2) for dwellings built after 20 June 1948, with state aid, the reasonable rent is cost covering, if the actual rent is lower, it can be raised to cost covering level but not by more than 0.3 DM/m^2. **Expiry date**: (1) liberalization of rents postponed to 1 January 1968 and (2) 2. BundesmietenG expires effective 31 December 1967.	BGBl, 969
21 December 1967	2. G zur Änderung des Schluß termins für den Abbau der Wohnungszwangswirtschaft und für weitere Maß nahmen auf dem Gebiete des Mietpreisrechts	**Rent updating**: (1) for dwellings built through 20 June 1948, basis rent can be raised by 10% and (2) no rent increase allowed in unhealthy, underground, and temporary dwellings. **Sphere of application**: cities Bonn, Freiburg, Hamburg, and Munich as well as in *Landkreise* (counties) Bonn, Göttingen, and Munich. **Expiry date**: in Landkreise Bonn, Göttingen, and Munich, the law expires effective 31 December 1968.	BGBl, 1251
20 December 1968	G zur Änderung mietpreisrechtlicher Vorschriften	**Rent updating**: (1) for dwellings built through 20 June 1948, basis rent can be raised by 20%; (2) no rent increase allowed in unhealthy, underground, and temporary dwellings. **Sphere of application**: (1) cities Hamburg, and Munich as well as in Landkreis Munich and (2) not applicable to large dwellings (6+ rooms including kitchen) from 1 January 1969. **Expiry date**: (1) in cities Bonn and Freiburg and in Landkreise Bonn and Göttingen, the law expires effective 31 December 1968 and (2) in cities Hamburg and Munich and Landkreis Munich, the law expires effective 31 December 1970.	BGBl, 1411
18 June 1970	G zur Änderung mietpreisrechtlicher und wohnungsrechtlicher Vorschriften in der Freien und Hansestadt Hamburg sowie in der kreisfreien Stadt München und im Landkreis München	**Rent updating**: (1) for dwellings built through 20 June 1948, basis rent can be raised by 10%; (2) no rent increase allowed in unhealthy, underground, and temporary dwellings. **Sphere of application**: cities Hamburg and Munich as well as in Landkreis Munich. **Expiry date**: The law expires effective 31 December 1972.	BGBl, 786

(Continued)

Table 7. (Continued)

Date	Law title	Summary	Source
04 November 1971	G zur Verbesserung des Mietrechts und zur Begrenzung des Mietanstiegs sowie zur Regelung von Ingenieur- und Architektenleistungen	**Rent setting**: setting excessive rents and asking excessive agency fees is forbidden. Unreasonably excessive rent (*unangemessen hoher Entgelt*) is the rent resulting from exploiting the housing shortage and substantially exceeding typical local rents negotiated in the region or similar regions for dwellings of comparable type, size, equipment, quality, and location.	BGBl, 1745
25 November 1971	G über den Kündigungsschutz für Mietverhältnisse über Wohnraum	**Rent updating**: rent can be increased, if it remained unchanged for 1 year and desired rent does not exceed the typical rent in the region or similar regions for dwellings of comparable type, size, equipment, quality, and location.	BGBl, 1839
30 October 1972	2. G zur Änderung mietpreisrechtlicher und wohnungsrechtlicher Vorschriften in der Freien und Hansestadt Hamburg sowie in der kreisfreien Stadt München und im Landkreis München	**Rent updating**: (1) for dwellings built through 20 June 1948, basis rent can be raised by 10%; (2) no rent increase allowed in unhealthy, underground, and temporary dwellings. **Sphere of application**: cities Hamburg and Munich as well as in Landkreis Munich. **Expiry date**: The law expires effective 31 December 1974.	BGBl, 2054
18 December 1974	2. G über den Kündigungsschutz für Mietverhältnisse über Wohnraum	**Rent updating**: (1) rent can be increased, if it remained unchanged for 1 year and desired rent does not exceed the typical rent in the region or similar regions for dwellings not subject to price controls of comparable type, size, equipment, quality, and location; (2) in case of modernization increasing the practical value of housing, the landlord may charge 14% of modernization cost to tenants; (3) if interest rate increases, the landlord may charge the resulting additional cost to tenants; and (4) in cities Hamburg and Munich and Landkreis Munich, until 31 December 1976, the rent for dwellings with >6 rooms including kitchen can be raised at most by 10% of basis rent. **Measurement of typical rents**: (1) survey of typical rents in the region or similar region conducted or recognized by the municipality or by representatives of landlords' and tenants' associations; (2) report by a sworn expert; and (3) rents in three dwellings of other landlords.	BGBl, 3603

(*Continued*)

Table 7. (Continued)

Date	Law title	Summary	Source
20 December 1982	G zur Erhöhung des Angebots an Mietwohnungen	**Rent updating**: (1) rent can be increased, (a) if it remained unchanged for 1 year; (b) required rent does not exceed the typical rent in the region or similar regions for dwellings of comparable type, size, equipment, quality, and location negotiated in the last 3 years; and (c) the rent within 3 years is not raised by > 30% and (2) stepwise increase (*gestaffelter Mietzins*): provision up to 10 years, automatic rent increase once in a year by an amount indicated in the contract. **Rent setting**: setting excessive rents and asking excessive agency fees is forbidden. Unreasonably excessive rent is the rent resulting from exploiting the housing shortage and substantially exceeding typical rents negotiated within the last 3 years in the region or similar regions for dwellings of comparable type, size, equipment, quality, and location. **Measurement of typical rents**: (1) survey of typical rents in the region or similar region conducted or recognized by the municipality or by representatives of landlords' and tenants' associations (first mention of *Mietspiegel*), which should be updated every 2 years; (2) report by a sworn expert; and (3) rents in three dwellings of other landlords.	BGBl, 1912
21 July 1993	4. G zur Änderung mietrechtlicher Vorschriften	**Rent updating**: (1) rent can be increased, (a) if it remained unchanged for 1 year; (b) required rent does not exceed the typical rent in the region or similar regions for dwellings of comparable type, size, equipment, quality, and location negotiated in the last 4 years; and (c) the rent within 3 years is not raised by > 20% for rents >8 DM/m^2 and >30% for rents $\leq$ 8 DM/m^2, the resulting rent cannot exceed 9 DM/m^2; (2) stepwise increase: provision up to 10 years, automatic rent increase once in a year by an amount indicated in the contract; and (3) indexation of rent by CPI without housing happening once a year. **Rent setting**: setting excessive rents and asking excessive agency fees is forbidden. Unreasonably excessive rent is the rent resulting from exploiting the housing shortage and substantially exceeding typical rents negotiated within the last 4 years in the region or similar regions for dwellings of comparable type, size, equipment, quality, and location by >20%. Rent is reasonable, if it covers current expenses and the dwelling is built after 1 January 1991. **Measurement of typical rents**: (1) survey of typical rents in the region or similar region conducted or recognized by the municipality or by representatives of landlords' and tenants' associations, which should be updated every 2 years; (2) report by a sworn expert; and (3) rents in three dwellings of other landlords.	BGBl, 1257

(*Continued*)

Table 7. (Continued)

Date	Law title	Summary	Source
25 June 2001	G zur Neugliederung, Vereinfachung und Reform des Mietrechts (MietrechtsreformG)	**Rent updating**: (1) rent can be increased, (a) if it remained unchanged for 1.25 year; (b) required rent does not exceed the typical rent in the region or similar regions for dwellings of comparable type, size, equipment, quality, and location negotiated in the last 4 years; and (c) the rent within 3 years is not raised by > 20% (*Kappungsgrenze*); (2) stepwise increase: provision up to 10 years, automatic rent increase once in a year by an amount indicated in the contract; (3) indexation of rent by CPI once a year; and (4) in case of modernization increasing the practical value of housing, the landlord may charge 11% of modernization cost to tenants. **Rent setting**: setting excessive rents and asking excessive agency fees is forbidden. Unreasonably excessive rent is the rent resulting from exploiting the housing shortage and substantially exceeding typical rents negotiated within the last 4 years in the region or similar regions for dwellings of comparable type, size, equipment, quality, and location by >20%. Rent is reasonable, if it covers current expenses. Measurement of typical rents: (1) survey of typical rents in the region or similar regions conducted or recognized by the municipality or by representatives of landlords' and tenants' associations, which should be updated every 2 years (introduction of a survey based on scientifc principles, the so-called *qualifizierter Mietspiegel*); (2) report by a sworn expert; and (3) rents in three dwellings; (4) rent databank.	BGBl, 1149
11 March 2013	G über die energetische Modernisierung von vermietetem Wohnraum und über die vereinfachte Durchsetzung von Räumungstiteln (MietRÄndG)	**Rent updating**: rent can be increased, (a) if it remained unchanged for 1.25 year; (b) required rent does not exceed the typical rent in the region or similar regions for dwellings of comparable type, size, equipment, quality, and location negotiated in the last 4 years; and (c) the rent within 3 years is not raised by > 20% (in the area, where sufficient supply of rental dwellings under reasonable conditions is endangered, the upper limit for rent increases is 15%).	BGBl, 434
21 April 2015	G zur Dämpfung des Mietanstiegs auf angespannten Wohnungsmärkten und zur Stärkung des Bestellerprinzips bei der Wohnungsvermittlung (MietNovG)	**Rent setting**: the rent for a dwelling located in an area with a tight housing market (*angespannter Wohnungsmarkt*) can be at most 10% higher than the typical local rent. Federal states are empowered to establish such areas for a period of at most 5 years. **Criteria for tight market**: (1) local rents grow faster than at the national level; (2) local average rent-to-income ratio is significantly higher than the national average; (3) population grows, whereas new housing construction does not create enough dwellings; or (4) vacancy rate is low, while demand is high. **Sphere of application**: (1) not applicable if dwellings are used and let for the first time after 1 October 2014 and (2) not applicable for the first letting after an extensive modernization.	BGBl, 610

Notes: (1) 'G' denotes 'Gesetz' (primary law); (2) 'VO' denotes 'Verordnung' (secondary law, or ordinance); (3) 'RGBl' stands for 'Reichsgesetzblatt' (Law Gazette of German Reich); (4) 'BGBl' stands for 'Bundesgesetzblatt' (Law Gazette of Federal Republic Germany); and (5) In column 'Date', the dates format DD-MM-YYYY is used.

Table 8. Regional legislation on capping limit.

Bundesland	Law title	Date	Date active	Date cancel	Municipalities
Baden-Wrttemberg	KappungsgrenzenVO Baden-Württemberg	09 June 2015	01 July 2015	30 June 2020	44/1101
Bavaria	WohnungsgebieteVO	15 May 2012	01 July 2012	30 June 2022	90/2056
Bavaria	MieterschutzVO	10 November 2015	01 January 2016	31 July 2020	90/2056
Bavaria	KappungsgrenzesenkungsVO	03 May 2013	15 May 2013	14 May 2018	90/2056
Bavaria	WohnungsgebieteVO	15 May 2012	01 July 2012	30 June 2022	90/2056
Bavaria	Zweite KappungsgrenzesenkungsVO	23 July 2013	31 July 2013	31 December 2015	90/2056
Berlin	Kappungsgrenzen-VO	07 May 2013	19 May 2013	10 May 2018	1/1
Brandenburg	VO zur Bestimmung der Gebietskulisse zur Senkung der Kappungsgrenze	05 August 2014	01 September 2014	31 August 2019	30/419
Bremen	Kappungsgrenzen-VO	05 August 2014	01 September 2014	31 August 2019	1/2
Hamburg	KappungsgrenzenVO	30 August 2013	01 September 2013	31 August 2018	1/1
Hessen	Hessische KappungsgrenzenVO	08 October 2014	18 October 2014	17 October 2019	29/426
North Rhine-Westphalia	KappungsgrenzenVO	20 May 2014	01 June 2014	31 May 2019	59/396
Rhineland-Palatinate	KappungsgrenzenVO	04 February 2015	13 February 2015	12 February 2020	4/2306
Saxony	Kappungsgrenzen-VO	10 July 2015	31 July 2015	30 June 2020	1/468
Schleswig-Holstein	Schleswig-Holsteinische KappungsgrenzenVO	14 November 2014	01 December 2014	30 November 2019	15/1116

states took advantage of this option, identifying municipalities where it applies, see Table 8.

The rental brake was introduced in 2015 (Table 7). Like the capping limit, it is a region-specific regulation: Federal states may identify areas with a tight housing market (*angespannter Wohnungsmarkt*), where rental brake shall be implemented. Typically, the areas are municipalities, see Table 9. Unlike capping limit, it constrains the rent setting for new contracts. Two exceptions from this rule are the newly built dwellings (housing completed after 1 October 2014) for all contracts to follow and substantially modernized dwellings for the first contract after modernization. For all other dwellings, the newly negotiated rent cannot exceed by more than 10% the typical local rent. Since the federal law came into force, nine federal states implemented it (as of May 2016).

For both capping limit and rental brake, municipality-specific binary variables are created. They are aggregated to the national level by multiplying them by the shares of the respective municipalities in the national housing stock as of 2011. In 2011, the most recent census of housing stock was conducted, which makes it appropriate as a basis for the weighting scheme. The resulting nationwide indices are plotted in Figure 6. The vertical axis reflects the share of national housing stock subject to respective regulations. Two years after their introduction, capping limits cover more than a quarter (28.5%) of the housing in 338 municipalities, covering 22.5 million inhabitants. The rental brake, in the first 12 months of its existence, was extended to 26.8% of dwellings in 310 municipalities with 21.0 million persons. In 384 municipalities, covering 30% of national housing stock, at least one of these regulations is valid, while both are in force across 264 municipalities, making up 25% of German dwellings. The areas subject to these regulations are significantly larger than the national average (66,625–67,698 inhabitants vs. 7,159) and have a substantially lower homeownership rate than Germany as a whole (29% vs. 43%).

4.4.2. Evolution of rent controls

The evolution of the intensity of rent controls between 1913 and 2016 is displayed in Figure 7. In 1922, federal law introduced the first generation of rent controls in Germany. Under this regulation, the rents for the so-called old housing (*Altbau*) were frozen at peacetime levels, that is, those prevailing on 1 July 1914. This meant that rents could not be raised, neither during the rental contract nor after its expiry. The definition of old housing changed with the passage of time: Initially, it encompassed dwellings built prior to 1 July 1918. After WWII, it was extended to cover housing constructed through 20 June 1948. Rent controls were very strong between 1922 and 1933 as well as between 1936 and 1950. Almost all rent updates were executed by the state, which from time to time ordered countrywide rent increases or even decreases, as was the case in 1931.

Due to a huge housing shortage following WWII, rents remained frozen. However, starting in the early 1950s, the coalition governments composed of Christian democrats[14] and liberals set a long-term objective of completely removing rent controls. The rent liberalization resulted from two different developments. First, Germany experienced a massive spurt of private housing construction, unsupported by state aid. Consequently, as dwellings built without state aid were not subject to rent controls, it became less relevant as time passed.[15] Second, since 1960, rent controls could be abandoned in cities (*kreisfreie Städte*) and counties (*Landkreise*) where the housing market was normalized. As an indicator for normalization, a ratio between effective households and housing stock was used as defined in Equation (7). As soon as the excess demand went below 3% in an area, the rents for all dwellings in that area were no longer subject to any limitations.

Table 9. Regional legislation on rental brake.

Bundesland	Law title	Date	Date active	Date cancel	Municipalities
Baden-Wrttemberg	MietpreisbegrenzungsVO Baden-Württemberg	29 September 2015	01 October 2015	30 September 2020	68/1101
Bavaria	MietpreisbremseVO	14 July 2015	01 August 2015	31 July 2020	144/2056
Bavaria	MieterschutzVO	10 November 2015	01 January 2016	31 July 2020	9/2056
Berlin	MietenbegrenzungsVO	28 April 2015	01 June 2015	31 May 2020	1/1
Brandenburg	MietpreisbegrenzungsVO	08 December 2015	01 January 2016	31 December 2020	31/419
Bremen	Mietenbegrenzungs-VO	17 November 2015	01 December 2015	30 November 2020	1/2
Hamburg	MietpreisbegrenzungsVO	23 June 2015	01 July 2015	30 June 2020	1/1
Hessen	Hessische MietenbegrenzungsVO	17 November 2015	27 November 2015	30 June 2019	16/426
North Rhine-Westphalia	MietpreisbegrenzungsVO	23 June 2015	01 July 2015	30 June 2020	22/396
Rhineland-Palatinate	MietpreisbegrenzungsVO	28 September 2015	08 October 2015	07 October 2020	3/2306
Schleswig-Holstein	MietpreisVO Schleswig-Holstein	11 November 2015	01 December 2015	30 November 2020	12/1116
Thuringia	Thüringer MietpreisbegrenzungsVO	10 March 2016	01 April 2016	31 January 2021	2/913

Notes: (1) 'VO' denotes 'Verordnung' (secondary law, or ordinance); (2) In column 'Municipalities': number of municipalities with regulation/total number of municipalities; (3) In column 'Date', the dates format DD-MM-YYYY is used.

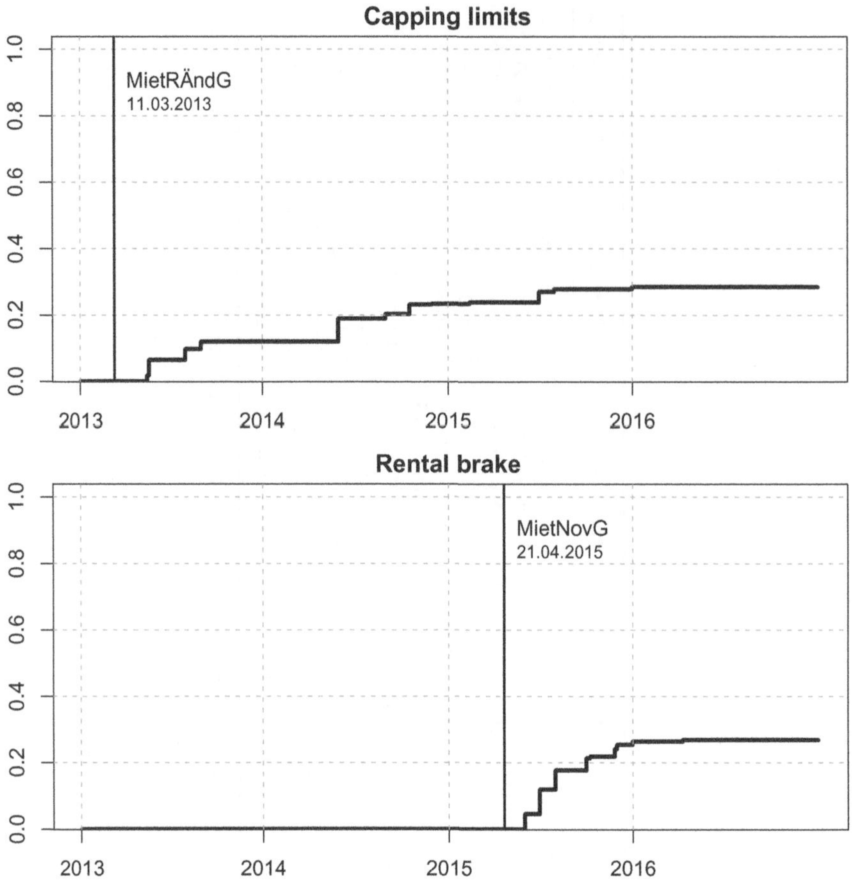

Figure 6. Capping limits and rental brake, 2013–2015.

Nevertheless, the liberalization process was neither steady nor rapid. On the one hand, very soon a notion of 'reasonable rent increases' was introduced. It implied imposing upper limits on rents increases. On the other hand, in large settlements – such as West Berlin, Hamburg, and Munich – the removal of the first-generation rent controls was postponed many times. For example, in Hamburg and Munich rent controls were removed in 1976; while in West Berlin, it was only in 1989. In 1971, a second generation of rent controls was introduced. Rents were no longer frozen at some past level; instead rents were and are anchored to some typical local rent for dwellings of comparable type, size, equipment, quality, and location. When updating rents within old contracts and setting rents for new contracts, landlords must keep an eye on the typical local rent. Otherwise, they might be sued for asking too high rent. As a result, a whole battery of measures was developed in order to gauge typical local rents.

By 2001, the housing market situation had relaxed. Lower birth rates and outmigration from city centers to the periphery contributed to this development. However, in 2010, a new trend emerged[16]: big cities and university towns became more attractive. This was reflected in the following migration flows.

First, between 2004 and 2013, a net internal migration (inflow minus outflow) to the top seven cities (Berlin, Cologne, Düsseldorf, Frankfurt, Hamburg, Munich, and Stuttgart)

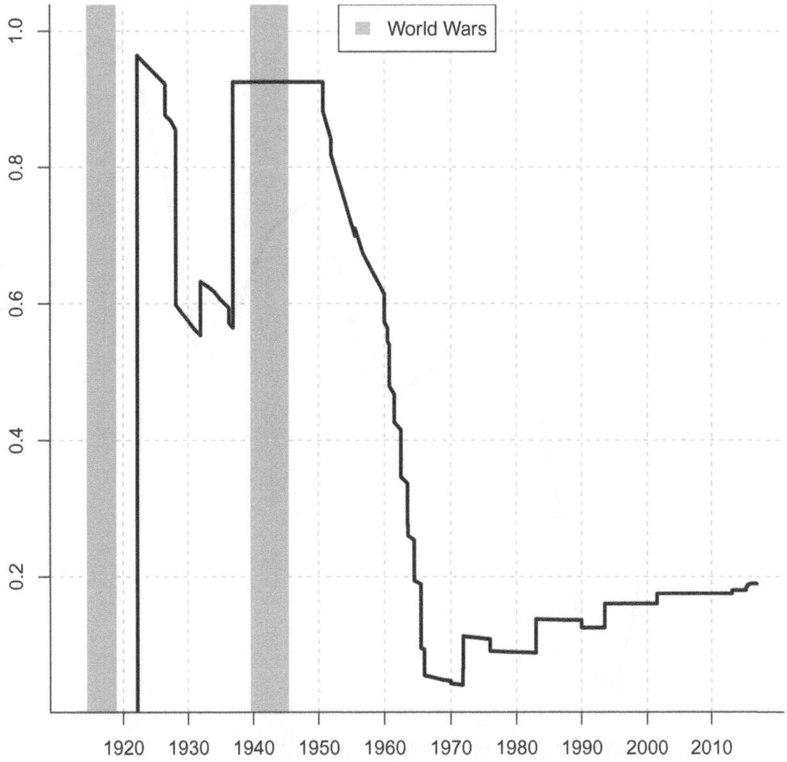

Figure 7. The index of rent controls regulations, 1913–2015.

across municipality borders strongly increased, see Figure 8. At its peak, in 2006, the net internal migration attained 50,000 persons, which makes up over 0.5% of the total population of the top seven cities (9.5 million as of 2013). In the 1990s, the internal net migration went in the opposite direction – toward suburban areas.

Second, since 2010, in the wake of the Great Recession, the net foreign migration (those who came from abroad minus those who went abroad) to the top seven cities dramatically surged, as shown Figure 8. To a large extent, it can be explained by immigration from other European countries, where economic perspectives are much worse than in Germany. In 2014, the net foreign migration to the top seven cities was over 100,000, accounting for more than 1% of the annual population growth of those cities.

Together these factors lead to a locally concentrated scarcity of rental housing. However, urban population represents the majority of German population. According to the Statistical Yearbook for Germany 2015, the largest cities (with population exceeding 100,000) alone make up 31% of German population. Moreover, the homeownership rate is substantially lower in urban areas than in the countryside: according to 2011 Census data, the tenant occupancy rate (share of tenant-occupied dwellings in total housing stock) was on average 70% in urban areas (*kreisfreie Städte* plus city states Berlin and Hamburg) and about 42% in countryside (*Landkreise*). This implies that a vast majority of tenants live in the urban areas. Furthermore, the cities are also the centers where legislative and executive powers are located and political decisions are made. Thus, a relative housing shortage in the cities affects many tenants leading to political protests and eventually to

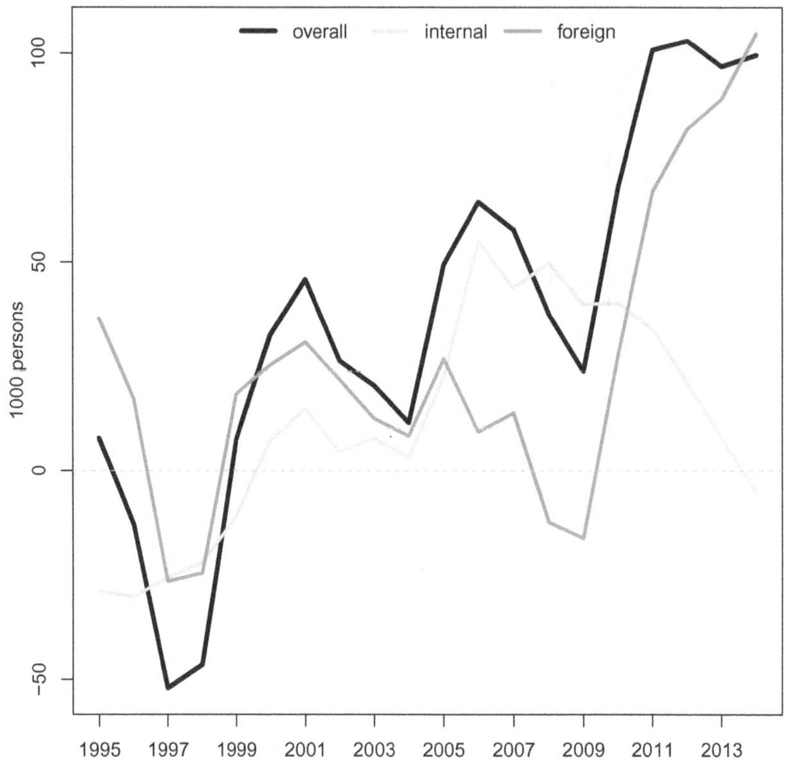

Figure 8. Net overall, internal, and foreign migration in top seven German cities, 1995–2014.

adoption of new legal acts trying to reflect the increased concerns of the numerous tenant population.

Therefore, in 2013, federal authorities began issuing stricter regulations with regard to housing rents: lower capping limits could be introduced in areas with tight housing market. Further, in 2015, the rental brake was implemented. It revived the almost forgotten notion of old housing: Now, it includes the dwellings completed prior to 1 October 2014. In the municipalities with tight housing markets, the rental brake restricts the growth of rents for such dwellings.

Starting from fall 2015, further deterioration in the housing market situation can be expected. The reason is that in 2014 and 2015, a huge wave of foreign refugees, especially from the Middle East and North Africa, superimposed upon the previous two inflows. According to some estimates, alone in 2015, about 900,000 refugees came to Germany.[17] Out of these, 79,034 came to and about 54,325 remained in Berlin,[18] making up about 1.6% of its population. This is an impressive number compared both to the net internal and foreign migration, not to speak of a tiny natural growth rate.[19] The refugees tend to concentrate in big cities, where the employment chances are higher and communities of the refugees' compatriots are larger.

4.5. Composite index

The composite housing regulation index is computed as an average of individual regulation class indices: (1) rent controls; (2) tenant eviction protection; (3) housing rationing;

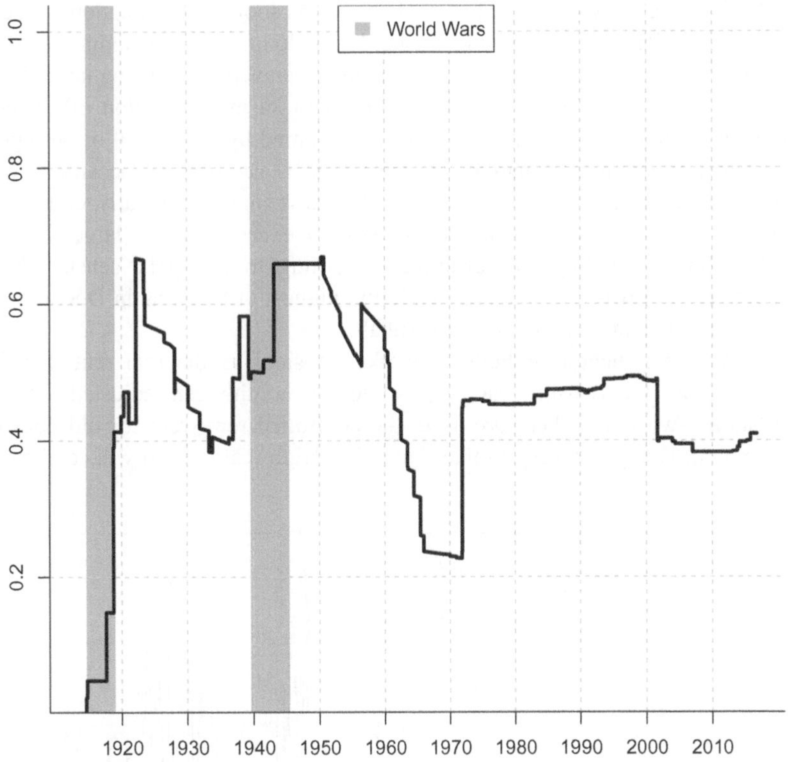

Figure 9. Composite index of housing market regulations in Germany, 1913–2015.

and (4) social housing policy. It is shown in Figure 9 as a sum of its four components. It covers the period between 1913 and 2015.

It can be seen that Germany experienced five housing market regulation waves since 1913. The first wave started during WWI and ended in the mid-1930s. The second wave began with the outbreak of WWII and lasted until the mid-1950s. The third encompassed the period between the late 1950s and early 1970s. The fourth wave lasted between the mid-1970s and early 2000s. Since the early 2010s, Germany entered in upward phase of the fifth wave of regulations. An average duration of regulation waves is about 20 years. During crisis times, the first stage is characterized by a swift and strong increase in regulations, followed by their gradual removal. In peaceful times, both regulation and deregulation occur at a slower pace.

Different types of regulations have various degrees of persistence. Thus, tenant protection, which initially was introduced as emergency measure, has remained in place continuously. By contrast, housing rationing and social housing constructions are sometimes completely eliminated. The rationing of housing causes considerable inconveniences to both landlords and tenants and, therefore, is more difficult to justify. Social housing construction requires large-state investment and, hence, is abandoned as soon as the housing market situation improves or the government runs into financial troubles. Rent controls occupy an intermediate position: Unlike tenant protection – now considered to be a basic element of social market economics in Germany – rent controls are regarded as a distorting intervention in the economy. Therefore, during the periods of no excess demand for housing, they can be reduced. However, as soon as the situation worsens, they are reintroduced. Panel (a) of Figure 9 shows the long-term development of housing vacancy rate.[20] The higher the vacancy rate the more relaxed the housing market. It can be seen that the market tightening in 1933–1939 led to an intensification of all regulation classes, while its relaxation after 1950 was accompanied by a removal of all regulations, except tenant protection. The national vacancy rate is not perfect, because it hides the mismatch in the housing market: The areas with excess supply (typically, countryside and small towns) may coexist with the areas with extreme excess demand (large cities) and the latter drives housing policy. For example, according to the 2011 census, the lowest vacancy rate (1.6%) was in Hamburg, while the highest (14%) was in Dessau-Roßlau, a small city in the federal state of Saxony-Anhalt.

An alternative indicator of housing market tensions is the real rent. Panel (b) of Figure 10 displays the year-on-year growth rates of monthly rent adjusted for consumer price inflation. Two rent indices are used: the controlled rent (rent for old housing) and free market rent. Both have very similar dynamics. High real rent growth can be observed

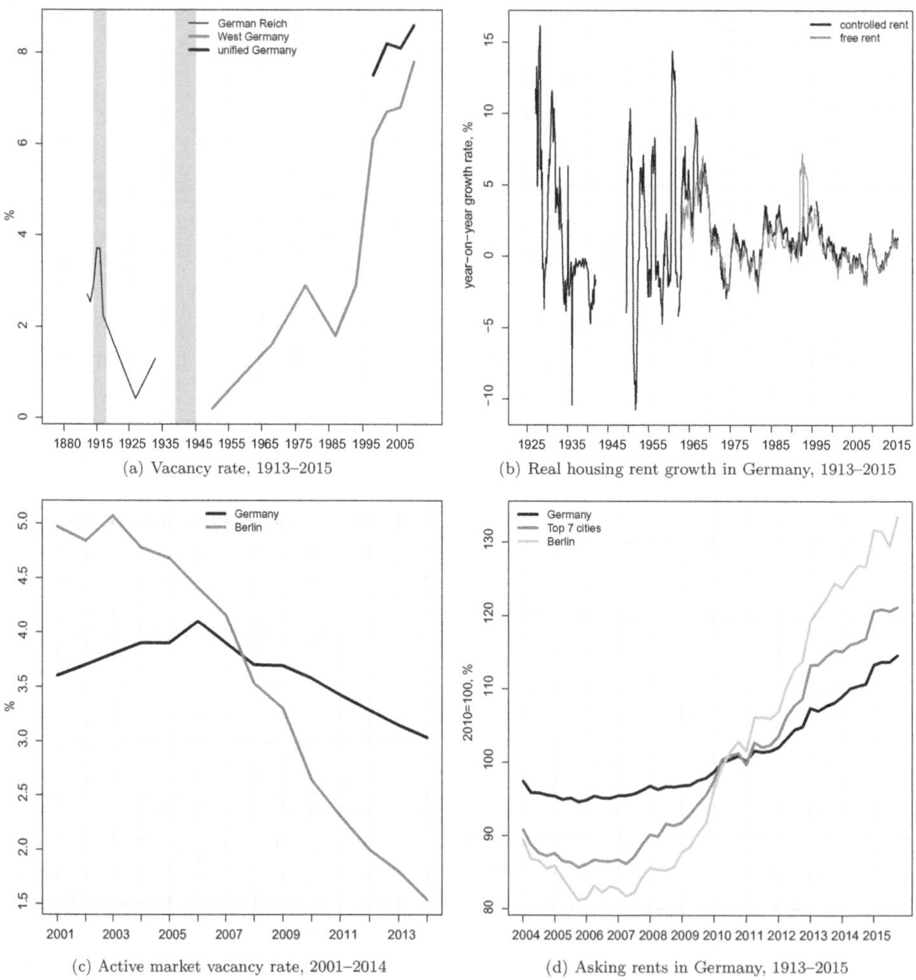

(a) Vacancy rate, 1913–2015

(b) Real housing rent growth in Germany, 1913–2015

(c) Active market vacancy rate, 2001–2014

(d) Asking rents in Germany, 1913–2015

Figure 10. Stylized facts of German housing market.
Sources: (a) Federal Statistical Office; (b) Federal Statistical Office and own calculations; (c) empirica ag; and (d) empirica ag.

from 1926 through 1961, despite the fact that most of the time they were virtually frozen. After most of the time, they were below 5% and often negative.

In 2016, a deterioration of the housing market can be observed, see Figure 10. It is not very visible in the latest available value of the national vacancy rate as shown in panel (a): 8.6% in 2010. However, there is a strong geographical housing market mismatch: the countryside, Ruhr area, and East Germany are losing people, who are heading for larger cities with better education and employment opportunities.[21] Thus, their regions of origin show large housing vacancy rates, while destination regions experience a relative housing shortage. Additional evidence of housing shortage is provided in panel (c) of Figure 1, which shows an active market vacancy rate (*marktaktiver Leerstand*), that is, the share of vacant dwellings in apartment buildings that can be rented out immediately or in the midterm.[22] Starting from 2003 in Berlin and 2006 in Germany, the vacancy rate has been sharply decreasing. Especially, strong decreases can be observed in Berlin.

In addition, there is a moderate nationwide[23] increase in real rents that started in the late 2013; see panel (b) of Figure 10. The index is a part of the consumer price index and, therefore, includes rent values of existing contracts negotiated in part over long period. Panel (d) of Figure 10 displays the evolution of asking rents that reflect the newest market developments. As seen, since 2007, rents in Berlin and in top seven cities (Berlin, Cologne, Düsseldorf, Frankfurt, Hamburg, Munich, and Stuttgart) have been growing strongly. Between 2007 and 2015, in Berlin, asking rents increased by over 60%, while in top seven cities by almost 40%. Germany-wide, asking rent also grew, albeit at a much slower pace.

As a result, three of the regulation classes are being strengthened. The *rationing of housing* expands: An ever-growing number of cities and federal states introduce social conservation areas and prohibitions of housing misuse. These measures are accompanied by a relaxation of land use and building standards. Since October 2015, the federal legislation created favorable conditions for building refugee shelters. The prescriptions of land use plans can be overseen, issuance of building permits is facilitated, and energy efficiency standards are lowered for the shelters.[24] Similar processes are taking place at the regional level. A law facilitating the construction of refugee shelters was promulgated in Lower Saxony.[25] In Berlin, a *Law on acceleration of housing construction*[26] is passed, which should simplify bureaucratic procedures regarding the issuance of building permits for dwellings in general. *Rent controls* are made more restrictive. In 2013, the possibility to raise rents under existing contracts was further reduced: Now, in areas with tight housing market, the rent increase can be at most 15% over 4 years, that is, approximately 3.6% a year. In other areas, it can be raised by 20% within 4 years, that is, roughly 4.7% a year. In 2015, the rental brake law imposed restrictions on the rent setting by new contracts for dwellings completed before 1 October 2014 and located in areas with tight housing markets. In May 2016, almost a quarter of the housing stock is subject to the rental brake. In 2016, the German Federal Minister for Justice plans to implement stronger rent controls.[27] *Social housing policy* is also being intensified. At the federal level, the amount of money assigned for the purposes of social housing construction was doubled from 518.2 to 1018.2 million euros in October 2015; see Table 1. Federal states are also expanding their social housing policy. For example, in November 2015, the Berlin Government promulgated a *Law on provision of housing* that aims at extending the construction of social housing.[28]

5. Conclusion

In this paper, we develop a set of new indices reflecting the intensity of the rental housing market regulations in Germany. They stretch over the period from 1913 through 2015 and cover four major regulation classes: tenant protection from eviction, rationing of housing, rent controls, and social housing fostering.

The indicators are mainly based on the federal regulations. However, some of more recent regulations are measured at the federal state (prohibition of housing misuse) or even municipality level (social conservation areas, capping limits, and rental brake). It would be desirable to examine the regional dimension of the earlier regulations. However, it is precluded by the unavailability of the necessary data. Overall, more than 170 legal acts – including 102 federal laws and ordinances with more than 700 pages – were analyzed.

The developed indices seem to be in a close relation with actual indicators of the housing market: total and social housing construction, vacancy rate, and rent growth. All four indices are especially high between 1920 and 1965, pointing out to a strong state intervention, see Figure 9. Initially, introduced during and shortly after WWI, the regulations were gradually reduced until the mid-1930s. The outbreak of WWII led to a new surge in the intensity. Following the war, the liberal coalition governments tried to withdraw from rent controls and housing rationing, which is reflected in a declining intervention intensity, which attained its low point in the late 1960s. Starting from the early 1970, social-democrats-led coalition governments raised the degree of intervention that stabilized at a relatively high level until the end of twentieth century. In the early 2000s, the relaxed housing market permitted the reduction of government intervention in the rental housing market. However, since 2013, a new, albeit yet small, surge in the regulatory intensity can be observed.

Both class-specific indices and the composite index can be used to investigate the impact of formal institutions on the evolution of various aspects of the housing market. These can also be used to assess the effectiveness of housing regulations. It would facilitate their cost-benefit analysis, for their consequences could be quantified.

The approach presented in this paper can be developed in at least two directions. First, other regulations related to housing market can be analyzed: for example, tax treatment of rental and owner-occupied dwellings. Second, it can be extended to the housing policy of other countries in order to allow cross-country comparisons. It could, thus, be identified, to what extent the performance and structure of the housing market are shaped by the formal institutions.

Acknowledgments

I thank the participants at the research seminars of the Leontief Centre in St. Petersburg, Russia on 23 January 2016, and the LISER, Esch-sur-Alzette, Luxembourg on 10 February 2016. The standard disclaimer applies.

Disclosure statement

No potential conflict of interest was reported by the author.

Notes

1. See, for example, Kettunen and Ruonavaara (2015).
2. An alternative would be, for example, to use a weighted average based on the standard deviations of individual indices. In the case under inspection, the composite indices based

on a simple and weighted average are very similar (correlation coefficient almost 1), since the standard deviations are very close to each other.

3. For more details on its computation, see So (1959).
4. See Destatis (1964, 6–25).
5. As pointed out by a referee, recovery costs may have increased over time, thereby deflating actual values too much. However, a comparison of the recovery costs to the construction costs (*Baukostenindex*) between the 1st quarter of 2000 and 4th quarter of 2015 shows that both grew at a similar rate: 30% and 32%, respectively. Thus, it can be assumed that recovery costs correctly reflect the construction costs.
6. Reich's Post (*Reichs-Postverwaltung*), Reich's Navy (*Reichs-Marineverwaltung*), Reich's Railways (*Reichseisenbahnverwaltung*), and the Administration of Kaiser-Wilhelm's canal (*Verwaltung Des Kaiser Wilhelm-Kanals*).
7. Interestingly, it is in this decree that the notion of 'social housing' (*sozialer Wohnungsbau*) is mentioned for the first time.
8. For a detailed and very systematic account on housing market regulations in 1914–1924 in 17 countries, see International Labour Office (1924).
9. It was the first postwar coalition government that included social democrats. The coalition remained in power from 1969 through 1983.
10. Similar regulations exist in other countries, for example, in Canada (Toronto) and the USA (District of Columbia and Seattle).
11. For explanation of the difference between *Gesetz* and *Rechtsverordnung* in German law, see Schmidt-Eichstaedt (2005, 5–6).
12. For some examples of such modernizations in Berlin, see 'Die Beurteilung von Anträgen auf Rückbau, Änderung oder Nutzungsänderung baulicher Anlagen in den Erhaltungsgebieten des Bezirks Pankow gemäß § 172 Absatz 1 Satz 1 Nummer 2 des Baugesetzbuchs' Bekanntmachung vom 20. Dezember 2012.
13. In Hamburg, on 2 October 2015, a law on accommodation of refugees (*Gesetz zur Flüchtlingsunterbringung in Einrichtungen*) was promulgated, which permits the state to confiscate the private property in order to accommodate refugees. In Bremen, a similar law (*Gesetz zur vorübergehenden Unterbringung von Flüchtlingen und Asylbegehrenden*) was adopted on 20 October 2015, which, unlike its Hamburg counterpart, explicitly excludes small properties (area $<300\ m^2$) from seizure. Thus, according to our estimates based on the data from Statistisches Landesamt Bremen (2014), 25–30% of buildings and 60% of dwellings potentially fall under this regulation.
14. Christian democrats remained in the government without interruption between 1949 and 1969.
15. It should be mentioned, however, that at that time social housing accounted for a large part of the newly built housing stock. The rents in the social dwellings were specifically subject to controls.
16. Geppert and Gornig (2003, 2010).
17. http://www.zeit.de/news/2015-11/27/deutschland-bundesregierung-geht-von-mehr-als-900000-fluechtlingen-aus-27124202.
18. http://www.rbb-online.de/politik/thema/fluechtlinge/hintergrund/zahlen-und-fakten-fluechtlinge-in-berlin-und-brandenburg.html.
19. For example, in 2014 in Berlin, the surplus of births over deaths accounted for just 0.15% of its total population.
20. A share of vacant dwellings in the total housing stock.
21. Braun (2014).
22. For more details on construction of the indicator, see Braun and Schlatterer (2015).
23. The rents are growing much more rapidly in large and university cities with large inflow of internal migrants.
24. *Asylverfahrensbeschleuningsgesetz*, 20 October 2015, BGBl, 1722 and *Verordnung zum Asylverfahrensbeschleuningsgesetz*, 24 October 2015, BGBl, 1789.
25. *Niedersächsisches Gesetz zur Erleichterung der Schaffung von Unterkünften für Flüchtlinge oder Asylbegehrende (NEFUG)*. 12 November 2015, Nds. GVBl., 311.
26. *Gesetz zur Beschleunigung Des Wohnungsbaus*. 4 February 2016, Gesetz und Verordnungsblatt Berlin (2016, 26).

27. Among other things, it is planned to reduce the share of modernization cost that can be charged to tenants from 11% to 8% and to compute local typical rents based on the contracts concluded over the last 10 years, an increase from 4 years; see Messelken (2015).
28. *Gesetz über die Neuausrichtung der sozialen Wohnraumversorgung in Berlin (Berliner Wohnraumversorgungsgesetz – WoVG Bln)*, 24 November 2015, Gesetz- und Verordnungsblatt für Berlin, 422.

References

Alesina, A., S. Ardagna, G. Nicoletti, and F. Schiantarelli. 2005. "Regulation and investment." *Journal of the European Economic Association* 3 (4): 791–825. doi:10.1162/jeea.2005.3.issue-4.

Andersen, H. S., R. Andersson, T. Wessel, and K. Vilkama. 2016. "The impact of housing policies and housing markets on ethnic spatial segregation: Comparing the capital cities of four Nordic welfare states." *International Journal of Housing Policy* 16 (1): 1–30. doi:10.1080/14616718.2015.1110375.

Andersson, R., and L. Magnusson Turnerc. 2014. "Segregation, gentrification, and residualisation: From public housing to market-driven housing allocation in inner city Stockholm." *International Journal of Housing Policy* 14 (1): 3–29. doi:10.1080/14616718.2013.872949.

Andrews, D., A. C. Sánchez, and Å. Johansson. 2011. "Housing markets and structural policies in OECD countries." Economics Department Working Paper No. 836.

Blumenroth, U. 1975. *Deutsche Wohnungspolitik seit der Reichsgründung. Darstellung und kritische Würdigung*. Münster: Institut für Siedlungs- und Wohnungswesen, Universität Münster.

Braun, R. 2014. "Mietanstieg wegen Wohnungsleerstand! Kein "zurück-in-die-Stadt", sondern "Landflucht"." empirica paper Nr. 219.

Braun, R., and M. Schlatterer. 2015. *CBRE-empirica-Leerstandsindex 2009–2014. Ergebnisse und Methodik*. Berlin: empirica ag.

Brauns, H. 1922. "Bericht des Ausschusses über den Entwurf eines Gesetzes zur Abänderung des Gesetzes über die Erhebung einer Abgabe zur Förderung des Wohnungsbaues vom 26. Juni 1921 (Reichsgesetzblatt S. 773)." Reichstag 1. Wahlperiode 1920–1924 Drucksache Nr. 3472. Berlin: Reichstag.

Cuerpo, C., S. Kalantaryan, and P. Pontuch. 2014. "Rental market regulation in the European Union." *European Economy* - Economic Papers 515.

Dawson, J. W., and J. J. Seater. 2013. "Federal regulation and aggregate economic growth." *Journal of Economic Growth* 18: 137–177. doi:10.1007/s10887-013-9088-y.

Destatis. 1964. *Fachserie E "Bauwirtschaft, Bautätigkeit, Wohnungen" Gebäudezählung vom 6. Juni 1961, Heft 3 "Hauptergebnisse nach Kreisen"*. Stuttgart: W. Kohlhammer Verlag.

El-Shagi, M., C. Michelsen, and S. Rosenschon. 2014. "Regulation, Innovation and Technology Diffusion. Evidence from Building Energy Efficiency Standards in Germany." DIW Discussion papers 1371.

Führer, K. C. 1995. *Mieter, Hausbesitzer, Staat und Wohnungsmarkt: Wohnungsmangel und Wohnungszwangswirtschaft in Deutschland 1914–1960 (Vierteljahrschrift für Sozial- und Wirtschaftsgeschichte. Beihefte)*. Stuttgart: Franz Steiner Verlag.

Geppert, K., and M. Gornig. 2003. "Die Renaissance der groß en Städte — Und die Chancen Berlins." Wochenbericht des DIW Berlin Nr. 26.

Geppert, K., and M. Gornig. 2010. "Mehr Jobs, mehr Menschen: Die Anziehungskraft der groß en Städte wächst." Wochenbericht des DIW Berlin Nr. 19.

Geβner, M. 2008. "Leistungsfähigkeit des städtebaulichen Instruments Milieuschutz für die Stadtentwicklung in Berlin." Technische Universität Berlin. Dissertation zur Erlangung des akademischen Grades Doktor der Ingenieurwissenschaften.

Gyourko, J., A. Saiz, and A. Summers. 2008. "A new measure of the local regulatory environment for housing markets: The Wharton residential land use regulatory index." *Urban Studies* 45 (3): 693–729. doi:10.1177/0042098007087341.

Heylen, K. 2013. "The distributional impact of housing subsidies in Flanders." *International Journal of Housing Policy* 13 (1): 45–65. doi:10.1080/14616718.2013.764660.

International Labour Office. 1924. *European housing problems since the war*. Geneva: Imprimeries réunies S.A.

Kerner, F. 1996. *Wohnraumzwangswirtschaft in Deutschland. Anfänge, Entwicklung und Wirkung vom Ersten bis zum Zweiten Weltkrieg*. Frankfurt am Main: Peter Lang. Europäische Hochschulschriften: Reihe 3, Geschichte und ihre Hilfswissenschaften. Bd. 720.

Kettunen, H., and H. Ruonavaara. 2015. "Discoursing deregulation: The case of the Finnish rental housing market." *International Journal of Housing Policy* 15 (2): 187–204. doi:10.1080/14616718.2014.990774.

Kofner, S. 1997. "Das Wohnraum-Mietrecht in Deutschland: Zeittafel zu seiner historischen Entwicklung, Teil I: 1896 bis 1945." *Deutsche Wohnungswirtschaft* 49: 321–332.

Kofner, S. 1999. "Das Wohnraum-Mietrecht in Deutschland: Zeittafel zu seiner historischen Entwicklung, Teil II: 1946 bis 1998." *Deutsche Wohnungswirtschaft* 51 (9): 275–289.

Kofner, S. 2004. *Wohnungsmarkt und Wohnungswirtschaft*. München: Oldenbourg.

Malpezzi, S., and G. Ball. 1993. "Measuring the urban policy environment: An exploratory analysis using rent controls." *Habitat international* 17 (2): 39–52. doi:10.1016/0197-3975(93)90003-U.

Messelken, S. 2015. "Noch mehr Schutz für Mieter: Justizminister Heiko Maas will Mietrecht weiter verschärfen." *immowelt.de*, November 26.

Mezler, J., and M. Seyfried. 2010. "Neue Datenbasis zur Wohnraumförderung." *Bundesbaublatt* 11: 12–15.

Nguyen, M. T. 2015. "The intersection of immigration and housing policies: Implications for the U. S. housing market and economy." *Housing Policy Debate* 25 (4): 796–798. doi:10.1080/10511482.2015.1043084.

Nicoletti, G., S. Scarpetta, and O. Boylaud. 2000. "Summary Indicators of Product Market Regulation With an Extension to Employment Protection Legislation." OECD Economics Department Working Papers, No. 226.

Noam, E. M. 1983. "The interaction of building codes and housing prices." *AREUEA Journal* 10: 394–404. doi:10.1111/1540-6229.00271.

Reichsamt des Innern. 1904. *Die Wohnungsfürsorge im Reich und in den Bundesstaaten*. Berlin: Reichsdruckerei.

Schmidt-Eichstaedt, G. 2005. *Städtebaurecht. Einführung und Handbuch*. Stuttgart: Verlag W. Kohlhammer.

Schmidthuysen, F. 1928. "Die Entwicklung der Wohnungsbauabgabe und des Geldentwertungsausgleichs bei bebauten Grundstücken (Hauszinssteuer) in Deutschland." *Finanzarchiv* 1: 162–255.

So. 1959. "Zur Frage des Wohnungsdefizits." *Wirtschaft und Statistik* 6: 302–304.

Statistisches Landesamt Bremen. 2014. "Zensus 2011." GebäGeb und Wohnungen sowie Wohnverhältnisse der Haushalte. Bundesland Bremen am 9. Mai 2011.

SVR. 2013. "Gegen eine rückwärtsgewandte Wirtschaftspolitik. Jahresgutachten 2013/14." Sachverständigenrat zur Begutachtung der gesamtwirtschaftlichen Entwicklung.

Witt, P.-C. 1979. "Inflation, Wohnungszwangswirtschaft und Hauszinssteuer." In *Wohnen im Wandel: Beiträge zur Geschichte des Alltags in der bürgerlichen Gesellschaft*, edited by L. Niethammer, 385–407. Wuppertal: Peter Hammer Verlag.

The Role of Nonprofits in Meeting the Housing Challenge in the United States

Rachel G. Bratt*

Housing owned by nonprofit housing organizations comprises one of the two components of the U.S.'s social housing sector, the other being public housing. After providing relevant background about affordable rental housing programs in the United States (including federal, state, and local strategies); the overall size of the U.S. social housing sector; and the level of direct and indirect subsidies for housing, the article focuses on the key challenges facing the nonprofit housing sector. Details also are provided about the difficulties involved in navigating the Low Income Housing Tax Credit program for both nonprofit and for-profit developers. The final section offers suggestions for how nonprofits could be better supported through a series of 'nonprofit-centric' public policies and programs. Despite the ongoing need for more federal involvement in affordable housing, and the important role that nonprofit housing organizations are able to play, the current political situation in the United States means that an expanded federally supported affordable housing agenda is highly unlikely in the foreseeable future.

1. Introduction and definitions

Although the term social housing is little used in the United States, it consists of two main types of programs: public housing and nonprofit-owned housing. 'Public housing' refers primarily to housing that has been built under the U.S. Public Housing Act of 1937 or, in a few cases, through a similar program operated at the state level.[1] Local housing authorities (LHAs) have produced public housing with a federal subsidy for the development and management of public housing; long-term ownership is retained by the LHA, with regulatory oversight provided by the U.S. Department of Housing and Urban Development (HUD).

This contrasts with the definition of public housing used in some other contexts: any housing that is developed, regulated, and/or funded by the government to provide affordable housing for the public, whether or not it is managed by the government. Thus, this broad view of public housing includes housing that is developed and owned by private for-profit and nonprofit entities, using federal subsidies. It also includes, for example, housing produced by developers in compliance with local or county government regulations, such as inclusionary zoning statutes. However, in the United States, none of these forms of housing is considered 'public housing.' Housing that is owned by nonprofit organizations, which can have a variety of unique characteristics, is considered the second component of the social housing sector.

Housing units that are owned by for-profit firms and that are either subsidized by the federal government or produced as a result of local regulatory provisions are not considered part of the social housing stock. Only actual housing units that are slated to be affordable over the long-term are so designated.[2] The 'long-term' is typically defined as more than the 30 years that is currently required in the Low Income Housing Tax Credit (LIHTC) program. Since nonprofit and public owners of housing strive for affordability in perpetuity, units owned by these sponsors are viewed as part of the social housing sector; housing built by for-profits typically does not meet this standard. Thus, although some public housing units have, over time, been lost from the public housing stock, the **intent** is for such units to be affordable in perpetuity. Also excluded from the 'public housing' category is private market housing that is rented to income-eligible households using a Section 8 Housing Choice Voucher. Such housing, too, is not under long-term affordability restrictions.

Given the challenges facing housing nonprofits, as discussed later in this article, a key question is: What are the compelling reasons for supporting nonprofit organizations as producers and managers of affordable housing? [3] There are at least three responses: First, nonprofits typically share a clear mission to produce and maintain affordable housing over the long-term. While it is essential that they be able to cover their costs, the desire to maximize returns for themselves or investors or to generate profits is absent. This means that their work is focused on maximizing benefits for the residents of the housing, rather than for the organization.

Second, nonprofits, particularly those that are community-based, provide opportunities for residents to become involved with the effort. This, in turn, not only increases the likelihood that the housing will fit in with the general neighborhood, but it also promotes resident involvement in day-to-day decision-making and, in some cases, may even provide ultimate control of the housing.

Third, since new funding for public housing development is even less likely to be forthcoming than funding for public–private initiatives that could include nonprofit organizations, the only way to increase the size of the social housing sector and to assure the availability of a stock of long-term affordable housing is through the work of nonprofits. As competition for housing continues to be intense in strong market areas, social housing is a key and, perhaps, the best, mechanism for providing low-income residents with security against unwanted displacement. Unless housing is separated from the private, speculative market, low-income tenants always are faced with the possibility that rents will increase and that they will need to move.

This article's focus on nonprofit housing should not be interpreted as a condemnation of the federal public housing program, the other major form of social housing. Indeed, many researchers (myself included) have argued that the record is far better than popular perceptions (Connerly 1986; Bratt 1989; Bloom 2008; Vale 2002; 2013) and the many reasons for the problems that have plagued public housing (e.g., poor management, stigmatizing design, and inadequate federal funding for capital repairs and day-to-day maintenance) are unrelated to the public housing concept. Nevertheless, any future deep federal funding for affordable housing would almost certainly require substantial private contributions, as in the LIHTC program, thereby eliminating the likelihood of a revised public housing program, where the entire subsidy came from the federal government. Nonprofit organizations, that work by leveraging public funds with private investments would, however, be able to participate in such a public–private funding initiative.

Although nonprofit organizations represent a key vehicle for producing affordable housing, these groups also have been blamed for undermining grassroots organizing and advocacy initiatives; instead, nonprofits' efforts have been channeled into more mainstream activities, such as housing development. For example, as a result of changes in New York City's Charter, local residents were given a stronger voice in articulating community needs and in decisions related to land use and neighborhood development. But, at the same time, the funding that became available for community groups 'helped to move groups that started as community organizers and tenant advocates more firmly into the development and ownership of low-income housing' (Wylde 1999, p. 79).[4]

There is also, by now, a fairly extensive literature critiquing the structural contradiction arising from the need for nonprofits to work closely with financial institutions and equity investors to acquire capital for development projects, while also trying to fulfill their mission to serve the community (as summarized in Bratt 2006). In short, as Stoecker has stated: 'CDCs manage capital like capitalists, but do not invest it for a profit. They manage projects but within the constraints set by the funders. They try to be community oriented while their purse strings are held by outsiders' (1997, p. 5).

A case study of decades of activism by public housing residents in New Orleans presents a critical analysis about the role of nonprofits, both in undermining community activism and in trying to mediate between capital and resident interests. As resident leaders became involved with 'a government and foundation-funded nonprofit complex,' they lost their accountability to their grassroots base. This led activists to:

> abandon direct action as their key political weapon for coercing concessions and defending the interests of public housing residents. The political allegiances and financial benefits of the nonprofit model moved these activists into a strategy of insider negotiations that prioritized the profit-making agenda of real estate interests above the housing and other material needs of black public housing residents. (Arena 2012, pp. xviii–xix)

In short, according to this view, former activists became co-opted.

Another perspective acknowledges some of the limits of nonprofits, while also providing an appreciation for their contributions. A case study of San Francisco revealed the extent to which there had been an 'NGO-ization of community-based movements' and the development of 'quasi-corporatist insider interests' (Beitel 2013, p. 167). However, at the same time, the author acknowledges significant contributions of The Council of Community Housing Organizations (whose origins date back to protests surrounding Urban Renewal), which channels funding to local nonprofits. Indeed, the work of this citywide coordinating body and local nonprofits has 'led to a significant increase in the supply of low-income affordable housing' (Beitel 2013, p. 34).

As someone who has been a close observer and strong supporter of the community-based housing movement, I take the several criticisms seriously. I acknowledge the concerns about the extent to which nonprofits can find themselves in the awkward role of trying to mediate corporate versus community interests and the potential for grassroots activism to become diverted. Indeed, I am also aware of the complexity of trying to represent the 'community' when that is far from a homogeneous construct.

On balance, though, I am impressed and heartened by the real contributions that these organizations have made in improving the lives, in concrete and observable ways, for millions of low-income people. Over the years, I have advocated for a role for private nonprofit entities, as well as for-profit entities, in producing affordable housing. The key questions relate to whether the guidelines that govern the participation of the private sector, assure the long-term affordability of the developments and promote good living environments. To what extent are these public purpose goals undermined by the developer's goal to maximize profits?. Larger more conceptual and theoretical questions about how best to create a more just economic system are obviously very important, but from a pragmatic standpoint, the pressing set of housing problems being confronted at the present time demand immediate responses. For me, it is not a question of whether community action and protest is preferable to a nonprofit-based affordable housing agenda. Clearly, both are essential components of social movements that are promoting greater social and economic opportunity, while also striving to guarantee the basic necessities of life.

2. Overview of the U.S. housing system

2.1. Federally supported rental housing programs

Consistent with many other countries, the U.S. federal government has been retreating from providing deep, direct subsidies for the development of rental housing targeted to lower income households, which had been the hallmark of the U.S.'s public housing program. Starting in 1959 and continuing during the 1960s and 1970s, a series of other federal programs were implemented that depended on private for-profit and nonprofit developers to build and manage a new generation of federally assisted housing – not considered public housing in the U.S. context.

The first federal public–private housing partnership program was enacted in 1959, in the form of below-market interest rate (BMIR) loans to private nonprofit developers for the production of housing for low-moderate income elderly renters (Section 202 program). This was followed by programs that provided BMIR loans to both nonprofit and for-profit developers for the construction of housing targeted to low- and moderate-income households. These were known as the Section 221(d)(3) and Section 236 programs, which were legislated in 1961 and 1968, respectively. The Section 514 and 515 programs are similar to the other BMIR programs, except that they target rural areas and are funded through the U.S. Department of Agriculture. These initiatives were followed by the Section 8 New Construction and Substantial Rehabilitation program (1974), which was another federal public–private production initiative that encouraged the participation of private developers, both for-profit and nonprofit. The LIHTC program, created in 1986, further cemented the role of private developers in affordable housing development.

Although the focus here is on the nonprofit sector, it is important to underscore that it is the for-profit sector that is currently the largest producer of federally assisted housing in the United States. For-profit developers produced about 78 percent of the LIHTC projects placed in service between 1987 and 2014 (Lew 2016).

The contradiction between the public purpose of maintaining affordable housing over the long-term and the desire for private sector profit became a key concern as the affordability restrictions on developments built through the BMIR programs began to expire, starting in the 1980s. The 'expiring use' problem, as it came to be known, resulted from the terms in the original contract between HUD and developers. The contracts typically gave the latter the option of prepaying the outstanding principal balance on their mortgage after 20 years, and converting the buildings to market-rate rental units or condominiums. Favorable locations of the developments could encourage such conversions, since profits could be substantial in strong market environments. By 2002, a total of 110,132 units in 953 federally subsidized developments were lost from the affordable housing stock due to the 'expiring use' problem (as cited in Schwartz 2015, p. 209). A series of public sector interventions attempted to preserve these homes for lower income occupancy. Similar problems have arisen concerning expirations on affordability restrictions on the Section 8 New Construction and Substantial Rehabilitation portfolio (Achtenberg 2006).

Table 1 presents an overview of the various types of assisted rental housing initiatives in the United States, including the traditional public housing program, and shows that there are over 8 million active assisted housing units; 71 percent are within developments, and the remainder are subsidized with Housing Choice Vouchers. Figure 1 presents a schematic view of the progression of the federal housing direct subsidy programs.

2.2. Attributes of the U.S.'s approach to subsidizing housing and ongoing needs

Four additional observations round out this overview and provide important background for understanding the context and challenges currently facing nonprofit housing organizations. First, federal funding for housing for low-income households was substantially reduced during the 1980s, when President Reagan cut back the amount of new budget authority (funding for additional housing subsidies) by 70 percent. Between 1977 and 2012, new budget authority for HUD programs declined 52 percent, in constant dollars (Schwartz 2015, p. 56).[5] The low-point came in 1997 and, since then, there has been a modest upward trend. But just looking at two key programs, the numbers are not encouraging: the public housing capital fund was reduced by about 25 percent from \$2.5 billion in FY 2010 to \$1.9 billion in FY 2016 and the HOME program, which provides a flexible source of funds for housing, has been nearly cut in half from an appropriation level of \$1.825 billion to \$950 million in FY 2016 (National Low Income Housing Coalition 2016a, Section 2, p. 6). On balance, the decline over more than four decades has been significant and damaging. This is not likely to change in the near-term, as funding during the Trump administration could result in a particularly sharp decrease in HUD funding. The President's first budget, for 2018, requested \$40.7 billion in gross discretionary funding for HUD, which is a \$6.2 billion or 13.2 percent decrease from the 2017 annualized Continuing Resolution (CR) level (U.S. Office of Management and Budget 2017).

Second, while there have been overall declines in new funding for low-income housing, subsidies for individuals who are eligible for various kinds of tax breaks through the income tax system have been on an upward trajectory. In 1967, the first year the U.S. Congress published estimated costs of tax deductions, the combined value of mortgage interest and property tax deductions (also known as the homeowners' deduction[6]) totaled \$3.7 billion (Treasury Department and Joint Committee on Internal Revenue Taxation 1972, p. 4). By 2016, these two subsidies alone cost the U.S. government about \$90 billion (see Table 2).[7]

Table 2 also shows that the level of direct federal housing assistance, which is targeted to lower income households, is much less than the subsidies provided through the tax system, with the latter consuming nearly three-quarters of the more than \$174 billion total amount of housing assistance. Stated another way, subsidies through the tax system are nearly three times the budgeted amount for all of HUD's major programs and just the homeowners' deduction alone is nearly twice the entire HUD budget (\$47 billion in 2016), which focuses on housing assistance targeted to lower income households (Joint Committee on Taxation 2017; National Low Income Housing Coalition, 2016b; U.S. Department of Housing and Urban Development, 2017).

Table 1. **Major components of U.S. assisted rental housing sector.**[a]

Project-based programs	No. of units[a]	Percentage of total assisted housing stock	Percentage of project-based programs
Public housing	1,156,839	14.1	19.9
Below-market interest rate programs (public subsidy/ private ownership)	1,404,589	17.1	24.1
Section 8 production programs (public subsidy/private ownership)	590,774	7.2	10.1
LIHTC (public subsidy/private ownership)	2,100,000	25.6	36.1
USDA Below-market interest rate programs	571,000	7.0	9.8
Subtotal	**5,823,202**	**71.0%**	**100%**
Rental subsidies			**Percentage of rental subsidies**
Housing Choice Vouchers (also known as Section 8 vouchers)	2,100,000	25.6	88.5
USDA Rental Assistance	273,000	3.3	11.5
Subtotal	**2,373,000**	**28.9%**	**100%**
TOTAL	**8,196, 202**	**100% (rounded)**	**100%**

Sources: Schwartz (2015, pp. 144, 164, 218 and 232); National Low Income Housing Coalition (2016a).

Another source estimates that, as of 2015, some 5,106,000 households were receiving rental housing assistance through a HUD program (Center on Budget and Policy Priorities 2015b). This does not include LIHTC and USDA units. Thus, this estimate is quite close to the estimates presented in this table. When there were discrepancies between various sources, I used the number that appeared to be the most up-to-date. Most discrepancies, however, were quite small.

[a]Includes only still active units; many public housing and other project-based units are no longer in the assisted housing inventory.

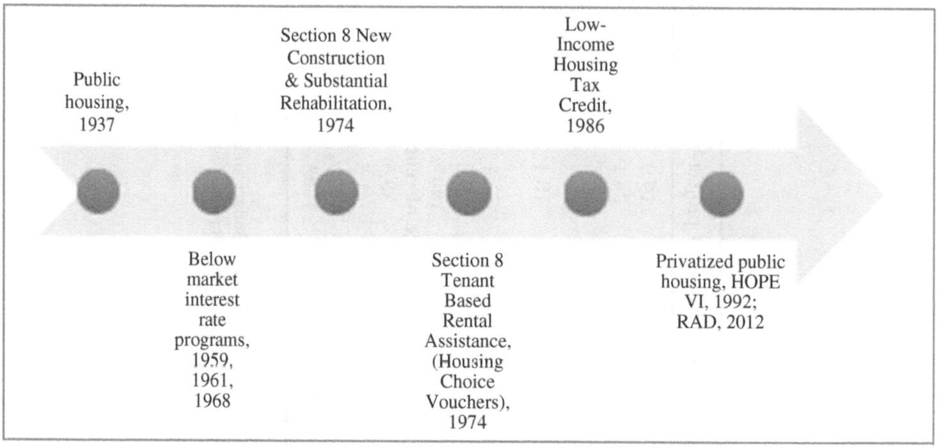

Figure 1. Progression of major federal rental housing subsidy programs targeted to lower income households.

Also important is that housing subsidies through the tax system disproportionately benefit moderate- and high-income households – 81 percent of the total amount of this subsidy goes to households earning $100,000 or more; 42 percent of the benefit goes to households with incomes over $200,000 (National Low Income Housing Coalition 2016a, Section 3, p. 20; see also; Bernstein 2013; Fischer and Sard 2013).

Third, federal rental housing strategies are, increasingly, tending to rely on the workings of the private market to raise revenues for affordable housing or to increase opportunities for lower income households to gain access to homes that otherwise would not have been built. The implications of all these changes are becoming clear: the public role in the development and management of assisted housing is dwindling and, with that, there are many unknowns about the extent to which the housing that is produced will be able to be maintained over the long-term.

Figure 2 presents a summary of how each of the four major types of federal rental housing programs operated in relation to several key factors: the ownership of the development; how the subsidy is provided; who manages the development; and how governmental regulatory oversight is implemented. In the traditional public housing program, all four components are in the public domain. In the BMIR and Section 8 New Construction/Substantial Rehabilitation programs, there was a shift to private ownership and private management. This is also true for the LIHTC program, but in that case, regulatory oversight is no longer handled by HUD, the nation's housing agency. Instead, the governmental body with responsibility for overseeing that program is the Internal Revenue Service, within the U.S. Department of Treasury; the incomes of tenants must be validated to fall within a certain range in order to safeguard the tax credit benefits for private investors. In the LIHTC program, many of the functions that HUD performed, such as overall compliance with federal regulations and determining which developers should be awarded subsidies are, instead, handled through state housing finance agencies. In addition, in both the HOPE VI and Rental Assistance Demonstration programs, which are derivatives of the public housing program, there has been a similar shift away from the pure public ownership/management/subsidy/oversight model. Instead, in both of these programs, private owners, managers, and investors are involved (Fischer 2014).

Table 2. Major indirect and direct U.S. subsidies for housing, 2016(in millions).

Program	Amount	Percentage of total housing subsidies	Percentage of subtotal tax subsidies
Major tax subsidies[a] (indirect)			
Homeownership			
Mortgage interest deduction	$ 59,000	33.9	46.3
Deduction of state and local property taxes	31,200	17.9	24.4
Exclusion of capital gains on home sales	29,200	16.8	22.9
Rental housing			
Low Income Housing Tax Credit	8200	4.7	6.4
Subtotal major tax subsidies	**$127,600**	**73.3%**	**100%**
			Percentage of subtotal direct subsidies
HUD programs[b] (direct)			
Tenant-based rental assistance	$19,629	11.3	42.2
Project-based rental assistance	10,620	6.1	22.8
Public housing (capital and operating funds)	6,400	3.7	13.8
Community development fund	3060	1.8	6.6
Homeless assistance grants	2250	1.3	4.8
Other HUD programs	3036	1.7	6.5
Subtotal HUD programs	**$44,995**	**25.9%**	**96.8% (error due to rounding)**
Subtotal USDA rural housing programs (direct)	**$1487**	**0.8**	**3.2**
Subtotal direct programs	**$46,482**	**26.7**	**100%**
TOTAL Tax and Direct Subsidies	**$174,082**	**100%**	

Sources:
[a]Tax figures are for calendar year 2016 (Joint Committee on Taxation 2017, p. 34).
bHUD and USDA figures are for fiscal year 2016 (National Low Income Housing Coalition 2016b).

Program	Ownership	Government Subsidy	Private Investors	Management	Regulatory Oversight
Public Housing (traditional)	Local housing authority— public entity	Covers cost of construction with additional funds allocated for management and capital repairs/modernization.	No	Local Housing Authority	HUD
Below Market Interest Rate (BMIR) programs	Private for-profit or nonprofit developers	Federal government made up the difference between prevailing interest rates and interest rates of 3 percent and 1 percent (HUD Section 221(d)(3) and 236 programs, respectively. USDA Section 515 program also with a 1 percent interest rate; Section 515 is the only BMIR program that is still active). In addition, various tax incentives provided additional subsidies to limited partners in the project.	Yes	Private for-profit or nonprofit owner or separate management firm.	HUD
Section 8 New Construction, Substantial Rehabilitation	Private for-profit or nonprofit developers	Deep federal subsidy to cover cost of actual costs (both development and management) and what lower income households can pay @ 30 percent of income. In addition, various tax incentives provided additional subsidies to limited partners in the project.	Yes	Private for-profit or nonprofit owner, or separate management firm.	HUD
Low Income Housing Tax Credit	Private for-profit or nonprofit developers	Tax credits, which provide a dollar-for- dollar reduction in tax liability, are bought by private investors. Proceeds from the sale of these tax credits are used to cover development costs.	Yes	Private for-profit or nonprofit owner or separate management firm.	Diminished federal role. Oversight no longer performed by HUD. Instead, this role is carried out by the Internal Revenue Service (IRS), U.S. Department of Treasury
Public Housing Variations, HOPE VI and RAD	Public housing converted to private ownership	LIHTC or Section 8 contracts replacing public housing subsidy.	Yes	Private for-profit or nonprofit owner or separate management firm.	HUD and Internal Revenue Service (IRS), U.S. Department of Treasury

Figure 2. Changes in the public role in U.S. federal housing programs.

The fourth and final general comment about the U.S. housing system is that the net result of reduced new funding for housing can be seen in the estimates of housing needs; there continue to be longstanding and serious housing problems in the United States, particularly facing very low-income renters.

> Between 2007 and 2011, the number of income-eligible renters rose by 3.3 million while the number of assisted housing units was essentially unchanged . . . securing housing assistance is increasingly difficult. At last count in 2011, more than three-quarters of low-income households that qualified for subsidies were left to find housing in the private market. For the nation's 11.5 million extremely low-income renters (defined as household income of less than 30 percent of AMI), this meant competing for a dwindling stock of just 3.2 million units that were both affordable and available. (Joint Center for Housing Studies 2014, pp. 5–6; also see; National Low Income Housing Coalition 2016a, section 1, pp. 10–11)

In addition:

- Housing affordability is a concern that faces tens of millions of households, including many with middle incomes. One estimate is that more than one-third (40.9 million) of all U.S. households have housing costs that exceed their means.

- More than four out of five households with incomes below $15,000 – about equivalent to full-time work at the federal minimum wage – paid more than 30 percent of those incomes for housing, with more than two-thirds paying over 50 percent. In the next-lowest income group (earning $15,000–29,999), three-quarters of renters were cost burdened compared with 52 percent of owners.
- The incidence of severe cost burdens remains particularly high among minority households; 27 percent of black households were severely burdened, along with 24 percent of Hispanic households and 21 percent of Asian households. In contrast, only 14 percent of white households paid more than half their incomes for housing (Joint Center for Housing Studies 2014, pp. 27–28).

The intensity of the housing problem was captured in a story about the 10,000 applicants for one of the new 73 rental vouchers available. One of the applicants was a 31-year-old single mother who had been living in a hotel for 2 years with her young child, one of nearly 5,000 families Massachusetts has been housing in emergency shelters and motels. Although she knew that the odds of landing a rental voucher were long, she was hoping for a 'little bit of normalcy,' so she and her son wouldn't have to be crammed into one tiny little room... (Johnston 2014).

Before proceeding with a more detailed exploration of some of the key issues facing the United States's nonprofit housing sector, the following section presents a brief discussion of the array of state and municipal-level strategies that promote housing affordable to lower income households. These efforts have been critical, particularly in view of the federal government's trajectory of reduced funding for deep, direct housing subsidies for lower income households.

3. State and local housing initiatives[8]

Responding to the reductions in federal housing assistance, and in an attempt to address local needs, an array of state and local housing programs have encouraged and stimulated the participation of the private for-profit and nonprofit sectors. Many of these efforts started in the 1980s, as federal funding for housing programs began to be cut significantly. But a few have longer standing origins. The following is a brief summary, not an exhaustive catalogue, of the dozens of state and local initiatives that promote the development and preservation of housing that is affordable to lower income households. This information is presented under two main categories: New programs and revenue sources for affordable housing; and regulatory strategies. Data on state and local programs, which do not use a federal subsidy program, are often not available in an aggregated form, so estimates concerning numbers of units produced are not presented.

3.1. New programs and revenue sources for affordable housing

This first category encompasses the many types of efforts aimed at directly producing affordable housing by creating new programs or new dedicated revenue streams. A handful of states, including Connecticut, Hawaii, New York, and Massachusetts developed state-based public housing programs; the latter two states, as well as others, also have an extensive history of implementing their own subsidized public–private partnership programs, as well as unique initiatives targeting specific subpopulations, such as the homeless or elderly. A few states, such as New Jersey, Illinois, and Massachusetts also have state-based rental voucher programs.

Beyond creating programs through direct appropriations, state and local governments also are creative in figuring out how to raise additional funding for affordable housing. Seventeen states have a supplementary Low Income Housing Tax Credit program (Novogradac 2017). Housing Trust Funds – income from a particular source earmarked for housing – are another important strategy for generating revenue. Strategies may include special taxes, such as land transfer taxes; interest on escrow accounts; or revenue generated from sales of abandoned or publicly owned property.[9] Massachusetts has created an innovative mechanism to raise funds, through the Community Preservation Act, which enables localities to develop their own programs for affordable housing, as well as for historic preservation and open space acquisition or improvements, through a surcharge on the property tax, with some matching state funds.

Two additional Massachusetts initiatives are also noteworthy. First, in 1990, the state passed an Interstate Banking Act, which requires companies that acquire Massachusetts banks to make funds available to a quasi-public agency, the Massachusetts Housing Partnership, for affordable housing. Second, in 2012, the Community Investment Tax Credit was created to raise private funds by offering tax credits, to help support the work of community development corporations (CDCs).

Although not widely used, regional revenue sharing is another potentially effective strategy, whereby each city in the region contributes to a pool, based on the growth in its tax base. The revenues may then be redistributed to low-growth areas, as well as to high-growth areas that may be particularly resistant to developing affordable housing.

A number of cities and states have leveraged their own funds to encourage banks to meet the credit needs of low-income households and communities, which can include providing financing for affordable housing developments. While the federal government has created an important tool through the Community Reinvestment Act (which has been supplemented by similar legislation in at least three states – Connecticut, Massachusetts, and New York), localities also have created 'linked deposit' programs. Financial institutions that meet a certain standard of lending to targeted groups and communities may be given preferential treatment by governments seeking to invest public funds (Davis 2006, p.369).

A final type of initiative that is aimed at raising additional funds for affordable housing involves the use of tax increment financing. Under such a program, increased tax revenues expected from new development are typically pledged to cover the costs of, for example, new roads and schools; but a minimum percentage of the anticipated new revenues can also be earmarked for affordable housing (Lubell 2006).

3.2. Regulatory strategies[10]

Programs within this second category typically create incentives, sanctions, and sometimes both, for noncompliance with a particular statute. But the overriding goal is to create a framework for cities, towns, and developers to promote affordable housing development.

The New Jersey experience is particularly noteworthy. The Supreme Court in that state issued two groundbreaking rulings, known as Mt. Laurel I and II, in 1975 and 1983, respectively. Based on these cases, all communities in New Jersey are directed to create zoning to accommodate housing for low- and moderate-income people. A so-called 'builder's remedy' allows a developer, who demonstrates that a municipality's zoning is exclusionary and who commits to a set aside of low-to-moderate-income units, to seek permission from the court to build more market-rate units than allowed under existing zoning, as long as the site and project meet certain planning and environmental standards. A municipality whose zoning cannot accommodate a range of housing options could be subject to a court mandate, which might include voiding its existing zoning, as well as other sanctions. Any community that has not met its 'fair share' of affordable housing is vulnerable to a court-ordered directive (trumping any town objections) that the builder be granted the right to build, so long as the specified number of affordable units are part of the deal.

Even before the New Jersey court cases, Massachusetts had enacted a law that had many of the same components as the New Jersey 'fair share' requirement. Since 1969, Massachusetts' Chapter 40B has required that all cities and towns have no less than 10 percent of their housing stock designated as affordable to lower income households. Under the statute, developers that are willing to set aside 20–25 percent of the units being built in a given development for households earning less than 80 percent of AMI, may be able to bypass town zoning requirements concerning minimum lot sizes, density, and other non-health and non-environmental-related provisions. Several other states, including Connecticut, California, Rhode Island, and New York have adopted variations on the New Jersey and Massachusetts programs (for a comparison of several of these state-based initiatives, see Bratt and Vladeck 2014).

Voluntary 'density bonus' programs, such as one adopted in Virginia in 1990, can also be effective. Developers are allowed increases in the density for either single family or multifamily units in exchange for the inclusion of a fixed percentage of affordable units. Such programs may be most effective when they are combined with a mandatory set-aside program that grants density bonuses as a form of 'compensation' to participating developers (Salsich, 2003, p. 16).

Massachusetts' Chapter 40R program, enacted in 2004, encourages municipalities to create special zoning overlay districts that allow for increased densities of single family, townhouses, and condominiums/apartments, so long as the zoning includes the requirement that at least 20 percent of the units are affordable and that they include a mix of uses. As an incentive for creating such a zoning district and creating a streamlined process for development within these areas, cities and towns can receive between $10,000 and $600,000 in state funding, as well as $3000 for each new home created.

Many localities, nonetheless, continue to be resistant to accepting their 'fair share' of affordable housing. Among the reasons frequently cited are increased traffic, potential negative environmental impacts, and added school costs. To address the latter concern, Massachusetts enacted Chapter 40S in 2005, whereby state subsidies are provided to local governments to cover the net increase in education costs resulting from children living in the affordable housing developments built under the Chapter 40R program.

Inclusionary zoning and linkage are two popular strategies for harnessing growth in 'hot market'[11] areas for the benefit of affordable housing. Under the former approach, localities mandate the provision of a certain percentage of affordable housing in all new privately built developments over a particular size (Nenno 1991; Graddy and Bostic 2010; Salsich 1999). While inclusionary zoning policies are able to produce affordable housing units without public subsidy, the costs of the market rate units need to be high enough to offset the cost to the developer of providing the lower rent units, thereby creating upward pressure on private housing market costs. This means that, in reality, it is the market rate renters and homeowners who are covering the costs of including the below-market units.

Under linkage programs, a developer of a commercial property is typically required to either make a contribution to a designated fund for housing or directly construct or rehabilitate affordable housing units at another location. In 'hot' housing markets, city officials are in a good position to create or increase fees being charged as a way to offset the price rises created by new development (Adams 2015; Logan 2015). Linkage programs can also be a source of capital for a local housing trust fund.

Less of a 'stick' than linkage requirements, some local governments have offered various types of tax abatement 'carrots.' This enables developers to make payments in lieu of taxes for developments that include affordable housing. Funds generated in this way from Battery Park City in New York, for example, have helped support thousands of affordable units elsewhere in the city.

A number of cities and states have also included various long-term use restrictions in connection with funding initiatives for subsidized development. Affordability on such projects may be guaranteed for several decades, for the 'useful life' of the property, or in perpetuity. Vermont has been a pioneer in developing mechanisms to preserve access for low-income households to federally subsidized developments where 'use restrictions' were expiring (Davis 2006).

Thus, the federal government's reduced involvement with housing programs has stimulated a wide array of state and local programs, some of which have very low levels of any type of public involvement, thereby continuing the trend of federal retrenchment in subsidized rental housing programs, discussed earlier. Looking at one example, inclusionary zoning, that is, perhaps, the most prevalent of the local regulatory strategies, there is virtually no public role (other than the adoption of the original statute by the legislative body and approval of the specific plan by the local planning board). Ownership and management of these developments is fully in private hands. And, once they are built, there is little or no regulatory oversight related to the continued requirement that a certain number of units remain affordable. Sometimes, a public or private monitoring agency may be given the task for oversight, but often the continued affordability of these units comes through long-term, unmonitored deed restrictions.

Taken together, the state and local approaches, while producing units in many locations, only have been able to make modest dents in the overall problem – they are not a proverbial 'magic bullet.' Although there is a considerable amount of enthusiasm for inclusionary zoning, for example, largely because it produces affordable housing without public subsidies, the extent to which these programs let the government 'off the hook' for being responsible for a 'decent home' for all is troubling.[12] And, although state and local initiatives have helped to fill the gap between housing needs and the supply of decent, affordable housing, the cumulative outcomes are far from robust.

Regardless of relative levels of success (an analysis that is beyond the scope of this article), these approaches, along with federal strategies, comprise the 'toolkit' that nonprofits (as well as for-profit developers) use to develop and preserve affordable housing. Although many innovative programs and ideas are being utilized, the overall system is still presenting complex challenges for nonprofits.

4. U.S. housing nonprofits: overview and key challenges

Nonprofit housing organizations continue to be a critical part of the post-public housing era in the United States. As shown in Table 3, total cumulative production by various types of nonprofit housing organizations comprises about 70 percent of the overall U.S. social housing sector; public housing comprises virtually all the remaining total of the approximately 5,000,000 social housing units. Among nonprofits, CDCs are the single largest nonprofit producer, accounting for nearly one-quarter of all social housing units and 35 percent of the social housing units produced by nonprofits.

Table 3. Components and approximate size of the U.S. social housing sector, 2016.[a]

	Number of units	Percentage of total social housing units	Percentage of public housing
Public housing			
Federal (family and elderly) (local PHAs *N* = 3095)[b]	1,156,839[b]	22.9	76.3
Department of Defense (for military households)	300,000[c]	5.9	19.8
Other programs (state and local)	59,629[d]	1.2	3.9
Subtotal public housing	**1,516,468**	**30.0%**	**100%**
			Percentage of nonprofit housing (adjusted total)
Nonprofit housing			
Community development corporations (including housing development organizations) (*N* = 4,600)[e]	1,252,000[e]	24.8	35.5
Housing partnership network members (*N* = 97)[f]	219,300[f]	4.3	6.2
Community land trusts (*N* = 220)[g]	59,813[g]	1.2	1.7
Limited equity cooperatives	425,000[h]	8.4	12.1
Federally subsidized housing for the elderly	400,000[i]	7.9	11.3
Habitat for humanity (*N* = 1,400)[j]	130,523[k]	2.6	3.7
Mutual housing and other nonprofit organizations	240,000[h]	4.8	6.8
Estimated additional production since data was collected for each type of organization, as presented above	800,000[l]	16.0	22.7
Subtotal nonprofit housing	**3,526,636**	**69.9%**	**100%**
TOTAL ALL SOCIAL HOUSING UNITS	**~5,043,104**	**100% (rounded)**	

Sources:

[a]Table updated from Bratt (2012, p. 442). This version also appears in Bratt, Rosenthal and Wiener (forthcoming).

The various notes, below, describe some variations from prior presentations. Attempting to compile this type of data is very difficult and subject to errors.

[b]Cited in Schwartz (2015, p. 164).

[c]http://www.acq.osd.mil/housing/ct97_congress.htm (accessed 14 February 2016)

[d]Stone (2006) had estimated 700,000 other state and local public housing units and this was the number presented previously (Bratt 2012, p. 442). However, my subsequent efforts to confirm this number have proven unsuccessful. Based on the information I have been able to find, I believe that a more accurate number of 'other state and local public housing' is 59,629 units. According to Linda Couch, Senior Vice President for Policy, National Low Income Housing Coalition, there are only four states with state-based public housing programs, Connecticut, Hawaii, Massachusetts and New York (email communication, 26 February 2015). Connecticut = 11,500 units (Michael C. Santoro, CD Specialist, Office of

Policy, Research and Housing Support, Connecticut Department of Housing, Private email communication, 3 March 2016). Hawaii = 864 units. A report states that there is 'no subsidy' associated with these units (Hawaii Public Housing Authority, 2015, p. 10). However, in a follow-up phone call to the agency a staff member, Mari Car, clarified that this means that there is no federal subsidy (4 March 2016). Massachusetts = 45,484 units. (Number provided by Margot LeClair, Massachusetts Department of Housing and Community Development, 1 March 2016 (telephone call). As of 30 June 1997, there were 50,285 state-aided public housing units (Citizens' Housing and Planning Association, 1999), meaning that 90 percent of this portfolio has remained under state control. New York = 1,781. In all, New York State financed the construction of some 66,123 public housing units (New York State, Homes and Community Renewal, 2016). Thus, nearly all of New York State's state-funded public housing units have been 'federalized' – transferred to the federal public housing stock.

e. This number comes from the last national census of CDCs (National Congress for Community Economic Development 2005). However, according to the National Alliance of Community Economic Development Associations (2010) the production by community development corporations (CDCs), large nonprofit housing producers and other types of nonprofits totaled 1,614,000 units. In this chart, an effort is made to break out the different types of nonprofits. However, there may be some double counting in the number of units listed for CDCs, Housing Partnership Network members, and other types of nonprofits. This is one reason why the figures in the chart should be viewed as approximations.

f. Housing Partnership Network, Membership Profile (2014 data).

g. The total number of CLTs is an estimate offered by Emily Thaden (private email communication, 16 February 2016). The production data is based only on the number of members in the CLT Network (N=136).

However, since 24 of these organizations did not have any rental units in their portfolio as of 31 December 2014, the production number in the chart is based only on 112 CLTs. 'Of members with residential units (N = 112), one member stewarded 32,000 cooperative units, which accounted for 53.5 percent of all member units' (Thaden and Webb, 2015, p. 9). The production figure of 59,813 was calculated from this information.

h. The numbers for 'limited equity cooperatives' and 'mutual housing and other nonprofit organizations' are from Stone (2006).

i. See the National Low Income Housing Coalition (2016a, Section 4, p. 24). Schwartz (2015) cites a slightly lower number, 360,000, and also notes that some sources estimate only 270,000.

j. http://www.habitat.org/where-we-build/united-states (accessed 14 February 2016).

k. Private email communication from Angie Kuhlmann, Habitat for Humanity, 10 March 2015.

l. Several of the figures in the chart are outdated, particularly production by CDCs. CDCs produced some 602,000 units in the seven years between 1998 and 2005, for an annual average of 86,000/year. One estimate could be that about this number of units has been produced by CDCs in each of the eleven years since the 2005 CDC census (National Congress for Community Economic Development 2005), for a total of 946,000. Additional nonprofit production, by groups other than CDCs is also not known. In particular, as noted above, the data for 'limited equity cooperatives' and 'mutual housing and other nonprofit organizations' are more than ten years old. On the other hand, nonprofit production was likely reduced significantly during the worst years of the recession, so it is reasonable to assume that annual nonprofit production was reduced for several years. On balance, I am estimating that the nonprofit sector has added at least 800,000 units, since the data cited for this chart were collected. Based on the estimates of the total number of nonprofit organizations in the U.S. presented in this figure, there are more than 5,000 nonprofit organizations producing housing. The calculation of un-counted units assumes that, in the eleven years starting in 2006 and continuing through 2016, there was an average annual production of less than 20 units/year/organization, a number that is consistent with the average annual CDC housing unit production between 1998 and 2005, which ranged between 18 and 23 units per organization, per year (calculated from figures presented in National Congress for Community Economic Development 2005). The total size of the social housing sector presented here is roughly the same as that presented previously (Bratt 2012), but some of the production, by program or organizational type, has shifted.

The origin of CDCs dates back to the 1960s, as a community-based response to urban problems. Grassroots protest and advocacy movements, which often formed around arson, redlining by financial institutions, displacement due to urban renewal, and dilapidated housing, transformed into a more positive set of initiatives aimed at producing new or rehabilitated affordable units for local residents. As noted earlier, some observers have been critical of this reorientation from protest to housing development, since it channeled community-based activism into the need to master the complexities of housing development. In short, this new agenda involved community groups working within the existing system, as opposed to the activism that, at least in part, was based on a more fundamental critique of the prevailing market-based housing system.

During the 1970s and 1980s, the nonprofit housing movement began to take shape, with large numbers of organizations forming during this period. As of late 1990, there were an estimated 2000 CDCs; seven years later, the estimated number skyrocketed to 3600 (National Congress for Community Economic Development 1991; 1999). The last census of CDCs, which is now more than a decade old, placed the number of CDCs at 4600 (National Congress for Community Economic Development 2005). While the number of organizations has grown considerably during the past five decades, we also know that many organizations have gone out of business or merged with other nonprofits. The above estimates are not able to capture the kind of more nuanced fluctuations that have occurred.

Momentum for CDC growth was also fueled by the creation of several national intermediary organizations, which began to provide technical and financial resources to nonprofits (e.g., NeighborWorks America, 1978 – formerly Neighborhood Reinvestment Corporation; Local Initiatives Support Corporation, 1979; and Enterprise Community Partners, formerly Enterprise Foundation, 1982). The current period, dating from the 1990s, can be characterized as increasing professionalism of the sector, a greater focus on training programs, and efforts to work closely with for-profit entities, social services providers, and public officials in collaborative development efforts. The various entities and supports for CDCs have been characterized as being part of a community development system (Bratt 1989; Frisch and Servon 2006; Mayer and Keyes 2012).

Although CDCs are the single most prevalent type of nonprofit housing organization, this sector encompasses several different forms, as noted in Table 3, each of which has various attributes, strengths, and weaknesses (Davis 1994; Stone 2006). Even within the CDC sector, there are many different types, with small 'mom and pop' store-front groups with only a few employees, to large organizations with hundreds of staff members (Vidal 1992). And the extent to which any one group will encounter specific challenges is, at least in part, dependent on their size, asset base, organizational capacity, and the local context in which they work.

The variety of nonprofit groups notwithstanding, most of the research in this area has focused on CDCS. There has been a great deal of interest in understanding the various challenges that CDCs face and the kinds of capacities needed for them to be productive producers and managers of affordable housing (see, for example, Bratt 2006; Glickman and Servon 1998). Often cited are the long hours of work required and the frequency of staff burn-out, accompanied by generally lower salaries than would be available in other settings; the need for strong leadership, both by the board and the executive director; the difficulty of covering basic overhead and operations costs; and the need to have on staff, or have access to, a team of highly skilled development professionals, who are able to carry out a variety set of tasks that include legal work, financial analysis, community organizing, and delivery of resident services.

In terms of putting together development deals, nonprofits work in an environment of scarce resources, both for subsidies and for gap financing from conventional and public lenders. Then, too, there is the complexity of packaging deals with layers of funding all having different requirements. Also challenging is that affordable housing development demands a great deal of collaboration with a range of public, private, and nonprofit organizations in order to bring deals to fruition and to provide the desired level and types of services. Finally, nonprofits are typically eager to work with their local community and to be responsive to their needs. But, as noted previously, communities are not homogeneous entities, with different groups of residents and business owners likely having different ideas and goals for any given proposal. Not surprisingly, all these challenges can result in enormous frustration, since any given development deal is likely to take a long time to complete.

In addition to fulfilling their mission to develop long-term, affordable housing, CDCs also typically work in a number of other areas: neighborhood revitalization, citizen engagement, and providing social supports and other services aimed at promoting economic security and well-being for their residents. But, here too, projects are certain to take a very long time and measurable results may be very difficult to identify and a great deal of patience is needed.

A further challenge, also mentioned earlier, is that the very structure of CDCs may be problematic. Bratt has summarized the potential conflict as follows: 'To what extent can CDCs, organizations whose names includes the word "corporation," and who are forced to work closely with financial institutions and city governments, really be advocates for low income interests' (2006, p. 348)?

4.1. CDCs in the context of local housing markets and land use regulations

The workings of the private real estate market impact nonprofit, as well as for-profit, affordable housing developers, and can make it easier or harder for them to do development deals or to manage existing properties. Housing markets can present problems both in areas where the market is weak and where it is 'hot.' Weak markets are characterized by high vacancy rates, abandoned or boarded up buildings, vandalism/crime in the area, and long periods that homes and apartments stay on the market, un-rented or un-sold. In such areas, construction and management costs may be higher due to the need for extra security. In addition, in weak markets low cost market-rate housing is likely to compete with any existing or planned social housing, in terms of attracting tenants. Although the latter approach is likely to include a long-term affordability component, the roughly comparable rents make alternatives to social housing attractive. In addition, in terms of for-sale homes, if a market rate home is not much more expensive than the subsidized unit, most would-be homeowners would opt for the former, since the latter would likely include a long-term deed restriction controlling the inflationary value of the home.

In contrast, in hot markets, desirable land and buildings are costly and rarely stay on the market for long (also see footnote #11). Although a competitive development environment in these areas can be healthy, the need for nonprofits to compete with other nonprofits and for-profit developers for market-priced land and buildings, which can be used for affordable housing, can also make development very difficult or impossible for some groups (Bratt 2009b). Even if the property is feasible from a development perspective, the nonprofit may have difficulty assembling the needed funds quickly enough to, perhaps, outbid a for-profit developer.

Data on the extent to which nonprofits see competition from other nonprofit or for-profit developers comes from surveys from both the U.S. and abroad. Based on a survey completed by members of the U.S. Housing Partnership Network (*N* = 49 respondents), and from counterparts in Australia (*N* = 15), Canada (*N* = 10), and the United Kingdom (*N* = 14), Walsh and Davidson-Sawyer (2014) concluded that the nonprofit CEOs surveyed from the U.S. 'experienced the most change in the competitive environment with for-profits over the past three years' (pp. 9, 10). Nonprofit CEOs from other countries also reported changes in the competitive environment they were facing or anticipate facing in the future (see also Milligan, Hulse, and Davison 2013)

Another survey effort, one in which I was engaged, assessed organizational behavior and strategies among nonprofits in two U.S. locales – the Boston area of Massachusetts and the San Francisco Bay Area of California. Most organizations in our very small sample (a total of 12 organizations, 6 in each locale) have reported a decrease in the availability of suitable land for building. In addition, all 12 organizations reported a change in the pressure in their local housing market(s) and one-half (or slightly more) of the groups reported a change in the level of competition by nonprofit and for-profit housing organizations. In all the above examples, groups reported that the changes were important drivers in their operations (Bratt, Rosenthal and Wiener, forthcoming).

Another key aspect of how local housing markets affect housing development relates to the constraints created by local 'exclusionary' zoning that is prevalent in many suburban locales. Indeed, without available land, there can be no housing development, whether affordable or not.

Zoning that is exclusionary, whether by intent or by outcome, typically requires large lots (often in excess of one acre) for the construction of single-family homes. Also, many cities and towns have no zoning at all for multifamily dwellings, thereby precluding opportunities for producing dwellings, which could accommodate lower income households (Glaeser, Schuetz, and Ward 2006; Fisher 2007). This problem has been well understood for decades. For example, the 1968 Report of the National Commission on Urban Problems recommended that state governments take actions to amend planning and zoning enabling statutes to ensure 'the provision of adequate sites for housing persons of all income levels and to require that governments exercising the zoning power prepare plans showing how the community proposes to carry out such objectives in accordance with county or regional housing plans. . ..' (pp. 213, 215, 242).

Nearly five decades later, the exclusion of affordable housing in suburban areas is hardly a thing of the past. Indeed, 'exclusionary land-use regulations are still commonplace, and even in those states that have housing appeals or fair share statutes, the process of overcoming local regulations is often slow and expensive' (Mallach 2009, p. 174). An examination of various types of interventions aimed at countering exclusionary zoning revealed that: 'there has been an increase in the number of municipalities producing and/or experiencing a net increase in affordable housing. . .' However, attainment of the state-mandated goals in Massachusetts, Rhode Island, and New Jersey is a 'work in progress. In the two locales that have a 10 percent affordable housing goal (Massachusetts and Rhode Island), only a minority of municipalities has attained the goal (11 percent and 28 percent, respectively). In New Jersey, with its "fair-share" goal, only 30 percent of municipalities have attained the state goal' (Bratt and Vladeck 2014, p. 624).

The fact that municipalities are not meeting their goals for affordable housing production likely is a combination of there not being sufficient land for this purpose and/or that adequate subsidies to make the developments work are inadequate. Nonprofit developers of affordable housing (as well as for-profits), all must work within the land use frameworks of each particular locale. And, in many suburban areas, these frameworks can prohibit building homes on small lots and developing multifamily housing.

5. Specific challenges of using the LIHTC program for nonprofit (as well as for-profit) affordable housing developers

Beyond the various challenges discussed in the prior section, the LIHTC program, as the current major vehicle for developing affordable housing, is neither an easy to use nor an efficient development subsidy. Even if a developer has a thorough understanding of the program and has an ability to navigate its requirements, nonprofits (as well for-profits) will encounter some important constraints when working with this program. The following summarizes eight of the most compelling concerns related to the LIHTC.[13]

5.1. Stiff competition for 9 percent tax credits

The LIHTC program offers two types of tax credits. The 9 percent tax credit is the most sought after and is awarded to developments through a competitive process, usually administered through the state's housing finance agency. The amount of 9 percent tax credits that can be allocated by any given state per year is based on population. A developer who is awarded a 9 percent tax credit is able to raise equity equal to the present value of 70 percent of the eligible costs of the project. In the case of 4 percent tax credits, which are not awarded on a competitive basis, the developer is only able to raise 30 percent of the project's eligible costs. In short, the higher the tax credit rate the more equity that can be raised and the lower the amount of gap dollars required to close a deal. Across the country, there are about three to four applications for every 9 percent tax credit awarded (Serlin 2016). The award of the 4 percent tax credit is automatic, so long as the development is utilizing tax exempt financing. All LIHTC developments must set aside at least 40 percent of the units for renters earning no more than 60 percent of AMI or 20 percent of the units for renters earning 50 percent or less of AMI.

5.2. The value of the tax credit fluctuates with local and national investment markets

In order for developers to utilize the LIHTCs, they must be sold to investors. In exchange for their investment, investors enjoy a tax credit ($1 reduction in tax liability for every $1 of tax credit) for a period of 10 years. If, for example, the eligible basis[14] of the project is $10 million dollars, tax credit investors would receive tax credits equal to $10 million × 9% or $900,000 per year for 10 years.

In the early years of the LIHTC program, investors were wary about this new investment opportunity and looked for high rates of return. As a result, the amount of equity that could be raised per tax credit dollar provided hovered around $0.50. Over time, investors became more comfortable with the program, which was further boosted when Congress made the program permanent, in 1993. Since then, the value of the tax credit has typically ranged from around $0.80 to more than one dollar, for every dollar of tax credit provided. During the economic downturn in the late 2000s, the LIHTC was less sought after by investors and saw a decline in its value. Since then, however, there has been a general return to a valuation of more than one dollar for every dollar of tax credit. However, the value of the tax credit varies by region, with the more competitive housing markets on the east and the west coasts attracting the highest prices for each dollar of tax credit (Schwartz 2015). In addition, although still called 9 percent and 4 percent credits, there is no guarantee that these rates will prevail and, in fact, in recent years, the rates for each type of tax credit have been somewhat lower and are currently 'floating.'

With tax reform likely to be on the Trump administration's agenda, the entire LIHTC program may be vulnerable. In addition, the attractiveness of tax credit investments could be in jeopardy if changes in the tax code reduce marginal income tax brackets. If, for example, the top corporate tax rate is reduced from 35 percent, the amount of equity that could be raised through the program would be significantly reduced (Wallace and Novogradac, 2016).

5.3. To reach the lowest income households, multiple subsidies are needed

LIHTCs, by themselves, are not able to assist the lowest income households, since the LIHTC does not provide deep enough subsidies to make the units affordable to these groups. To make the units affordable to households earning below the targeted income levels of 50–60 percent of AMI,[15] additional subsidies must be accessed. Often, development deals involve six or more funders, which create a very cumbersome, time-consuming process.

Data from a number of sources indicate that LIHTC developments do, indeed, manage to reach lower income households. Several studies concluded that most LIHTC residents have incomes in the range of 40–50 percent of AMI (summarized by Schwartz 2015, p. 145), while another found that 45 percent of LIHTC tenants have incomes at or below 30 percent of AMI (O'Regan and Horn 2013, p. 598). Lower income households living in LIHTC developments are either the beneficiaries of multiple subsidies (e.g., almost like winning the lottery twice) or they are paying more than 30 percent of their income for rent. Again, looking to Schwartz's summary of relevant studies, he notes that researchers found that about: '47 percent of the [LIHTC] properties placed in service from 1995 through 2006 house one or more tenants with rental vouchers... [and] 7–13 percent of all voucher holders reside in tax-credit housing' (2015, p. 145). A comprehensive study, which looked at LIHTC developments in 18 states, totaling nearly 40 percent of all LIHTCs in the country, found that among households earning 30 percent of less of AMI, 70 percent receive an additional rental subsidy (O'Regan and Horn 2013, p. 598).[16]

There is no suggestion here that the households benefiting from the double subsidy are unworthy or that they do not deserve this level of assistance. Rather, the concern is that, from a public policy perspective, with only about one-quarter of low-income renter households receiving federal rental housing assistance (Center on Budget and Policy Priorities 2017a), the fact that so many of the households who get **any** assistance actually get double assistance, may be viewed as an unfair distribution of scarce resources.

With the costs of building high-quality housing rising, and the need to cobble together sufficient subsidies from a number of sources, it is not surprising that the final per unit cost can be very high. Critics, and even proponents, sometimes question themselves quietly and 'off the record' about whether it is justifiable to provide a single household with a home costing $350,000 (or more), when they are able to cover only a small fraction of the capital and operating costs, with the rest coming from public subsidy. How should the amount of this subsidy be viewed in relation to other competing and compelling uses of that money – health care, education, employment training, and other needed services? Alternatively, the funds also could be channeled for infrastructure improvements in roads, bridges, and other public facilities. One of the responses on the part of the housing community is to present data on the ripple effects that good housing can have on a community and, conversely, how much bad housing or no housing can cost, in terms of additional health costs, losses of productivity, and the need to provide shelter housing for homeless families.

5.4. *Narrow size range of LIHTC developments*

In addition to a fairly narrow band of income eligibility, it is nearly impossible to use the LIHTC program to produce smaller projects (less than about 30 units) and when building on scattered sites. This often means that the LIHTC cannot be used in many inner city locations, which may have a large stock of one to three family homes in need of rehabilitation or small, buildable vacant lots. Assembling these types of parcels into a single development package using the LIHTC program has proven to be extremely challenging. As Boston attorney Roberta Rubin explained:

> If a development has fewer than 30 units, it is tough to do a LIHTC project because of the fixed costs (including legal, accounting and consulting costs) associated with LIHTC investment, many of which are the same whether you have a large project or a small one. At the same time, it can be hard to generate investor interest in a small scattered-site LIHTC project, which may result in a lower amount of equity that can be raised.[17]

LIHTC projects are predominantly in the range of 50–60 units, with the average development having 58 units (Schwartz 2015). Thus, a substantial amount of work, which is required to do a LIHTC deal, goes into developing a fairly modest number of homes and many potential smaller projects are not feasible with this subsidy.

5.5. *Location of LIHTC developments*

Questions have been raised about how the location of LIHTC-funded developments impacts residential segregation patterns, both in terms of race and income. Summarizing the existing data, Schwartz (2015) notes that there has been a 'disproportionate percentage of tax-credit housing located in minority and low-income neighborhoods,' resulting in a perpetuation of racial and economic segregation (p.148). Countering this view, McClure (2006) argues that LIHTC developments may provide enhanced opportunities, compared with housing vouchers for low-income tenants to move to low-poverty areas. Although HUD guidelines concerning 'affirmatively furthering fair housing' suggest that localities should give priority to affordable housing development located in high opportunity areas, there needs to be sufficient interest and concrete proposals coming from the development community for housing to get built in those areas. Indeed, HUD and other funders cannot give priority to projects if suitable, high-quality proposals are not forthcoming. And, as discussed earlier, the relative scarcity of LIHTC projects in higher income suburban locales often is related to restrictive land use patterns in these areas.

5.6. *Subsidies are not deep enough to cover operating costs of the development*

If AMIs are not increasing, or increasing only slightly, the maximum rents that can be charged in LIHTC developments remain flat. Operating costs, however, will likely continue to rise. As a result, LIHTC developments often have inadequate operating income. Projects may need to cut back operating budgets to dangerously low levels with repair needs going unmet and even basic maintenance suffering. Without more rental subsidies (or explicit operating subsidies), the system could break down if rents cannot cover operating costs.

> There are no sources of funds that can make up the difference in what ELI [extremely low income] households can afford to pay for rent and the long-term operating costs of rental housing… Even if there is no debt encumbering a project because other programs have provided grants for property acquisition and development, ongoing operating costs can still present a burden if tenant rents are not sufficient to meet those costs. This is the overarching challenge that affects every single developer trying to serve ELI households. (Bolton, Bravve, and Crowley. 2014, p. 21)

Thus, the current situation with the LIHTC program is similar to that faced by the public housing program (both in the past and currently) and the earlier BMIR programs. In those cases, the original subsidy formula failed to include operating subsidies. As a result, the discrepancy between the actual cost of operating the housing and what tenants could pay kept increasing and, in the public housing program, in particular, there were (and still are) serious repair backlogs. Until additional operating subsidies were provided, the housing stock continued to deteriorate. And, even with this additional funding the unmet capital and operating needs of public housing are substantial. It is not yet known the extent to which LIHTC properties will face the same kinds of problems, but there are reasons to be concerned.

5.7. Residents may end up paying more than 30 percent of income for rent

Unlike the Section 8 program, where rents are based on tenants paying an 'affordable' level of their income, the LIHTC program's subsidy is not similarly linked to what a specific household can afford, based on a payment of 30 percent of their income. Any LIHTC household earning below 50–60 percent of AMI, that is not receiving another subsidy, would almost certainly need to pay more than 30 percent of its income for rent. Indeed, one study found that 41 percent of the LIHTC households in 14 states are paying more than 30 percent of their income for rent; 16 percent are severely rent burdened, paying more than 51 percent for their housing (O'Regan and Horn 2013, p. 606). Without additional rental or operating subsidies, either tenant affordability suffers, or maintenance and repair needs are not adequately addressed, as discussed above.

5.8. Potential for a repeat of the 'expiring use' problem

Similar to the early project-based rental housing subsidy programs (BMIR and Section 8 New Construction and Substantial Rehabilitation), LIHTC developments are safeguarded for low-income occupancy for a specified number of years, typically 30. At the end of this period, owners have the right to convert units to market rate rentals or to sell them as condominiums. While this is likely of future concern, so far, only about 5 percent of LIHTC units are no longer monitored and have left the program (Schwartz, 2015, p. 152). In addition, a comprehensive study carried out for HUD concluded that properties with mission-driven owners, who are committed to long-term affordability, and where market rents are no higher than LIHTC rents, will likely continue to remain affordable beyond the restriction period. In contrast, owners that are non-mission-driven for-profit entities, with developments in strong markets, where there is an opportunity to convert LIHTC properties to higher rent or homeownership units, may choose to opt out of the program as soon as they are able to do so (Khadduri et al. 2012). The extent to which there will be a

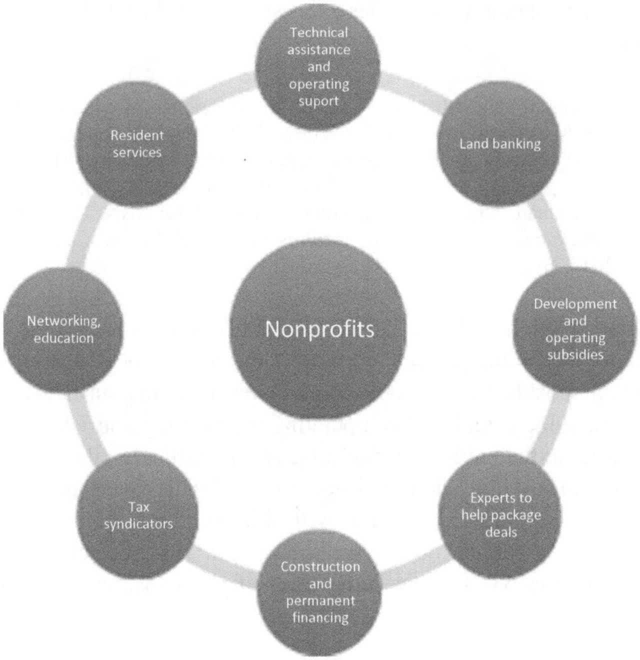

Figure 3. Functions and services contributing to a 'nonprofit-centric' system for affordable housing development.

significant LIHTC expiring use problem is not yet known and will likely depend on: the availability of a new round of tax credits (which would enable developments to undertake major repairs and to continue to maintain the developments at a high level); markets that are favorable for LIHTC developments; and owners interested in maintaining the affordable rent levels.

6. Moving the U.S. nonprofit housing agenda forward

Over the past 50 years, a variety of supports and programs – at national, state, and local levels – have been created to make the development of affordable housing by nonprofits more feasible and productive. Several of these programs could form the basis of what I have called a 'nonprofit-centric system' for affordable housing development. Unfortunately, past programs to support the work of nonprofits 'have formed a discontinuous series of initiatives, which have not generally built on the experiences of their predecessors… we have never had a coherent set of federal policies aimed at supporting nonprofit programs' (Bratt 1998, pp. 140 and 153). To remedy this, an affordable housing system is needed that understands the unique attributes of nonprofit housing organizations, appreciates their strengths and capacities, and creates the appropriate interventions to help overcome constraints and challenges, thereby promoting more optimal productivity. At the very least, a model support system (Bratt 1989) or, a 'nonprofit-centric system' would, as shown in Figure 3, include:

- technical assistance and operating support to help address the organizational needs of nonprofits;

- a clearinghouse of experts in land use, architecture, engineering, law, real estate development, and housing management, who, for example, would be available to help nonprofits package deals, at low (or no) cost;
- land-banking programs that would encourage local and state governments to set aside land and buildings suitable for affordable housing development;
- construction and long-term debt financing at attractive interest rates;
- if tax subsidies are involved, syndicators that can package the deals at low costs;
- adequate development and operating subsidies, both to bring the projects to fruition and to enable developments to be managed efficiently over the long-term;
- on-site resident services programs that would promote opportunities for households to move toward greater economic stability; and
- opportunities for nonprofits to share information and lessons learned through trade, educational, and support networks.

To be sure, many of these components exist in many parts of the country or, in some cases, at the national level (e.g., support and technical assistance provided by the nonprofit intermediaries such as LISC, NeighborWorks and Enterprise Community Partners). But, in no part of the country are all the pieces in place, particularly the deep subsidies needed to make affordable housing deals work, without layering a number of financial resources. While a 'nonprofit-centric system' would, of course, be geared to nonprofits, such a system would also greatly benefit and enhance the productivity of for-profit developers who share the commitment to providing long-term affordable housing.

As part of creating a comprehensive system of supports for nonprofit housing organizations, there are a number of changes in the affordable housing system that are needed. First, in view of the fact that the LIHTC is not suitable for small-size developments, there is a need to experiment with, and develop a subsidy mechanism that is fine-tuned for this type of project. More broadly, a thorough review of the LIHTC program could provide information on how this initiative could be enhanced, such as by assuring affordability to existing tenants, whether it would be feasible to package additional subsidies to expand the targeted income range, and how it could be made more useful for smaller-scale and scattered-site projects.

Second, there is a continuing need to explore mechanisms for overcoming restrictive local zoning practices. Without a better supply of land that is available for development in many locales, the work of all affordable housing developers, whether nonprofit or for-profit, will be significantly constrained.

Third, a consistent source of subsidy dollars to support comprehensive resident services programs is a critical missing ingredient of current affordable housing initiatives. In order for housing to serve as a platform for promoting economic opportunity, a range of support and training programs are essential.

Fourth, in view of the general opposition to discretionary domestic spending of all types in the United States, there is a need to develop and communicate creative and persuasive arguments about why proactive investments in affordable housing are essential. Housing is not an isolated area. The ability of a household to live in a safe, secure, affordable dwelling has implications for health costs, and employability. In addition, a household that is not able to secure housing will likely enter the homeless shelter system, which, we know, comes at a significant public cost. Additionally, people who are frustrated about a lack of affordable housing may need to resort to illegal activities that can create costs for society and also result in public expenditures for incarceration. Finally, on this point, employers often note that a supply of affordable housing is critical for attracting a suitable workforce. Advocates and others need to make the case that the public sector will end up paying one way or the other and, for many reasons, it is far better to be proactive, rather than needing to spend large sums of money to clean up messes that could have been avoided.

Fifth, advocates need to keep pointing out that the level of indirect housing subsidies that advantage higher income groups far surpass the level of direct housing subsidies that benefit those with the greatest needs – households at the lower end of the income distribution. Suggesting parity in expenditures for housing between indirect and direct approaches may be one way to articulate the issue and highlight the current enormous disparities.

Sixth, we need to do a better job of learning from some of the largest producers of affordable housing in the United States – for-profits that utilize the LIHTC. What lessons can they share with nonprofit affordable housing producers and how might these lessons be translated into new public policies?

Seventh, although this paper has not focused on issues of race, housing problems in the United States are inextricably tied to racial factors. Neighborhoods across the country are still often highly segregated, with the corresponding link to more limited school and employment opportunities, as well as the lower self-esteem often experienced by residents who feel excluded from racially mixed areas. Compliance with fair housing laws, overseeing banks to assure that they are not engaging in discriminatory lending practices, and continuing the national dialogue about race are all part of the housing challenge in the United States.

To conclude, as mentioned earlier, there has been a trend toward an increasing reliance on state and local housing strategies, and, connected to that, a greater reliance on the private sector in producing affordable housing. This is having the subtle but clear result of giving the federal government a 'pass' on fulfilling the national housing goal, first articulated by the U.S. Congress in 1949: 'a decent home and a suitable living environment for every American family.' Although the public–private partnership programs are important, without a strong and committed federal partner, they are not nearly sufficient to address the nation's housing needs. Advocates need to keep articulating the message that decent housing is a federal responsibility and that the government must be held accountable for assuming the leadership role in defining a responsive, robust affordable housing agenda. Ideally, this would place nonprofits in a central position, but it would also embrace and support the work of high performing, mission-oriented for-profit developers who are similarly committed to assuring top quality, long-term affordable housing.

At the same time, housing advocates also need to coordinate efforts with other groups that are promoting innovative and energy-efficient forms of public transportation. In many locales across the U.S., rapid transit, in particular, is lacking or inadequate and traffic congestion can be severe. The need for additional housing development must be seen in the context of how infrastructure improvements can be made to enhance mobility and access to opportunities. In view of the current political climate in the United States, with Republicans in charge of both the Executive and Legislative branches of government, and with possibly deep cuts to the housing budget during the Trump administration, there is little chance, in the foreseeable future, that the kind of public assistance that is needed to create a comprehensive affordable housing system will be forthcoming Yet, the experiences in the United States, and the lessons learned from several decades of robust activity, offer potentially useful insights for other countries committed to developing a comprehensive approach for providing affordable housing. Also, I remain optimistic that when a U.S. president and Congress is elected that has a greater concern for alleviating poverty and promoting social justice, these observations and suggestions will become part of the effort to advance the social housing agenda. Moving forward, local activism combined with nonprofit affordable housing production are both essential.

Acknowledgments

Thanks to Professor Penny Gurstein for organizing and hosting the meeting for which this paper was written. Professor Sasha Tsenkova's efforts in bringing this special issue to fruition are much appreciated.

Notes

1. As discussed in a subsequent section, housing that is owned and operated for military personnel by the U.S. Defense Department, is also considered 'public housing.' However, these units are not typically considered part of the traditional public housing stock. This housing is, however, included as part of the social housing stock, as shown in Table 3.
2. In the federal HOPE VI program (1993–2011), which provided funding for the conversion of seriously distressed developments into mixed-income housing, only those units that are still under the control of the local housing authority would be considered part of the social housing stock. Market-rate units in the new development would not be so designated.
3. For a unit to be considered affordable in the United States, a household earning no more than 80 percent of area median income (AMI) would pay no more than 30 percent of income for rent or housing costs. Many programs, such as the Low Income Housing Tax Credit and the Section 8 Housing Voucher, target households at income levels lower than 80 percent of AMI. The rent payment of 30 percent of AMI threshold is somewhat arbitrary and, for the lowest income people, even that amount may be too high to enable the household to cover the costs of other necessities.
4. It should be noted that Wylde is not, herself, critical of this changed role of community residents, having played leadership roles in a number of nonprofit community development organizations.
5. Schwartz (2015) also points out that while there has been a marked decrease in new budget authority, actual annual expenditures for housing, or outlays, have increased over the same period. This is because outlays include prior budgetary commitments. The level of budget authority is, however, a more accurate gauge of the direction that federal support for housing is going. Only by providing new funding for housing – funding that is not already committed to supporting existing households and programs – can there be any progress in reducing the number of households needing housing assistance.
6. Homeowners who itemize their federal income tax deductions are able to deduct from their income the amount of money that they pay in interest on their mortgage, as well as the amount that they pay in local property taxes on their home. Although there are some caps on the amount of the interest deduction allowed (see footnote #7), this results in a substantial subsidy to homeowners, particularly for those with high incomes, and a corresponding loss of income to the Treasury Department.
7. Over the years, there have been suggestions about how to reduce the impacts of this preferential treatment for homeowners. The Tax Reform Act of 1986 limited the amount of interest that could be deducted from a couple's gross income to the first $1 million of debt used for acquiring, constructing, or substantially improving the home ($500,000 if filing individually). In addition, only the first $100,000 of home equity debt is now deductible. Current tax reform proposals could reduce the size of the homeowners' deduction by providing a larger standard deduction, resulting in fewer homeowners itemizing their taxes, including mortgage interest. Other elements of recent tax reform proposals would remove the ability of homeowners to deduct from their gross incomes the amount paid in property taxes and reduce the top marginal tax bracket to 33 percent. Both of these changes would result in less money lost to the Treasury specifically due to the homeowners' deduction. However, as with other efforts to modify the homeowners' deduction, there is vigorous opposition from the influential private sector interest groups, notably the National Association of Realtors and the National

Association of Homebuilders (Harney 2017). At the same time, affordable housing advocates would like any savings from changes in the homeowners' deduction to be earmarked for affordable housing.

8. This section is revised from Bratt (2009a). Given my familiarity with Massachusetts, many of the examples cited are from that state. Despite this bias, Massachusetts is recognized as a leader in promoting affordable housing.
9. At the federal level, a new National Housing Trust Fund (NHTF) could be an important mechanism for funding large-scale housing development projects. The major source of money for the NHTF comes from Fannie Mae and Freddie Mac. But with the economic downturn and the serious problems confronting these two entities, contributions to the NHTF were suspended from 2008 to 2014 and funds did not become available until late 2016. Over the long-term, it is not clear how much money will be available or how it will be distributed. In view of the uncertainty about the future of Fannie Mae and Freddie Mac during the Trump administration, the NHTF approach could be abandoned altogether.
10. Omitted from this discussion are regulatory approaches that are focused exclusively on the private market, such as rent control and condominium conversion ordinances.
11. 'Hot markets' are characterized by a strong demand for housing. In such markets, housing prices are rising rapidly; units are rented or sold almost immediately after they are made available; sales prices often exceed asking prices for homeownership units, with cash sales commonplace; and there is a very low vacancy rate in the rental sector. Inclusionary zoning programs can only work in such locales, since the demand for housing in the area has to be sufficiently strong to attract market rate tenants or home-buyers, who may, in fact, be paying somewhat more than they would for other available units in the area.
12. A thoughtful observation by an anonymous reviewer of this article is worth noting: 'It is implied that these [state and local programs] are popular since they are consistent with the neoliberal agenda, with the government being left "off the hook" for being responsible for a decent home for all. This same logic might also explain why the nonprofits, who similarly allow the government to off-load responsibilities, have also exploded over the last 30 to 40 years of the neoliberal era.'
13. An additional issue, not discussed here, is the possibility, perhaps even the likelihood, that the LIHTC financing mechanism is more costly than a direct capital grant approach for subsidizing affordable housing. Indeed, Congress recognized the financial advantages of direct capital grants in 1987, when it converted the funding for public housing into a capital grant, from debt-based bond financing mechanism that required federal repayment of the capital costs of building the developments over a 40-year period. Specifically, 'The capital grant method of financing... calls for much less budget authority because [it] provides for federal grants for these units "up front" rather than providing direct outlays and tax expenditures over the long period of time needed to retire the tax exempt bonds. The grant method of financing could also result in savings to the public housing authorities by eliminating the accounting and administrative costs related to servicing loans and reissuing short term bonds over a 40-year period' (as cited in Stone 1993, p. 259).
14. The eligible or qualified basis is the total development cost (–) cost of land (×) percent of units in the development that are affordable (×) any bonuses in the eligible basis, such as for building in a difficult area. The final number is the adjusted qualified basis and is the figure used for calculating the tax credits, over a 10-year period.
15. Another criticism of LIHTCs is that many households with incomes somewhat higher than 60 percent of AMI, who still face significant housing affordability problems, are unable to benefit from this strategy.
16. Among the 10 states providing the information, 31 percent of LIHTC tenants earning 30 percent or less of AMI are not receiving any additional rental assistance, which may mean that they are paying more than 30 percent of their income for rent (O'Regan and Horn 2013, p. 598).
17. Author's interview, January 2014.

Disclosure statement

No potential conflict of interest was reported by the author.

References

Achtenberg, E. P. 2006. "Federally-Assisted Housing in Conflict: Privatization or Preservation?" In *A Right to Housing: Foundation for A New Social Agenda*, edited by R. G. Bratt, M. E. Stone, and C. Hartman, 163–170. Philadelphia, PA: Temple University Press. 163–170.

Adams, D. 2015. "Walsh under Pressure to Hike Fees on Developers." *The Boston Globe*, April 2. Accessed 2 April 2015. http://www.bostonglobe.com/business/2015/04/01/walsh-under-pressure-hike-fees-developers/hhKgAPVhHSXJ5u5xrdASrL/story.html

Arena, J. 2012. *Driven from New Orleans: How Nonprofits Betray Public Housing and Promote Privatization*. Minneapolis, MN: University of Minnesota Press.

Beitel, K. 2013. *Local Protest, Global Movements: Capital, Community and State in San Francisco*. Philadelphia, PA: Temple University Press.

Bernstein, J. 2013. "Tax Expenditures: How Cutting Spending through the Tax Code Can Lower the Deficit, Improve Efficiency, and Boost Fairness in the US Tax Code." Testimony before U.S. Senate Budget Committee, March5. Accessed 25 March 2015. http://www.cbpp.org/cms/index.cfm?fa=view&id=3916

Bloom, N. D. 2008. *Public Housing That Worked: New York in the Twentieth Century*. Philadelphia: University of Pennsylvania Press.

Bolton, M., E. Bravve, and S. Crowley. 2014. *Aligning Federal Low Income Housing Programs With Housing Need*. Washington, D.C.: National Low Income Housing Coalition. Accessed November 8, 2016. http://nlihc.org/sites/default/files/Alignment_Report_1214.pdf.

Bratt, R. G. 1989. *Rebuilding a Low-Income Housing Policy*. Philadelphia, PA: Temple University Press.

Bratt, R. G. 2009b. "Challenges for Nonprofit Housing Organizations Created by the Private Housing Market." *Journal of Urban Affairs* 31 (1): 67–94. doi:10.1111/j.1467-9906.2008.00429.x.

Bratt, R. G. 2012. "The Quadruple Bottom Line and Nonprofit Housing Organizations in the United States." *Housing Studies* 27 (4): 438–456. doi:10.1080/02673037.2012.677016.

Bratt, R. G., and A. Vladeck. 2014. "Addressing Restrictive Zoning for Affordable Housing: Experiences in Four States." *Housing Policy Debate* 24 (3): 594–636. doi:10.1080/10511482.2014.886279.

Bratt, R. G. 1998. "Nonprofit Developers and Managers: Their Evolution of Their Role in U.S. Housing Policy." In *Shelter and Society: Theory, Research, and Policy for Nonprofit Housing*, edited by C. Theodore Koebel, 139–156. Albany, NY: State University of New York Press.

Bratt, R. G. 2009a. "Promoting Housing Affordability." In *Local Planning: Contemporary Principles and Practice*, edited by G. Hack, E. L. Birch, P. H. Sedway, and M. J. Silver, 377–385, An ICMA Greenbook. Washington, DC: ICMA Press.

Bratt, R. G., L. A. Rosenthal, and R. J. Wiener. (forthcoming). "Challenges Facing Social Housing Organizations in the U.S.: Insights from the Boston and San Francisco Regions." In *Innovations in Affordable Housing Governance and Finance*, edited by Gerard van Bortel and Vincent Gruis, New York: Routledge.

Bratt, R. G. 2006. "Community Development Corporations: Challenges in Supporting a Right to Housing." In *A Right to Housing: Foundation for A New Social Agenda*, edited by R. G. Bratt, M. E. Stone, and C. Hartman, 340–359. Philadelphia, PA: Temple University Press.

Center on Budget and Policy Priorities. 2015b. "United States. Fact Sheet: Federal Rental Assistance. Accessed 11 February 2017. http://www.cbpp.org/sites/default/files/atoms/files/4-13-11hous-US.pdf

Center on Budget and Policy Priorities. 2017a. "Policy Basics: Federal Rental Assistance." May 3. Accessed 11 February 2017. http://www.cbpp.org/research/policy-basics-federal-rental-assistance?fa=view&id=3890

Citizens' Housing and Planning Association. 1999. *Housing Guidebook for Massachusetts*. Boston, MA: Citizens' Housing and Planning Association.

Connerly, C. 1986. "What Should Be Done with the Public Housing Program?" *Journal of the American Planning Association* 52 (2): 142–155. doi:10.1080/01944368608976614.

Davis, J. E. 1994. "Beyond the Market and the State: The Diverse Domain of Social Housing." In *The Affordable City: Toward a Third Sector Housing Policy*, edited by J. E. Davis, 75–106. Philadelphia, PA: Temple University Press.

Davis, J. E. 2006. "Between Devolution and the Deep Blue Sea: What's a City or State to Do?" In *A Right to Housing: Foundation for A New Social Agenda*, edited by R. G. Bratt, M. E. Stone, and C. Hartman, 364–398. Philadelphia, PA: Temple University Press.

Fischer, W., 2014. "Expanding Rental Assistance Demonstration Would Help Low-Income Families, Seniors, and People with Disabilities." Center on Budget and Policy Priorities. November 7. Accessed 21 May 2015. http://www.cbpp.org/research/expanding-rental-assistance-demonstration-would-help-low-income-families-seniors-and-people

Fischer, W., and B. Sard. 2013. "*Chart Book: Federal Housing Spending Is Poorly Matched to Need Tilt toward Well-Off Homeowners Leaves Struggling Low-Income Renters without Help*." Center on Budget and Policy Priorities. December 18. Accessed 16 April 2015. http://www.cbpp.org/cms/?fa=view&id=4067

Fisher, L. 2007. "Chapter 40B Permitting and Litigation: A Report by the Housing Affordability Initiative." MIT Center for Real Estate. Accessed 30 April 2015. http://mitcre.mit.edu/wp-content/uploads/2012/11/40B-report_fisher_07-0618.pdf

Frisch, M., and L. J. Servon. 2006. "CDCs and the Changing Context for Urban Community Development: A Review of the Field and Environment." *Community Development Journal* 37 (4): 88–108. doi:10.1080/15575330609490197.

Glaeser, E. L., J. Schuetz, and B. Ward. 2006. *Regulation and the Rise of Housing Prices in Greater Boston: A Study Based on New Data from 187 Communities in Eastern Massachusetts*. Cambridge, MA: Pioneer Institute, Boston, MA and Rappaport Institute.

Glickman, N. J., and L. J. Servon. 1998. "More than Bricks and Sticks: Five Components of Community Development Corporation Capacity." *Housing Policy Debate* 9 (3): 497–539. doi:10.1080/10511482.1998.9521306.

Graddy, E. A., and R. W. Bostic. 2010. "The Role of Private Agents in Affordable Housing Policy." *Journal of Public Administration Research and Theory* 20(Suppl, 1): i81–i99. 1477-1498. doi:10.1093/jopart/mup036

Harney, K. R. 2017. "Popular Deductions for Homeownership are Targeted in Tax Plans." *The Washington Post*. April 5. Accessed 18 May 2017. https://www.washingtonpost.com/realestate/homeowners-might-be-tempted-to-give-up-popular-tax-deductions/2017/04/04/04a7fb8e-189b-11e7-9887-1a5314b56a08_story.html?utm_term=.a76da2779a87

Johnston, K. 2014. "Demand Soars for Affordable Housing in Boston Area." *The Boston Globe*. November. 28. accessed 13 May 2015. http://www.bostonglobe.com/business/2014/11/28/demand-for-affordable-housing-soars/hCb4RSkLTbpqdMJR1eCYTI/story.html

Joint Center for Housing Studies. 2014. *The State of the Nation's Housing 2014*. Cambridge, MA: Harvard University.

Joint Committee on Taxation. 2017. *Estimates of Federal Tax Expenditures For Fiscal Years 2016-2020*. Washington, DC:Congress of the United States, January 30. Accessed 12 February 2017. file:///Users/rachelbratt/Downloads/x-3-17.pdf

Khadduri, J., C. Climaco, K. Burnett, L. Gould, and L. Elving. 2012. *What Happens to Low-Income Housing Tax Credit Properties at Year 15 and Beyond?* Prepared for the U.S.: Department of Housing and Urban Development, Accessed 10 May 2015. http://www.huduser.org/publications/pdf/what_happens_lihtc_v2.pdf

Lew, I. 2016. Analysis of LIHTC Data from the Low-Income Housing Tax Credit Database, U.S. Department of Housing and Urban Development. Unpublished paper. Cambridge, MA: Joint Center for Housing Studies of Harvard University.

Logan, T., 2015. "Cambridge Seeks to Tie Building Boom to Affordable Housing." *The Boston Globe*. July 24. Accessed 14 February 2015. https://www.bostonglobe.com/business/2015/07/23/cambridge-set-triple-fees-for-affordable-housing/TUpiACk2dAc8CZRGFz7t0H/story.html

Lubell, J. 2006. *Increasing the Affordability of Affordable Homes: An Analysis of High-Impact State and Local Solutions*. Washington, DC: Center for Housing Policy.

Mallach, A. 2009. *A Decent Home: Planning, Building, and Preserving Affordable Housing*. Chicago, IL: American Planning Association.

Mayer, N., and L. Keyes. 2012. "City Government's Role in the Community Development System." In *The Community Development Reader*, edited by J. DeFilippis and S. Saegert, 158–166. New York: Routledge.

McClure, K. 2006. "The Low Income Housing Tax Credit Moves Mainstream and Moves to the Suburbs." *Housing Policy Debate* 17 (3): 419–446. doi:10.1080/10511482.2006.9521576.

Milligan, V., K. Hulse, and G. Davison. 2013. "Understanding Leadership, Strategy and Organisational Dynamics in the Not-For-Profit Housing Sector." AHURI Final Report No.204. Melbourne: Australian Housing and Urban Research Institute.

National Alliance of Community Economic Development Associations. 2010. Rising Above: Community Economic Development in a Changing Landscape." Accessed 5 March 2015. http://www.naceda.org/sites/default/files/Rising percent20Above_Final%20NACEDA%20Census%20Report.pdf

National Congress for Community Economic Development. 1991. *Changing the Odds: The Achievements of Community-Based Development Corporations*. Washington, DC: National Congress for Community Economic Development.

National Congress for Community Economic Development. 1999. *Coming of Age: Trends and Achievements of Community- Based Development Organizations*. Washington, DC: National Congress for Community Economic Development.

National Congress for Community Economic Development. 2005. *Reaching New Heights: Trends and Achievements of Community- Based Development Organizations*. Washington, DC: National Congress for Community Economic Development.

National Low Income Housing Coalition. 2016a. *Advocates' Guide*. Washington, DC: National Low Income Housing Coalition. Accessed 12 February 2017. http://nlihc.org/sites/default/files/2016_Advocates-Guide.pdf

National Low Income Housing Coalition, 2016b. FY 17 Budget Chart. Accessed 12 February 2017. http://nlihc.org/sites/default/files/NLIHC_HUD-USDA_Budget-Chart.pdf

Nenno, M. K. 1991. "State and Local Governments: New Initiatives in Low Income Housing Preservation." *Housing Policy Debate* 2 (2): 467–497. doi:10.1080/10511482.1991.9521061.

New York State, Homes and Community Renewal. 2016. "About the Public Housing Program." Accessed 13 June 2017. http://www.nyshcr.org/programs/publichousing/

Novogradac. 2017. "2017 State Tax Credit Information." Accessed 14 February 2017. https://www.novoco.com/resource-centers/affordable-housing-tax-credits/application-allocation/2017-state-tax-credit-information

O'Regan, K. M., and K. M. Horn. 2013. "What Can We Learn about the Low-Income Housing Tax Credit Program by Looking at the Tenants?" *Housing Policy Debate* 23 (3): 597–613. doi:10.1080/10511482.2013.772909.

Report of the National Commission on Urban Problems. 1968. *Building the American City*. Washington, DC.

Salsich Jr, P. W. 1999. "Thinking Regionally about Affordable Housing and Neighborhood Development." *Stetson Law Review XXVII* 28: 577–606.

Salsich, Jr, P. W., 2003. "The Impact of Land Use Laws on Affordable Housing." Unpublished manuscript, Saint Louis University, School of Law, MO. Accessed 13 May 2017. http://www.ewgateway.org/pdffiles/BluePrintDocs/LandUseLaws.pdf.

Schwartz, A. 2015. *Housing Policy in the United States*. 3rd ed. New York: Routledge.

Serlin, C. 2016. "2016 Predictions: What's Ahead for the Affordable Housing Industry?" *Affordable Housing Finance*. January 5. Accessed 14 February 2017. http://www.housingfinance.com/news/2016-predictions-whats-ahead-for-the-affordable-housing-industry_o

State, New York, Homes and Community Renewal. 2016."About the Public Housing Program." Accessed 13 June 2017. http://www.nyshcr.org/programs/publichousing/

Stoecker, R. 1997. "The CDC Model of Urban Redevelopment: A Critique and Alternative." *Journal of Urban Affairs* 19 (1): 1–22. doi:10.1111/j.1467-9906.1997.tb00392.x.

Stone, M. E. 1993. *Shelter Poverty: New Ideas on Housing Affordability*. Philadelphia, PA: Temple University Press.

Stone, M. E. 2006. "Social Ownership." In *A Right to Housing: Foundation for A New Social Agenda*, edited by R. G. Bratt, M. E. Stone, and C. Hartman, 240–260. Philadelphia, PA: Temple University Press.

Thaden, E., and J. Webb. 2015. "National Community Land Trust Network: 2015 Member Directory". Portland, OR; National Community Land Trust Network. Accessed 13 June 2017. http://cltnetwork.org/wp-content/uploads/2015/11/2015-Member-Report-final-11-30-15.pdf

Treasury Department and Joint Committee on Internal Revenue Taxation. 1972. *Estimates of Federal Tax Expenditures*. Washington, DC: Congress of the United States.

U.S. Department of Housing and Urban Development. 2017. "HUD's Proposed 2017 Budget, Fact Sheet". Accessed 14 June 2017. https://portal.hud.gov/hudportal/documents/huddoc?id=ProposedFY17FactSheet.pdf

U.S. Office of Management and Budget. 2017. "America First: A Budget Blueprint to Make America Great Again." Accessed 17 May 2017. https://www.gpo.gov/fdsys/pkg/BUDGET-2018-BLUEPRINT/pdf/BUDGET-2018-BLUEPRINT.pdf

Vale, L. J. 2002. *Reclaiming Public Housing: A Half Century of Struggle in Three Public Neighborhoods*. Cambridge, MA: Harvard University Press.

Vale, L. J. 2013. *Purging the Poorest*. Chicago, IL: University of Chicago Press.

Vidal, A. C. 1992. *Rebuilding Communities*. New York, NY: Community Development Research Center, New School for Social Research.

Wallace, D., and M. Novogradac. 2016. "Tax Reform Could Significantly Affect LIHTC Equity Market". December 29. Novogradac & Company. Accessed 15 June 2017. https://www.novoco.com/notes-from-novogradac/tax-reform-could-significantly-affect-lihtc-equity-market

Walsh, D., and D.-S. Jessica. 2014. *CEO Current and Future Strategy Survey 2014*. Boston, MA: Housing Partnership.

Wylde, K. 1999. "The Contribution of Public–Private Partnerships to New York's Assisted Housing Industry." In *Housing and Community Development in New York City*, edited by M. H. Schill. New York: SUNY Press.

The organizational challenges of mixed-income development: privatizing public housing through cross-sector collaboration

Mark L. Joseph, Robert J. Chaskin, Amy T. Khare and Jung-Eun Kim

One of the largely undocumented dimensions of public housing transformation in the United States is the multi-sector, multi-organizational collaborations whose charge is to manage the local implementation of mixed-income developments. In Chicago, private real estate developers entered into partnerships with the Chicago Housing Authority to finance, design, build, and manage the new developments. Key topics considered in this paper include the structures and processes of new organizational working relationships that have been established, how they are evolving over time, and the key operational challenges confronted in creating and sustaining them. We argue that these cross-sector collaborations within the context of the privatization of public housing generate complex organizational roles and dynamics that would benefit from far greater intentionality, clarity, and support to promote effectiveness and accountability.

I think really one of the key accomplishments of the Plan [for Transformation] ... is the degree to which collaboration is required to get this work done. I can't say that anyone would have predicted how much collaboration would be required to even get us to this point. . .it's an evolutionary process. Public housing executive in Chicago

Introduction

Beginning in the 1990s, in response to enduring challenges of concentrated urban poverty and the failures of large-scale public housing, government agencies at the federal and city levels across the nation embarked on a major program of public housing transformation. In an expansion of the neoliberal approach to urban policy that had already gained traction in arenas such as education and human services, subsidized housing provision became one of several areas in which the public sector turned to market mechanisms to capitalize and drive implementation (Hackworth 2007). A key provision in the federal Quality Housing and Work Responsibility Act of 1998 enabled public housing authorities to leverage federal funding with private financing to create mixed-income developments (Hanlon 2010). Public housing redevelopment and management has been completely reoriented in the United States with the signature HOPE VI program (now succeeded by the Obama Administration's Choice Neighborhoods program), and its reliance on mixed-finance redevelopment approaches represents 'an unprecedented departure from past practices'

(Hanlon 2010, 83). In cities across the nation, public housing authorities have entered into partnerships with private developers to demolish public housing developments and replace them with mixed-income, mixed-tenure developments (Cisneros and Engdahl 2009; Joseph, Chaskin, and Webber 2007; Kleit 2005; Popkin et al. 2004). As in other policy arenas, turning to the private sector for implementation does not necessarily mean the reduction of the role of the public sector, but rather a 'complex reconstitution' of its role (Brenner and Theodore 2005, 102; see also; Hanlon 2010; Khare 2016; Miraftab 2004; Wettenhall 2003). The cross-sector partnerships generated by these efforts place local governments, for-profit actors, and an array of non-profit partners into new, complicated, and often-evolving roles and responsibilities.

Chicago has implemented mixed-income public housing redevelopment on a scale far greater than any other city. Regaining control of the housing authority after a 4-year federal takeover, Mayor Richard M. Daley launched the Plan for Transformation in 1999 and set about to demolish most of the high-rise public housing in the city. The original plan aimed to generate 25,000 new or renovated units within 10 years, including building more than 5000 new public housing units within 10 mixed-income housing developments (CHA, 2000).

The Plan for Transformation fully leveraged the new flexibility in the 1998 federal Quality Housing and Work Responsibility Act. Each of the new mixed-income developments has been constructed, managed, and owned by private development companies. The developers are responsible not only for bricks-and-mortar development – land assembly, financing, construction – but also for marketing and property management as well as social service provision to the high-needs public housing population. Each developer must either provide outreach, case management, and referral services themselves or contract with local social service agencies to perform these functions. This has created a highly complex operational challenge with a high premium on effective cross-sector collaboration.

The implementation process is an underexamined dimension of mixed-income development practice, both in the United States and internationally. While the literature on the experiences and outcomes of residents of mixed-income developments is growing (see, e.g., Chaskin and Joseph 2012, 2012; Fraser, Burns, and Buzuin, 2013; Graves 2010; Joseph 2008; Joseph and Chaskin 2010, 2012; Levy, McDade, and Bertumen 2011; McCormick, Joseph, and Chaskin 2012; Tach 2009; Thurber, Bohmann, and Heflinger 2017), there has been little in-depth documentation and analysis of the operations of the public–private partnerships that have been formed to implement this approach (Fraser and Kick 2007; Khare 2016, Khare 2017). This paper draws on a multi-year, mixed-method study to answer the following research questions about the specific challenges and key implications of cross-sector collaboration in mixed-income public housing transformation efforts: In what ways did the roles of the Chicago Housing Authority (CHA) shift in the course of implementing the mixed-income public housing transformation? What was the scope and evolution of the roles played by the private development partnerships? What operational structures and processes were put in place at each site to manage this complex multi-year, multi-actor cross-sector collaboration?

The paper proceeds as follows. First, we present some guiding concepts for our analysis drawing from the literature on public–private partnerships and cross-sector collaboration. We next provide details on our data and methods. We then present our findings about evolving implementation across three sites in Chicago with a focus on the new and shifting roles being embraced by actors in the public, private, and non-profit sectors and on the new structures and processes within which those roles play out. We conclude with a discussion of implications for future policy and practice. Our findings suggest that these cross-sector collaborations within the context of the privatization of public housing generate complex organizational roles and dynamics that would benefit from far greater intentionality, clarity, and support to promote effectiveness and accountability.

Guiding concepts: shifting roles and new collaborative structures and processes

An extensive literature explores efforts by the public sector to engage private sector actors to confront societal issues that government has failed to address effectively alone (see, e.g., Bovaird 2004; Erie, Kogan, and MacKenzie 2010; Moskalyk 2008; Sagalyn 2007; Shaeffer and Loveridge, 2002). Common to these studies is a focus on ways in which actors with often fundamentally different motives, organizational cultures, and stakeholder obligations attempt to develop shared goals and operational principles, exert mutual influence, navigate conflicts in interests and priorities, manage power differentials, and negotiate the sharing of risk and rewards from joint investments.

Cross-sector collaborations can be distinguished as a subset within the broader universe of public–private partnerships in terms of four main factors: the integral and intensive involvement of all three sectors (public, for-profit, and non-profit), the evolution of multi-dimensional working relationships that include but may extend well beyond formal contracts and written agreements, a high degree of joint planning and management, and a long-term commitment to joint investment in and management of initiatives of considerable scope, complexity, public profile, and impact (Fosler 2002). To guide our investigation of cross-sector collaboration in the Plan for Transformation, we focus on two main elements: the shifting roles of key actors at the site level and the new structures and processes that shape their working relationships.

Role shift imperatives and challenges: differing motivations, strengths, and limitations across sectors

To anticipate and understand the roles played by the actors from various sectors and how these roles often shift and evolve over time, it helps to understand the motivations that lead these actors to enter into cross-sector collaboration, the strengths that organizations in each sector often bring, and the limitations that tend to inhere in each sector (Andrew and Entwistle, 2010; Ansell 2003; Ansell and Gash 2008; Bovaird 2004; Fosler 2002; Huxham et al. 2000; Linder 1999; Moskalyk 2008; Osborne and Gaebler 1992; Rosenau 1999; Wallis and Dollery 2006).

For public sector actors, for example, embracing cross-sector collaborations is often driven by decisions by elected and appointed officials to reduce the direct role of government, the need to leverage additional resources, and a quest for more disciplined and efficient strategic management. Perceptions of government inefficiency and corruption and the stigmatization of needs-based programs and the individuals that rely on them have provided a key justification for rolling back government intervention and turning to market-driven decision-making and implementation (Hackworth 2007).

What then, Is the public sector expected to contribute to these cross-sector collaborations? Key presumed strengths of actors in the public sector relative to the other sectors include the capacity to ensure a flow of resources at scale that can be sustained over a multi-year period, a predominant focus on the public interest, and openness to public scrutiny and accountability. On the downside, reliance on public sector resources and responsibility is often accompanied by susceptibility to narrow political agendas and timeframes as well as the delays and complexity created by cumbersome bureaucratic processes and government regulations.

For for-profit sector actors, these partnerships represent an opportunity for new market opportunities in arenas once considered the exclusive purview of government and non-profits. In addition, organizations in the for-profit sector may be responding to pressures to demonstrate corporate social responsibility by deploying their capacity and know-how in the service of responding to challenging social problems. The for-profit sector is expected to bring operational flexibility, an entrepreneurial drive for efficiency and innovation, and access to private market capital. The corporate sector's adherence to profit maximization, however, presents potential problems of goal dissonance with social benefit initiatives supported with public funding such as the Plan for Transformation.

The non-profit sector's interests in engaging in cross-sector collaboration often include a quest to diversify funding sources, the chance to advance a social or civic mission on a greater scale, and the opportunity to build the organizational capacity required to meet higher funder accountability and more rigorous performance expectations. The non-profit sector brings a mission-driven focus and resultant positioning to secure philanthropic and charitable resources and the ability to build trusting, intensive relationships with the intended beneficiaries of social initiatives. However, non-profits may have difficulty pivoting to the new demands for scale, efficiency, and measurable results and may fall prey to mission drift that draws them out of the areas in which they hold comparative advantage and capacity.

In our examination of the cross-sector collaboration in the Transformation in Chicago, we focus on the roles played by four core actors: the CHA, the private developers (all but one of which, in this case, are for-profit organizations), property management organizations (also mostly for-profit organizations), and social service providers (which are all non-profits). We explore the extent to which these actors' participation in the cross-sector collaboration required them to expand and shift their roles, the tensions inherent in making these shifts, and the implications for capacity needs and effectiveness.

Establishing new structures and processes: facilitating coordination, building trust, and managing competing institutional logics

Inherent in cross-sector collaborations is a high degree of ambiguity and complexity, placing a premium on the structures and processes put in place to facilitate more effective collective action. A central dynamic to any cross-sector collaboration is the potential for tensions to be generated by fundamental differences in the motivations and practices of actors in each sector, what Bryson and colleagues (2006) refer to as competing 'institutional logics.' Institutional logics establish the formal and informal rules of the game and guide actions and interpretations among actors. As Bryson and colleagues (2006, 50) explain, 'actions, processes, norms, and structures that are seen as legitimate from the vantage point of one institutional logic may be seen as less legitimate or even illegitimate from the perspective of another logic' (see also Babaik and Thibault, 2009; Bovaird 2004; Erie, Kogan and MacKenzie 2010; Moskalyk 2008). In a cross-sector collaboration, competing logics can often create tensions between accountability and efficiency, between hierarchy and flexibility, between regulation and innovation, and between adherence to a social mission and pursuit of a bottom line. Furthermore, the delegation of public responsibility to private actors generates a principal-agent problem characterized by information asymmetry, diverging preferences, and heightening the imperative for effective oversight and accountability (Van Slyke 2006). Differing priorities and definitions of success can create divergence and conflict. Establishing effective governance and decision-making across sectors can be difficult, and roles and responsibilities can often overlap and be unclear. Underlying these challenges are dynamics of power and control that grow in intensity with the stakes and scope of the collaboration.

Thus, to explore the workings of a particular cross-sector collaboration, several features of structure and process are critical to examine. These include the nature of decision-making and reporting relationships; how existing structures are modified and to what extent new structures are developed; the processes through which leadership, trust, and legitimacy are forged; the mechanisms in place to promote collaborative planning, help manage conflict, and navigate competing institutional logics.

Studies of cross-sector collaboration and public–private partnerships identify a number of factors that appear to facilitate success (Bovaird 2004; Fosler 2002; Moskalyk 2008). These include an explicit shared vision and goals that guide the joint enterprise, clarity about organizational roles and responsibilities, a well-defined structure for managing the work and facilitating communication and coordination, including effective leadership in each sector, an increasing degree of trust and understanding among partners, appreciation of and the willingness to make accommodation for the organizational constraints unique to each sector, strong performance measurement and accountability mechanisms, and adequate resources to execute individual organizational responsibilities as well as engage in shared processes.

To explore cross-sector collaboration in the Chicago case, we examine two key operational groups formed at each site to manage these dynamics – Working Groups and Management Committees (which will be described in detail below) – and investigate the functioning of these collaborative mechanisms.

Context, data, and methods

Our analysis of cross-sector collaboration in Chicago is based on in-depth interviews, field observations, and a review of documentary data concerning three mixed-income developments that are part of the CHA's Plan for Transformation (see Table 1). In addition to each being designed and implemented by different development partnerships, the three developments provide geographic diversity (two on the south side of the city, one on the west), demographic diversity (one having a predominantly African-American population post-occupancy and the other two having substantial non-black populations), and organizational diversity (two of the developers are for-profit firms and one is a non-profit developer). Oakwood Shores is the development taking the place of Ida B. Wells/Madden Park, one of the oldest public housing developments in the nation. Oakwood Shores has been developed by two organizations, The Community Builders, the largest non-profit urban housing developer in the United States, which has completed over 20,000 units of affordable, mixed-income housing over the past 40 years, and Granite Development, a local, for-profit, African-American-owned real estate development firm that is responsible for the for-sale housing development on site. The Community Builders is unique among the lead developers in our sample and across the full array of mixed-income sites in Chicago in having the three major functions – real estate development, property management, and social service provision – all in-house. The other lead developers in our sample have contracted out property management and social service provision.

Table 1. The three mixed-income developments.

	Oakwood Shores	Park Boulevard	Westhaven Park
Former public housing site	Ida B. Wells/Madden Park	Stateway Gardens	Henry Horner Homes
Original projected units	3,000	1,316	1,317
Relocated public housing units (#/%)	1,000 (33%)	439 (33%)	824[6] (63%)
Affordable units (#/%)	680 (23%)	421 (32%)	132 (10%)
Market-rate units (#/%)	1,320 (44%)	456 (35%)	361 (27%)
% For-Sale	27%	42%	23%
Social service providers	In-house resident services function	New non-profit created by developer	Initially contracted out to local non-profit service organization, then to for-profit property management company
Developer(s)	National non-profit (rental); local for-profit (for sale)	Four local for-profits	Two regional and national for-profits
Guiding legal authority for returning residents	Relocation rights contract	Relocation rights contract	Consent decree
Neighborhood	North Kenwood Oakland, Southside Chicago	Bronzeville, Southside Chicago	Near Westside, Westside Chicago
Neighborhood amenities and institutions	Near Lake Michigan, public parks, Hyde Park, and Univ. of Chicago	Near public transit corridor, IL Institute of Technology, White Sox stadium, major highway	Near downtown central business district, public transit stop, United Center

Note: Includes off-site, scattered-site units, and the villages, a ‘superblock’ of 100% public housing residences located in the middle of the mixed-income development.

Park Boulevard is being built in place of Stateway Gardens, a collection of eight high-rise buildings that were constructed as part of the 'State Street Corridor,' an area that had some of the highest poverty concentration levels in the entire country. The project was originally developed by a team of four private, for-profit firms, all of which were new to the mixed-income development field: Kimball Hill Homes, Mesa Development Group, Davis Development Group, and Walsh Construction.[1] The for-profit Urban Property Advisors, affiliated with Davis Development Group, manages the rental and for-sale properties. The development plan included the creation of a non-profit organization, Stateway Community Partners, dedicated to managing the social support and community building efforts in the new development.

Westhaven Park is the second phase of the redevelopment of Henry Horner Homes, the first phase of which started prior to the Plan for Transformation. Westhaven Park has been developed by Brinshore-Michaels Development, a joint venture of locally based Brinshore Development and national developer Michaels Development Company. The property is managed by the for-profit Interstate Realty Management (IRM) company (a subsidiary of Michaels Development Company). Social services have been provided by the non-profit organizations Near West Side CDC and Project Match, and since 2014 by IRM, the property management company that now employs resident services staff. All redevelopment at Horner Homes is governed by a consent decree that is the result of a successful class-action lawsuit brought against the CHA prior to the Plan for Transformation (Wilen 2006). The consent decree introduces two unique factors at Westhaven Park: a superceding layer of mandates that guide the mixed-income implementation (such as resident screening protocols) and additional actors and structures including the plaintiff's legal counsel and a resident council empowered to negotiate with the housing authority and the development team (Chaskin, Khare, and Joseph 2012).

The consent decree at Horner Homes is an important contextual factor. Early mixed-income implementation in Chicago unfolded in a highly litigious atmosphere and two high-profile lawsuits against the CHA delayed and shaped action across the sites. Decades of mistrust between residents and the CHA have generated an experienced cohort of legal activists and housing advocates who would play a formative role in the cross-sector collaboration to come. Several well-positioned non-profit legal organizations – including Business People for the Professional Interest (led by Alexander Polikoff, the renowned lawyer who successfully argued the Gautreaux case), the Sargent Shriver National Center on Poverty Law, and the Legal Assistance Foundation of Metropolitan Chicago – were integral to the design and implementation of the Plan for Transformation.[2] In addition, as a compromise with legal advocates over concerns about the need for objective, third-party oversight, and accountability over the Plan for Transformation, the CHA contracted with an independent monitor to provide periodic assessments and recommendations.

The primary source of data for the analysis in this paper is three waves of interviews conducted from 2007 to 2010, which was supplemented with an additional round of interviews in 2014. Most respondents from the first wave of interviews were interviewed again in subsequent waves of data collection, and new interviewees were added in subsequent waves. This method allows us to trace how the perspectives of key actors evolved over time as well as to capture the insights of key actors who got involved along the way. The main data collection period occurred once the three sites had completed their first phases of construction and the first residents had moved back on site. We asked respondents to reflect back on the early planning phases of the initiative as well as to describe ongoing collaboration dynamics. In the initial round of field work we interviewed a total of 84 key informants involved in some way in the Transformation, either as 'development-team' members (developers, service providers, and property managers), as 'community stakeholders' (such as service providers, community activists, and public officials active in the neighborhoods in which these developments are being built and residents in leadership positions within the developments), or as 'macro-level' actors – public agency staff, civic leaders, and other stakeholders operating at the city level in connection with the Transformation (including officials with the CHA and public housing advocates). We invited interviewees to participate in the study based on their level of responsibility and active engagement in the Transformation. In 2014, a final round of interviews was conducted with a similar cross-section of 61 respondents who had influence on Chicago's public housing reforms during the period of 2000–2016. About half of these interviewees had been previously interviewed for the study. New interviewees were selected because of their more recent involvement in the effort and for their knowledge about political and economic dimensions of the redevelopment efforts. These interviews focused specifically on the nature and implications of the privatization of public housing. Additional background information that provides context for the analysis here includes over 30 observations of Working Group and Management Committee meetings, ongoing review of relevant documents and interviews, and focus groups with residents of the three developments.

Interviews were semi-structured, recorded digitally, transcribed in their entirety and coded for analysis based on a set of deductively derived thematic codes and refined based on inductive interim analysis. Field notes from observations of community meetings, programs, events, and interactions allow us to contextualize interview data within the specific dynamics of each site and capture the cross-sector collaboration processes as they unfolded in private and public group settings. Field notes were coded for analysis, and for formal groups that meet regularly we also synthesized field notes into narrative memos that described the content, participation, and changing dynamics at these meetings over time. Coding and analysis was done using NVivo qualitative data-analysis software. The primary interviews for this study were initially double-coded to ensure inter-rater reliability, and then a periodic sample of coded interviews (every fifth transcript) was reviewed to ensure continued reliability.

Findings

Mapping the new landscape: shifting roles and responsibilities

The privatization of public housing redevelopment in Chicago fundamentally changed the implementation of subsidized housing provision. Given limited space we focus on the expansion and evolution of the roles of four main actors: the CHA, private developers, property managers, and service providers (Joseph, 2010). We describe three key facets of the evolved roles of each of these actors: (1) a core tension each had to resolve, (2) the ways in which their conventional responsibilities were expanded, and (3) the evolution in their understanding and execution of their roles over the course of the initiative.

The CHA

Privatization has had far-reaching implications for the CHA. The scale, scope, and purview of the agency have been greatly reduced. As one indicator, the agency staff was decreased drastically from over 2500 employees in 1999 at the launch of the Plan for Transformation to fewer than 430 15 years later (CHA, 2014). In our interviews, CHA staff consistently defined the new intended role for the agency as being focused on 'asset management.' As a senior executive explained:

> We're asset managers. Those [housing properties] are our assets. In some cases those are our assets one hundred percent. In other cases those are our assets through a partnership. And anyone who is or has been affiliated with our program, we still have ownership in making sure that they're treated with dignity and respect, that the processes are fair and consistent, and we just need to continue to work towards that.

But ultimately the implications of this fundamental change have been complicated and, to some extent, contradictory. On the one hand, transferring responsibility for the core functions of the site redevelopment to private development organizations has meant less control and involvement on the part of the CHA. On the other hand, while some responsibilities have been delegated through contracting relationships to developers and other organizations, in significant ways the CHA has faced *increased* responsibility and the challenges associated with it. For example, CHA staff have been responsible for overseeing the relocation and return process for residents, ensuring that policies are followed and keeping pressure on the private development teams to make progress. Overall, CHA staff have remained highly engaged in many facets of the redevelopment process. As another CHA senior executive described:

> We may not overall have changed that much, 'cause we're still very, very, very hands-on, and I think that when they were talking about asset management, it was like 'Well we would just end up being a holding company basically,' and it's not gone that way at all, yet, anyway. I think at this ten-year point...we're still very hands-on, and I think we need to be.

A service provider had the same perspective:

> Now CHA is saying, 'Okay, we are giving out these dollars...we want to make sure that this program is implemented the way we envisioned it, and we're going to have a direct, hands-on approach.'

The CHA has been faced with accomplishing clear objectives in a high-stakes context while relying on other entities to execute the process and achieve those goals. So the central role tension for the CHA has been delegation on the one hand versus sustained control and responsibility on the other. A CHA senior executive explained that they have had to increase the resources dedicated to compliance and oversight of the mixed-income development teams:

> I think when the plan was originally envisioned that we would hire private developers and they would go off and we would give them the rules and they would follow them and know how to do it and we wouldn't need as much oversight of the mixed-income as we do the traditional, the traditional public housing sites where we still retain ownership and direct contracting oversight of the property managers we hire at the traditional sites. And I think we have found that not to be the case.

According to both CHA staff and development team members, examples of the heightened role for the CHA include regular meetings with property managers to review the status of residents, closer scrutiny of reports, continued refinement of the services strategy, and direct engagement with residents through the CHA's Ombudsman's office.[3]

Key elements, then, of how the role of the CHA has evolved over time include slimming the size and scope of the bureaucracy, taking an active role in holding developers and their partners accountable for progress and adherence to the physical and social development goals of the Transformation, and sustaining a hands-on role in some vital areas of the effort. The shift to a market-driven approach to public housing in Chicago has in no way meant withdrawal of the public sector but a shifting and refining of its role. Given factors such as the size and scope of the Plan for Transformation and the strong role of legal and housing activists, there exists considerable leverage (and pressure) on the part of local government to hold itself and the private developers to commitments to the social goals of the Transformation. As we will discuss, the bigger questions are whether and how effectively the CHA has used that leverage on behalf of the low-income households it is charged to serve.

The private real estate developers

To carry out their designated functions in the Transformation, the private developers have been called upon to move well beyond a focus on bricks and mortar, adding the major responsibility of overseeing human services and community building. Though this was generally understood as they entered into contracts with the housing authority, the new roles resulted in unexpected demands and constraints. The central role tension faced by developers is between defining their role primarily as a straightforward real estate task – building mixed-income housing – versus defining it much more broadly as building a mixed-income *community.*[4]

It must be noted that even the task of housing development, which is the bread and butter of the real estate developers, is far more complicated in the context of mixed-income public housing transformation than in market-rate developments. For example, financing the developments, with their mix of subsidized and market-rate housing units, requires multiple layers of funding, each with different monitoring and reporting requirements. The number of partners – in the private sector, in local government, and at the community-level – with which the developers must collaborate is considerably increased. Phasing the development construction is complicated and highly consequential. For example, achieving the balanced roll-out of for-sale and rental units to promote and sustain a mixed-tenure environment with a critical mass of homeowners has been exceedingly difficult in Chicago and was made vastly more challenging with the 2008 housing market crash. The crash created major slowdowns at all three sites and froze construction of for-sale units. At Park Boulevard the master plans for the developments were significantly altered to incorporate several rental-only buildings, which was not a component of the original plans.

One of the most challenging new roles for the developers has been the responsibility for resident supports and services. This responsibility is wide-ranging, including preparing residents for relocation, supporting them through the process of relocation, preparing them for a possible return to the development, screening and selecting those eligible to return, and providing supportive services to help residents maintain their eligibility and improve their social and economic circumstances. It has also proven to be daunting, as the service population has turned out to be even more disadvantaged and unprepared for the relocation process than expected, with high levels of physical and mental health challenges, numerous barriers to employment including extremely low literacy and skills, and fragile, if any, connections to the labor market (Popkin 2016; Popkin, Cunningham, and Burt 2005). The historically low return rates in the federal HOPE VI program – a median 18% of original residents have returned in 259 HOPE VI-funded redevelopments – has raised concerns and pressure from affordable housing advocates (Gress, Cho, and Joseph 2016).

Developers' understanding of and approach to their roles has evolved considerably over the course of the Transformation, with the acceptance among most of a more comprehensive view of their role, greater investment of time and resources in the human development challenges, and more proactive attention, particularly as the population on site grows, to the task of post-occupancy support. One developer explains the higher vigilance and engagement required in this enterprise as follows:

> It's more than a quarterback's role. It's a quarterback role and a coach's role and the general manager's role. It's more than just strategizing how this works as a real estate endeavor... So until you know until this thing is done and five years later, I suspect that we're gonna have to spend a lot of time being really careful about everything that's happening here.

For The Community Builders, which had its own in-house service provision staff and considerably more experience with managing mixed-income developments around the country, this transition to a more comprehensive role on site was relatively easier but still challenged by city and site contextual factors that we will discuss below.

Central components, then, of how the role of the private developers has evolved over time include expanding their focus to address human needs beyond housing, managing complex mixed-finance efforts in order to establish a mixed-income, mixed-tenure environment, and meeting stipulations as subcontractors to the CHA while also maintaining their profit-driven financial imperative.

Property managers

In the pre-occupancy phase, property managers have the all-important task of screening and selecting which households to accept for residency in the new developments. Herein lays an initial role tension for the property managers, who sought to maintain high occupancy rates to help the developers avoid the costs and other problems caused by vacancies while at the same time adhering to stringent screening criteria in order to accept only those residents deemed most prepared to live successfully in a mixed-income development. This tension was heightened in the early phases of the Transformation when it proved far more difficult than expected to find eligible relocated public housing residents interested in returning to the new developments and some new units remained vacant for up to a year (Bushey 2008; Olivo 2005, 2006; Rogal 2005). These extended vacancies caused financial and political problems for the developers and the CHA. Financially, developers have been penalized for unoccupied tax-credit subsidized units. Politically, the CHA and the city came under tremendous criticism from affordable housing advocates and others for the vacancies in light of long waiting lists and a paucity of affordable housing in the city.

Property management in mixed-income developments is a highly complex venture. As a CHA senior executive acknowledged:

> I think property management is a very hard job.... There's layers of regulatory agreements on these sites that require a lot of skill to be able to manage in terms of tenant selection and lease enforcement, waitlist management, all of those things, social services, file, documentation. Are they in this income category or this income category? Did they do the drug test? Did we do the recertification on time? ... Did we get our audit done and pass these inspections, multiple inspections and reviews? So there's a lot to do.... I think it's been a shock to some how much there is to do.

Of all the actors in the Plan for Transformation property managers have the most regular contact with residents during the post-occupancy phase of development at each site and thus have a critical role at the front lines of the initiative. As the first point of contact in most cases, they often have the most current information about a resident's status or change in status. This broadens expectations regarding the support and networking role that they can play. In mixed-income developments property managers' roles are expanded beyond managing occupancy, lease compliance, rent collections, and building maintenance to also collaborating closely with social service providers and, more broadly, promoting community building. A property manager at one site, for example, noted the many roles involved in the job, acting 'as a leasing agent, property manager, resource specialist, [and] a resident services coordinator.' The developer at the site elaborated:

> So the theory is, our resource specialists are the persons that you walk in the door, you want to rent. You sit down with them. They tell you about all the wonderful things that we offer. They get you in a lease and they stay with you throughout your living experience. So when you come back a year later, you'll do the lease renewal with them, and in between, if you have a question about your dog or you want to get a dog, you talk to your resource specialist. If you have a question about what's going on for your young people in the summer in your house, talk to the resource specialist. If you're having a problem with your neighbor, talk to the resource specialist. And so that person stays connected ... it's a very much different kind of relationship that we want to broker and the job of the resource specialist is to really help families problem solve through things.

In summary, the property managers hold extensive influence over the day-to-day operations at the sites and are the first line of interaction with residents and thus play a critically important but often underestimated role in the functioning of these cross-sector collaborations.

Service providers

Social service providers that are a part of each development team have been challenged to meet high resident needs for support within multiple constraints of resources, time and resident non-responsiveness. The central role tension for the service providers has been working with large caseloads and moving households quickly toward preparedness for relocation on the one hand while focusing on sustained engagement with households in order to achieve lasting improvements and changes in their circumstances and outlook. The dispersion of relocated residents to multiple locations across the city and metro region during the demolition and relocation phase of the Transformation made the service providers' task of outreach and ongoing engagement with households highly challenging. Not able to simply serve those relocatees who take the initiative to find their way to a centrally located office, service providers are charged to meet with all households on their caseload wherever they may be located. Their expanded role includes this heightened focus on outreach and, given the early challenges of filling the public housing units, on the challenges of marketing the new developments to potential returnees.

Over time and as the populations of residents at the redeveloped sites have increased the service providers have seen their roles include a greater focus on post-occupancy support. Their charge has also evolved from the early phases of the Transformation when they were simply expected to assess residents' needs and provide service referrals, to greater responsibility for individual case management, to an additional focus on broader community building at the new sites.

New mechanisms for collaboration: working groups and management committees

While one level of adaptation to the task of cross-sector collaboration consists of the new roles played by key actors, a second important level includes the structures and processes put in place to facilitate collective action. We highlight here two mechanisms that have been key to the structure of cross-sector collaboration at each redevelopment site in Chicago: the Working Groups formed by the CHA and Management Committees formed by the development teams. As the critical staging arenas for deliberation, decision-making and problem-solving about implementation at the sites, these new structures provide important insight into how cross-sector collaboration is being operationalized in the Plan for Transformation, illuminating the shifting but still-central role of the state in this enterprise and revealing some key dimensions of conflicting agendas and institutional logics.

The working groups

The CHA created Working Groups as the principal collaborative governance mechanism at each mixed-income redevelopment to inform site design and oversee implementation, including selecting developers and establishing eligibility criteria for returning families (Chaskin and Joseph 2012; Chaskin, Khare, and Joseph 2012; Chicago Housing Authority, & U.S. Department of Housing and Urban Development 2000). Among cities with major HOPE VI and public housing transformation efforts, these formalized, site-focused collaboratives are unique to Chicago. Their formation was an indication of the scope of the Transformation in Chicago and the need for this layer of structure *at each site* to move multiple sites along simultaneously across the citywide initiative. It also indicates an effort to formally engage local community stakeholders in the redevelopment process. While some members of the development team found the Working Group process cumbersome, others found it to be ultimately a useful vehicle for input and planning. One developer expressed his increased acceptance over time:

> I find it very productive. . . .The Working Group environment certainly takes a lot to get used to. We don't have a working group anywhere else in the country. . . . So I find it's a great environment.

Each Working Group has been led by a CHA representative who serves as the development manager for that site and includes other CHA staff (project management, asset management, legal department), representatives of the development team (real estate developer, architects, property manager, service provider), representatives of other city departments (housing, planning, park district and, more recently, the school district), resident leaders representing the former public housing population, legal advocates, and other community stakeholders such as the Alderman representing the local city ward. Due to a federal settlement, a private real estate firm, The Habitat Company, has been the court-ordered receiver for all new public housing construction in the city between 1987 and 2011, and a representative of Habitat also sits on each working group.

During the course of our fieldwork there were fewer than 20 regular participants at Park Boulevard Working Group meetings, around 25 participants at Westhaven Park, and about 30 participants at Oakwood Shores. At both Park Boulevard and Oakwood Shores, the Working Group met monthly. At Westhaven Park the Working Group met less frequently. Similar topics were discussed at each meeting by the groups across the sites. These included building and landscape design, unit construction and delivery schedules (and, often, delays), unit mix in planned buildings, lease-up and sales progress, CHA policy changes and implications, and emerging challenges on the development site and in the neighborhood. Because each of the groups had representation from the resident-elected Local Advisory Council (LAC) from the original public housing development, there were often issues raised by LAC representatives purportedly on behalf of public housing residents waiting to be relocated or who have moved into the new developments, such as concerns about property management or problems with the new units.[5]

The management committees

The most extensive collaboration at each site took place among representatives of the three key organizational actors that made up the development team – the real estate developer, property manager, and social service provider. At each site, representatives of these entities attended regular management meetings, which ranged in frequency from weekly to monthly depending on the demands of the particular phase of development and occupancy. At Oakwood Shores and Park Boulevard development team members were joined by the CHA project manager for the site while at Westhaven Park the CHA was conspicuously absent, having been asked not to attend by the developer to avoid having to deal with 'their bureaucracy' at these meetings. At Park Boulevard and Oakwood Shores, a representative of the LAC also joined the meetings, and at Westhaven Park (due to the legal consent decree described earlier), a legal advocate represented the public housing residents in the meetings.

During our primary period of observation, whereas Working Group meetings were focused on broader issues of site redevelopment progress and challenges, Management Committee meetings focused in a very detailed way on the status and challenges of individual relocated public housing households. In all three committees, the bulk of each meeting was dedicated to walking through a list of individuals – either in pre-occupancy or post-occupancy – and discussing specific issues that were preventing residents from being ready to move in or putting them in danger of eviction. By extension, the meetings also involved frequent conversations about interpreting CHA policy and implications for decisions about households. There was also often discussion of plans for resident events and activities.

The operations and evolution of the Working Groups and Management Committees provide a concrete illustration of the complicated evolution of the CHA's role with both decreased and increased responsibility and control and spotlight some key areas of divergence among actors. Although responsibility for implementation at each site had been delegated to the private sector partners, the CHA was the lead facilitator for all three Working Groups and two of the three Management Committees. As a Working Group participant at Park Boulevard explained in 2007, several years into the Transformation:

> At the working group, a CHA employee chairs that meeting. At the table is the relocation manager, the asset manager from CHA, a couple of lawyers' groups, – so I guess what I'm saying is ... in this level of the process, CHA still drives it, and [all the] contracts are with CHA. The management's company contract, the developer's contract, the service provider's contract are all with CHA. So, ultimately, at this point, CHA drives the process... .When will that transformation [to other leadership] occur? We're not sure. But for now, that's who drives the process.

We observed the same level of facilitation and influence over the collaborative process at Oakwood Shores, and in both sites this role continued through the period of our on-site observations through 2011. Westhaven Park provides an instructive counterexample. In that site, not only did the Management Committee exclude the CHA from participation, but the Working Group, which was facilitated by a CHA representative, met infrequently. This lower level of control and influence by the CHA can be explained by three factors. First, Westhaven Park was at a more advanced phase of redevelopment than the other two sites, so arguably major issues had been resolved and the development was more 'on course.' Second, the legal consent decree in place provided clearer parameters for the redevelopment, constrained flexibility, provided more protection of tenants' rights, precluded site-specific criteria beyond lease compliance, and inserted an additional actor – the plaintiff's counsel – into on-site oversight. Third, the developer at Westhaven Park had a more assertive leadership style, demanding distance from the CHA and with the track record to achieve it. These factors appear to have been instrumental in keeping the CHA out of the week-to-week management process in Westhaven Park.

While agenda-setting and meeting facilitation was perhaps the most visible form of continued CHA control, the housing authority's influence also played out through policy setting, modification, and interpretation. We observed actors at all three sites forced to adjust implementation in response to evolving CHA policy. A prime example is policy regarding repercussions for residents who exceed 1 year of living in a new development without successfully meeting the site-specific criteria – usually employment – which changed to become more strictly enforced by CHA over the course of the Transformation.

Another key dynamic made apparent through the operations of the Working Groups and Management Committees was the emergence and resolution of differing institutional agendas and priorities. In some cases these differences were between the CHA and development team actors. In other cases they developed *within* the development team – between the developer and property manager, on the one hand, and the service provider on the other. In cases where residents or resident legal advocates were present, they often were aligned with service providers. One issue of contention, for example, was a push for achieving numerical targets such as levels of occupancy and numbers of households relocated (supported by CHA, the developer, and the property manager) versus a focus on case-by-case support, patience, and flexibility in order to achieve the best outcome for that particular household (often advocated by the service provider). Another example, particular to Park Boulevard, was a demand by the property manager that the service provider conduct 'clinical needs assessments' before a household could be considered for move-in. This was resisted by both the service provider and the CHA as overly intrusive and labor-intensive, and eventually the developer agreed to not require assessments as a condition for occupancy. A third example was the priority on the part of the service provider to get families resettled as quickly as possible in whatever housing location would work best for that family, be it a return to a mixed-income development or another option. This conflicted in most cases with the developer, property manager, and CHA imperatives to fill as many of the mixed-income development units as possible. The requirement that residents had to achieve a certain degree of preparedness often meant delays in a resolution of their relocation and more tensions and friction among the parties.

Key challenges and facilitators of progress

Having described the evolving roles and structural relationships of some of the key actors in the cross-sector collaboration in Chicago's Plan for Transformation, we focus now on some of the key challenges they experienced and consider the factors that helped address these challenges and promote operational progress over time.

Key challenges

As we have indicated, the sites encountered a variety of challenges, many of which are anticipated in the collaboration literature. Key among these challenges are what Bryson, colleagues (2006) referred to as differing institutional logics. We have provided examples of differing priorities and goals in our discussion of collaborative mechanisms above. One example is the question of public housing resident relocation, with service providers for the most part prioritizing the needs and aspirations of the relocating public housing resident across an array of housing opportunities and developers and, in some cases, CHA representatives prioritizing the need to fill vacant units at the mixed-income sites. An even sharper difference in priority often surfaced between property managers and service providers regarding tenants who have difficulty complying with property rules and fall behind in rent payments. While property managers shared the objective of keeping tenants in their units in order to avoid vacancies and the cost of unit turnover, they have also been keenly focused on the challenges that such tenants generate for their management of the development overall, and thus less patient than service providers to provide additional time and resources to try to resolve issues rather than move to eviction. As a service provider described:

> [T]he social service side is more hand holding. 'Hey, Miss Clark, we know you're behind. What can we do to assist you? What's going on?' [But] if someone doesn't have utilities, that's a lease violation. On property management side, that's eviction. On the social service side, it's go out and find some resources to help the family.

The cross-sector collaboration process has been greatly constrained by entrenched bureaucratic structures and processes within the public agencies, particularly the CHA. As a civic leader explained:

> [A]ccording to the plan CHA was going to devolve a lot of the functions that used to be under their umbrella to private developers, to experts, to community based organizations, etc. and CHA would be more of an asset manager or a public organization overseeing these functions. And that was the intent of the plan and I think that's what most of the people at CHA believed in. But again the CHA is an organization with what? 75 years of history behind it and an organization [is] very difficult to change and the change is always incremental. . . . And they kept in place the older structure. They went through political reshuffling and redesign of the organization but the culture remained for a while and that culture was one of keeping control and keeping in charge of a lot of things. . . . They still have to become comfortable with their new role which is one of overseeing and less micromanaging all these new functions.

Also highly challenging have been efforts to manage communication and coordination among multiple players in the midst of continually shifting circumstances and policies. As another civic leader observed:

> [The development teams] were given some very vague guidelines and very changing policies and plans and they had to react to that on a daily basis and they found many surprises and things that they didn't expect.

It took several years to get the housing relocation and offer process sorted out, and during this time the structure of the service provision strategy shifted from a broad set of agencies focused on referrals to a more limited set of agencies charged with case management and direct service provision. The policies about employment and move-in eligibility also evolved over the course of the Transformation. As we have noted, the housing market crash had dramatic impacts on the Transformation, stalling development across the sites and creating crises for the developers and challenges for the Working Groups. Resultant economic challenges faced by residents, particularly market-rate renters, increased turnover and eviction, while homeowners felt and expressed greater stress and vigilance about maintaining their property values.

A final major challenge has been high staff turnover across sectors at the executive levels as well as middle-management and front-line staff. Over the course of 18 years, there have been eight CEOs of CHA, a position that requires mayoral appointment. The turnover in CEOs has occurred more frequently under Mayor Emanuel than under Mayor Daley, with five CEO transitions since 2011. The lead private developers have been relatively stable, although one firm that was part of the joint venture at Park Boulevard (Kimball Hill Homes) has been dissolved due to housing crisis-related bankruptcy and there has been considerable turnover among senior staff at The Community Builders. The property management firms have experienced particularly high staff turnover, but this is characteristic of the industry as a whole. Given the critical value of a collective understanding of objectives and working processes and developing trusting relationships, this turnover among key staff has created setbacks in the collaboration process.

Facilitators of progress

Despite the reality of enduring and evolving challenges, a few key factors can be identified as helping to promote improved collaboration among cross-sector actors over time. Each of the organizations and new organizational mechanisms have adapted and grown more comfortable in their roles over time. In most cases this has meant that closer working relationships developed with repeated interaction and shared experience. In others, notably the Management Committee in Westhaven Park, this has meant that over time the CHA and development team grew more comfortable functioning with some distance between them. Progress has been most steady where there has been stability among key actors and an emergence of certain leaders who have been able to promote engagement and bridge-building across sectors. At two of the sites, Oakwood Shores and Westhaven Park, this leadership role has been played by a member of the development team; at Park Boulevard a long-serving service provider has played this bridging role. At Oakwood Shores a longstanding, respected community stakeholder from outside the development team also provided critical leadership. In some cases CHA representatives have helped with the process of role clarity, as described by this service provider:

> I also think, too, having clearly defined roles and responsibilities between the partners because there's a lot of things that could kind of get muddy between what's the developer's responsibility and what's the property manager's responsibility? What's the service provider's responsibility and what's the property manager's responsibility? And all those different things so having a, sort of, sense of accountability and a sense of roles and responsibilities really helped. I think that the best thing that CHA has done is to be able to help enforce those lines. And I really see that as, sort of, CHA's role in some ways.

Working relationships among various players strengthened over time both through repeated interactions and through the trust-building of shared crisis resolution and accomplishment. The early phases of the Transformation presented numerous challenges – legal battles, resident mistrust and anger, and construction delays, to recap a few. And just when the initiative was taking steam, the housing crisis hit. The actors who remained at the table through all of this gained confidence in one another through their work together. Real estate development of multifamily complexes is unique in its cycle of successive development phases – financing, design, relocation, construction, reoccupancy, and then repeat the process – which affords collaborators multiple opportunities to improve their joint efforts and adjust practices based on previous experience. Stakeholders cite an increased openness, sense of common purpose, and level of respect for one another's capacity and commitments as key to increasingly strong collaboration over time.

Discussion

Our examination of the case of cross-sector collaboration in the mixed-income public housing transformation in Chicago reinforces much of what the literature suggests in terms of motivating factors and ensuing dynamics. The city of Chicago and the CHA leveraged millions of dollars of private financing and greatly reduced the size of the public sector workforce employed to manage and support public housing while providing access to prime locations and subsidies for development. Under Mayor Daley, the original champion of the Transformation, public sector resources such as infrastructure investments, and housing subsidies were quite plentiful. Over time, however, and especially under the subsequent administration of Mayor Emanuel, these resources have been shifted to other priorities. Thus, as predicted in the cross-sector collaboration literature, the Transformation has certainly fallen prey to the challenges of political agendas and timeframes. Also as expected, development teams brought more flexibility and entrepreneurial problem-solving to the task while being greatly constrained by the delays and complexities created by government bureaucracy and regulation. The nonprofit service providers that sustained their engagement over time as subcontractors and partners in this cross-sector collaboration were able to broaden their funding sources and increase their capacity, though they faced considerable challenges engaging and serving residents due to considerable mistrust of the system and often deep challenges and barriers faced by the households.

As anticipated, there was some dissonance between the private sector goals of profit maximization and the social goals of maximizing benefits for low-income households (Chaskin and Joseph 2012). This was most apparent, for example, in choices about the proportion of low-income households, the screening and monitoring protocols, and the ultimately low return rates of original households. For their part, developers generally described an alignment between market and social goals. The inclusion of market-rate units was seen to make the overall mixed-income development financially feasible while attending to the social goals of stabilizing and supporting low-income households would make the development more marketable to residents paying market rates. However, the city and CHA's commitment to prioritizing the social benefits of the Transformation and maintaining openness to public scrutiny and accountability has been quite contested. For many affordable housing advocates, the housing authority relinquished its social responsibility in favor of catering to the needs and demands of the private developers.

Most of the key success factors delineated in the cross-sector collaboration literature were also relevant in these mixed-income partnerships. In particular, these include developing greater consensus around goals, increasing role clarity, establishing stronger structures for communication and coordination, increasing understanding of the constraints faced by actors from each sector, building increased trust, familiarity, and mutual accountability over time, and increasing resources and organizational capacity. Perhaps unique to the mixed-income public housing redevelopment context is the stark power differentials given the highly marginalized and vulnerable nature of the target population. This dynamic is reinforced by underlying issues of race and class, the heightened imperative of marketability to an affluent constituency and the stigma, and adverse institutional track record of the CHA as the core public sector partner.

Implications

In 1999 Mayor Daley fully embraced a neoliberal approach to public housing redevelopment and turned to public–private partnerships to implement the Plan for Transformation. Though the move generated tremendous resistance and criticism, including concerns that city was facilitating a lucrative 'land grab' of valuable real estate by the private sector, the undeniably abhorrent conditions in Chicago's public housing and surrounding neighborhoods, the isolation of the public housing population, decades-long dysfunction and corruption of the CHA, and shrinking federal resources provided a compelling case for turning to the private sector.

The Chicago case presents a particularly challenging context for the ensuing quest for effective cross-sector collaboration. The scale of the Plan for Transformation – first 10, then 12 major new mixed-income developments, 15 renovated public housing developments, and a total of 25,000 units to be replaced – as well the high stakes and profile of this initiative in this city, the deep legacy of racial and socioeconomic discrimination, marginalization and disenfranchisement, and, with the housing crisis, a national and local economy in free fall, all combined to increase the difficulty of the task. Well over a decade into full implementation, the prevailing sense among respondents at each of the three sites we studied was that they had ultimately developed ways of working effectively and collaboratively across sectors, but that the collaborative path had been arduous and had generated important lessons along the way.

Our analysis suggests some key implications to guide future mixed-income development policy and practice. First, armed with the knowledge about the nature and forms of organizational transformation necessary to undertake an enterprise of this complexity, lead stakeholders in the public, private, and non-profit sectors should look for means of targeting and accelerating the process of clarifying roles, establishing communication and decision-making procedures, and aligning expectations. Much is now known about the specific ways in which the roles of the various actors – particularly the developer, property manager, and service provider – must be expanded and the effective structure and functioning of site-level collaborative mechanisms. For future mixed-income initiatives, these implications are relevant to the selection of these key actors based on their demonstrated ability and willingness to play more expanded roles and also relevant to technical assistance needed to help them through this process. Given the extensive practical and technical experience across multiple mixed-income redevelopment efforts, there is plenty of information available for Department of Housing and Urban Development (HUD) or another housing entity to generate some type of standard operating procedures document that could provide guidance to those establishing future development partnerships and structures.

Second, rather than incrementally working toward shared clarity on goals and processes through successive phases of developing the cross-sector collaboration, lead stakeholders can be much more proactive in facilitating multi-phase planning and goal consonance. The respective phases of a mixed-income redevelopment initiative – relocation and demolition, design and construction, marketing, sales, screening and lease-up, post-occupancy property management, services and community building – can be better anticipated, and more is now known about the unique imperatives and constraints associated with each. It has proven particularly challenging to get development teams to focus together in a proactive way on their vision, expectations, and plans for the post-occupancy phase when the developments will be populated with a mixed-income population. Earlier deliberation and preparation for the specific challenges inherent in successive phases should promote goal consonance and sustain coordination. Well-timed and well-positioned technical assistance could be a key support to the parties initiating a mixed-income development initiative.

Third, much more must be done to consider and clarify public versus private responsibility for the overall enterprise and its components and to bolster accountability to a set of shared principles and objectives. Our findings demonstrate the sustained role of the CHA over time, despite the transition to private firms charged with ownership and operations of the housing. With these public–private partnerships, the role of the state does not disappear, rather it is reshaped in ways that require continued leadership on the part of the public agencies. There is a critical need to establish and maintain shared vision that balances social and market goals and to assert the influence to recruit and sustain public and civic commitment and resources. It would be helpful to designate a clear initiative leader with the positioning and authority to set overarching goals, facilitate coordination and communication across numerous public- and private-sector actors, and hold the various parties accountable to maintaining fidelity to the initiative's objectives. In most cases, placing this leader in the mayor's office with a clear designation as the mayor's delegated authority on the initiative could provide valuable sustained direction and coordination across city agencies and across sectors.

Finally, given the critical role of key leaders with strong collaboration skills as well as the value of longstanding individual working relationships, it is vital to nurture and support effective leaders and proactively implement retention policies that will reduce turnover and promote a greater degree of staff stability. Taken together, these findings elucidate the significant challenges of cross-sector collaboration in mixed-income development and provide a framework for bringing greater intentionality to this essential operational dimension of these efforts in order to increase their transformative impact on individuals and communities.

Acknowledgments

This research was supported with funding from the John D. and Catherine T. MacArthur Foundation and the Annie E. Casey Foundation. We are grateful to members of our research team including project director Sara Voelker along with Brenda Copley, Ranada Harrison, April Hirsh Urban, Matthew Maronick, and Florian Sichling.

Disclosure statement

No potential conflict of interest was reported by the authors.

Funding

This research was supported with funding from the John D. and Catherine T. MacArthur Foundation and the Annie E. Casey Foundation.

Notes

1. Kimball Hill Homes, the largest privately owned homebuilder in the nation at the time, declared bankruptcy in 2009 during the height of the housing market crisis and dropped out of the partnership.

2. For more on the Gautreaux case and the political and legal context surrounding the Plan for Transformation, see Polikoff (2006).
3. In 2008, the CHA requested a waiver of federal regulations in order to establish 'an alternate mechanism' to facilitate representation of relocated public housing residents who had moved into mixed-income developments (CHA 2008). In place of the elected LACs in these sites, the CHA established the Office of the Ombudsman at its central offices downtown, which mediates and responds to residents' concerns pertaining to their housing experience.
4. For more on the community building challenge in the mixed-income development and the various perspectives and strategies, see Chaskin and Joseph (2010, 2012).
5. For more on the LACs and their relationship to the Working Groups, see Chaskin, Khare, and Joseph (2012).

References

Andrews, R., and T. Entwistle. 2010. "Does Cross-Sectoral Partnership Deliver? An Empirical Exploration of Public Service Effectiveness, Efficiency and Equity." *Journal of Public Administration Research and Theory* 20: 679–701. doi:10.1093/jopart/mup045.

Ansell, C., and A. Gash. 2008. "Collaborative Governance in Theory and Practice." *Journal of Public Administration Research Theory* 18 (4): 543–571. doi:10.1093/jopart/mum032.

Ansell, C. 2003. "Community Embeddedness and Collaborative Governance in the San Francisco Bay Area Environmental Movement." In *Social Movements and Networks: Relational Approaches to Collective Action*, edited by M. Diani and D. McAdam, 123–144. Oxford: Oxford University Press.

Babiak, K., and L. Thibault. 2009. "Challenges in Multiple Cross-Sector Partnerships." *Nonprofit and Voluntary Sector Quarterly* 38 (1): 117–143. doi:10.1177/0899764008316054.

Bovaird, T. 2004. "Public-Private Partnerships: From Contested Concepts to Prevalent Practice." *International Review of Administrative Sciences* 70 (2): 199–215. doi:10.1177/0020852304044250.

Brenner, N., and N. Theodore. 2005. "Neoliberalism and the Urban Condition." *City* 9 (1): 101–107. doi:10.1080/13604810500092106.

Bryson, J. M., B. C. Crosby, and M. M. Stone. 2006. "The Design and Implementation of Cross-Sector Collaboration: Propositions from the Literature." *Public Administration Review* 66: 44–55. doi:10.1111/j.1540-6210.2006.00665.x.

Bushey, C. 2008. "Housing Agency Struggles to Speed up Residents' Return." *Chi-Town Daily News*, June 18. Accessed July 2 2008. http://www.chitowndailynews.org/Chicago_news/Housing_agency_struggles_to_speed_up_residents_return,14858.

Chaskin, R. J., A. T. Khare, and M. L. Joseph. 2012. "Participation, Deliberation, and Decision-Making: The Dynamics of Inclusion and Exclusion in Mixed-Income Developments." *Urban Affairs Review* 48 (6): 863–906. doi:10.1177/1078087412450151.

Chaskin, R. J., and M. L. Joseph. 2012. "Positive" Gentrification, Social Inclusion, and the "Right to the City" in Mixed-Income Communities: Uses and Expectations of Space and Place. *International Journal of Urban and Regional Research*, 37 (2), 480-502. doi: 10.1111/j.1468-2427.2012.01158.x.

Chicago Housing Authority. 2008. "Amended and Restated Moving to Work Agreement." Attachment D, No. 20. Chicago, IL: Chicago Housing Authority.

Chicago Housing Authority. 2014. "Comprehensive annual financial report for the year ended December 31, 2014." Chicago, IL: Chicago Housing Authority.

Chicago Housing Authority, & U.S. Department of Housing and Urban Development. 2000. "Moving to Work Demonstration Agreement." Chicago, IL: Chicago Housing Authority and U.S. Department of Housing and Urban Development.

Cisneros, H. G., and L. Engdahl, eds. 2009. *From Despair to Hope: Hope VI and the New Promise of Public Housing in America's Cities*. Washington, DC: Brookings Institution Press.

Erie, S. P., V. Kogan, and S. A. MacKenzie. 2010. "Redevelopment, San Diego Style: The Limits of Public-Private Partnerships." *Urban Affairs Review* 45 (5): 644–678. doi:10.1177/1078087409359760.

Fosler, R. S. 2002. *Working Better Together: How Government, Business and Nonprofit Organizations Can Achieve Public Purposes through Cross-Sector Collaboration, Alliances and Partnerships*. Washington, DC: Independent Sector.

Fraser, J. C., A. B. Burnes, and J. T. Bazuin. 2013. "HOPE VI, Colonization, and the Production of Difference." *Urban Affairs Review* 49 (4): 525–556. doi:10.1177/1078087412465582.

Fraser, J. C., and E. L. Kick. 2007. "The Role of Public, Private, Non-Profit and Community Sectors in Shaping Mixed-Income Housing Outcomes in the U.S." *Urban Studies* 44 (12): 2357–2377. doi:10.1080/00420980701540952.

Graves, E. M. 2010. "The Structuring of Urban Life in a Mixed-Income Housing "Community"." *City and Community* 9 (1): 109–131. doi:10.1111/j.1540-6040.2009.01305.x.

Gress, T., S. Cho, and M. Joseph. 2016. "HOPE VI Data Compilation and Analysis." Final report submitted to Office of Policy Development and Research, Washington, D.C: U.S. Department of Housing and Urban Development.

Hackworth, J. R. 2007. *The Neoliberal City: Governance, Ideology, and Development in American Urbanism*. Ithaca, NY: Cornell University Press.

Hanlon, J. 2010. "Success by Design: HOPE VI, New Urbanism, and the Neoliberal Transformation of Public Housing in the United States." *Environment and Planning A* 42 (1): 80–98. doi:10.1068/a41278.

Huxham, C., S. Vagen, C. Huxham, and C. Eden. 2000. "The Challenge of Collaborative Governance." *Public Management Review* 2 (3): 337–358. doi:10.1080/14719030000000021.

Joseph, M. 2010. "Creating Mixed-Income Developments in Chicago: Developer and Service Provider Perspectives." *Housing Policy Debate* 20 (1): 91–118. doi:10.1080/10511481003599894.

Joseph, M. L. 2008. "Early Resident Experiences at a New Mixed-Income Development in Chicago." *Journal of Urban Affairs* 30 (3): 229–257. doi:10.1111/j.1467-9906.2008.00394.x.

Joseph, M. L., and R. J. Chaskin. 2010. "Living in a Mixed-Income Development: Resident Perceptions of the Benefits and Disadvantages of Two Developments in Chicago." *Urban Studies* 47 (11): 2347–2366. doi:10.1177/0042098009357959.

Joseph, M. L., and R. J. Chaskin. 2012. "Mixed-Income Developments and Low Rates of Return: Insights from Relocated Public Housing Residents in Chicago." *Housing Policy Debate* 22 (3): 377–406. doi:10.1080/10511482.2012.680479.

Joseph, M. L., R. J. Chaskin, and H. S. Webber. 2007. "The Theoretical Basis for Addressing Poverty through Mixed-Income Development." *Urban Affairs Review* 42 (3): 369–409. doi:10.1177/1078087406294043.

Khare, A. T. 2016. "Privatizing Chicago: The Politics of Urban Redevelopment in Public Housing Reforms." Unpublished doctoral diss., University of Chicago.

Khare, A. T. 2017. "Privatization in an Era of Economic Crisis: Using Market-Based Policies to Remedy Market Failures." *Housing Policy Debate* 1–23. doi:10.1080/10511482.2016.1269356. Published online March 2017 http://www.tandfonline.com/doi/full/10.1080/10511482.2016.1269356

Kleit, R. G. 2005. "HOPE VI New Communities: Neighborhood Relationships in Mixed-Income Housing." *Environment and Planning A* 37 (8): 1413–1441. doi:10.1068/a3796.

Levy, D. K., Z. K. McDade, and K. D. Bertumen. 2011. *Effects from Living in Mixed-Income Communities for Low-Income Families. A Review of the Literature*. Washington, DC: Urban Institute.

Linder, S. H. 1999. "Coming to Terms with the Public-Private Partnerships: A Grammar of Multiple Meanings." *American Behavioral Scientist* 43 (1): 35–51. doi:10.1177/00027649921955146.

McCormick, N. B., M. L. Joseph, and R. J. Chaskin. 2012. "The New Stigma of Relocated Public Housing Residents: Challenges to Social Identity in Mixed-Income Developments." *City and Community* 11 (3): 285–308. doi:10.1111/j.1540-6040.2012.01411.x.

Miraftab, F. 2004. "Public-Private Partnerships: The Trojan Horse of Neoliberal Development?" *Journal of Planning Education and Research* 24 (1): 89–101. doi:10.1177/0739456X04267173.

Moskalyk, A. 2008. "The Role of Public-Private Partnerships in Funding Social Housing in Canada, Ottawa." Ontario: Canadian Policy Research Networks Report.

Olivo, A. 2005. "Report Hits Cha For Losing Residents: Many Former Tenants Are Now Off The Books." *Chicago Tribune* 22: 1.

Olivo, A. 2006. "Rules Leave New Cha Homes Empty: Strict Guidelines Draw Criticism." *Chicago Tribune* 16: 3.

Osborne, D., and T. Gaebler. 1992. *Reinventing Government*. Reading, MA: Addison-Wesley Publishing Company.

Polikoff, A. 2006. *Waiting for Gautreaux: A Story of Segregation, Housing, and the Black Ghetto*. Evanston, IL: Northwestern University Press.

Popkin, S. J. 2016. *No Simple Solutions: Lessons from Chicago's Public Housing Transformation*. Lanham, MD: Rowman & Littlefield.

Popkin, S. J., B. Katz, M. K. Cunningham, K. D. Brown, J. Gustafson, and M. A. Turner. 2004. *A Decade of Hope VI: Research Findings and Policy Challenges*. Washington, DC: Urban Institute and The Brookings Institution Press.

Popkin, S. J., M. K. Cunningham, and M. Burt. 2005. "Public Housing Transformation and the Hard-To-House." *Housing Policy Debate* 16 (1): 1–24. doi:10.1080/10511482.2005.9521531.

Rogal, B. J. 2005. "Uncertain Prospects: Displaced Chicago Housing Authority Tenants Wonder if They Will Qualify to Return to Rebuilt Public Housing." *Chicago Reporter*, March 1. Accessed December 2 2009. http://www.chicagoreporter.com/index.php/c/Inside_Stories/d/Uncertain_Prospects.

Rosenau, P. 1999. "Introduction: The Strengths and Weaknesses of Public-Private Policy Partnerships." *American Behavioral Scientist* 43 (1): 10–34.

Sagalyn, L. 2007. "Public-Private Development." *Journal of the American Planning Association* 73 (1): 7–22. doi:10.1080/01944360708976133.

Schaeffer, P. V., and S. Loveridge. 2002. "Toward an Understanding of Types of Public-Private Cooperation." *Public Performance and Management Review* 26 (2): 169–189. doi:10.1177/1530957602238261.

Tach, L. M. 2009. "More than Bricks and Mortar: Neighborhood Frames, Social Processes, and the Mixed-Income Redevelopment of a Public Housing Project." *City and Community* 8 (3): 269–299.

Thurber, A., C. R. Bohmann, and C. A. Heflinger. 2017. "Spatially Integrated and Socially Segregated: The Effects of Mixed-Income Neighbourhoods on Social Well-Being." *Urban Studies* . doi:10.1177/0042098017702840. Published online March 2017.

Van Slyke, D. M. 2006. "Agents Or Stewards: Using Theory To Understand The government – Nonprofit Social services Contracting Relationship." *Journal Of Public Administration Research And Theory* 17 (2): 157–187. doi: 10.1093/jopart/mul012.

Wallis, J., and B. Dollery. 2006. "Revitalizing the Contribution Non-Profit Organizations Can Make to the Provision of Human Services." *International Journal of Social Economics* 33 (7): 491–511. doi:10.1108/03068290610673261.

Wettenhall, R. 2003. "The Rhetoric and Reality of Public-Private Partnerships." *Public Organization Review* 3 (1): 77–107. doi:10.1023/A:1023000128175.

Wilen, W. P. 2006. "The Horner Model: Successfully Redeveloping Public Housing." *Northwestern Journal of Law and Social Policy* 1 (1): 62–95.

Non-profit housing, a tool for metropolitan cohesion? The case of the Vienna–Bratislava region

Aurore Meyfroidt

Non-profit housing has a long history both in Austria and in Slovakia, even if recent socio-economic and political transformations question this model born in the nineteenth century. This type of housing is considered as affordable housing according to a generalist conception in Austria and a residual one in Slovakia. But in spite of divergences in their national housing policies, both countries are facing common challenges which are epitomised in the Vienna–Bratislava region. This article analyses the role of non-profit housing in bringing more cohesion to a growing but fragmented metropolitan region.

1. Introduction

Housing appears both as a product and a matrix of current metropolitan dynamics: it is a tool for socio-spatial differentiation in metropolitan spaces but it also impacts metropolitan processes by creating and enhancing specific areas. Metropolisation is linked with competitiveness and ranking of agglomerations, which is demonstrated by an increasing concentration of populations, investments and capitals, but at the same time exclusion and segregative mechanisms (Lacour and Puissant 1999). In this context of generalised metropolisation, spatial effects are part of a tension between competitiveness and cohesion. To address these negative effects, metropolitan cohesion is becoming a norm, an agenda for spatial planning, at every scale. This concept is indeed often analysed from a top-down perspective through the European view of spatial integration amongst Member States and regions (Montabone 2011). Here, we will rather look at more local issues of metropolitan cohesion which we define as a process aiming at a balanced allocation of resources between metropolitan regions and also between the core of metropolises and their periphery.

When analysing the relation between housing and metropolisation, metropolitan regions appear as relevant perimeters. First, metropolisation is a space-consuming phenomenon which questions traditional administrative borders (Halbert 2009). Then, by studying metropolitan regions, one can better understand potential redistributive effects from the core to the peripheries and also daily mobilities creating functional integrated areas. All these dimensions are reflected in housing market dynamics. We choose to look specifically at the Vienna–Bratislava region since this is a growing cross-border metropolitan region which is still facing a lack of functional integration and the impact of administrative and national borders on spatial dynamics, which could be alleviated by an appropriate housing supply.

The selective geography of housing is often seen through segregative effects on the demand side which are increased in the current context of financialisation of real estate markets (Filippi 2011; Halbert 2013; Renard 2008): metropolises are increasingly products of a globalised capitalism which is epitomised by real estate markets but influences every circumstance of housing production. Therefore, even housing segments which do not appear to be linked with conventional private housing are affected: this is the case of social housing, facing a trend to residualisation which assumes that social housing is only aimed at disadvantaged populations and not at a large population spectrum (Desjardins 2008; Lévy Vroelant 2011). But one segment still appears to bring about a certain spatial justice through a generalist conception of social housing (Harloe 1995), the non-profit housing sector, often described as the 'third housing sector', between the social and private segments. It is mainly subsidised but built by private developers with various legal statuses (cooperatives, limited liability companies, corporations) and is also addressing evolutions of both sectors. Since the conditions of housing production seem characterised by financialisation and the ambiguous consequences of metropolisation, I assume that non-profit housing is devoted to other logics in order to ensure equal access to affordable housing for a broader population. This article aims to draw the metropolitan patterns of non-profit housing in a growing but differentiated region, but also to determine spatial logics regarding the pricing structure of this housing segment.

In the context of a fragmented region, to what extent is non-profit housing an effective tool to ensure the social and spatial cohesion of a metropolitan region in the making? We argue in particular that the added value of the non-profit housing sector is linked in particular with three factors: its adaptability to local socio-spatial contexts, its role as a compensatory measure for territories where the affordable housing supply is inadequate and its indirect benefices in terms of welfare and territorial solidarity.

This article is structured as follows: after an overview of the existing literature and the spatial context of the Vienna–Bratislava region, the methods, based on a quantitative approach, will be described. Then I will show how housing production matches the specific socio-spatial context of each municipality. Thereafter, we will discuss the relevance of the centre–periphery model in this region through the prism of housing prices and consequently the viability of such projects.

2. Theoretical underpinnings: non-profit housing and metropolitan cohesion

Non-profit housing and metropolitan cohesion are both products of social constructs. On the one hand, housing, as a good, is specific because of the combination of agents involved (Harloe 1995), on the other hand, metropolitan cohesion is shaped through the use of vocabulary specific of the European Commission (Tewdwr-Jones 2011) but I assume that it is also the spatial translation of welfare.

2.1. Characteristics of non-profit housing

In the European context non-profit housing refers to housing built by non-profit housing providers which refers to a specific segment between social housing and private housing market in order to insure a generalist form of social housing, focused on a broader population. In Austria, non-profit housing developers can have various legal status:

Limited Liability Company, Housing Cooperative or Shareholding Corporation. However developers with the status of cooperative are less and less characterised by a bottom-up approach which was present at their very beginning through the legacy of grassroots movements but seem always more commodified, which was analysed in the case of Vienna by contributions of Lang and Novy (2011); and Reinprecht (2014). Non-profit housing is deeply dependent on State intervention, at least for the beginnings, at the stage when the economic viability of non-profit developers is not completely guaranteed (Lang and Roessl 2013; Scanlon and Whitehead 2008). This model is regulated with the obligation for non-profit associations to set rents which are fair for the tenants but cover costs; all profits are then reinvested for maintenance of the stock or further construction of units (Kemeny, Kersloot, and Thalmann 2005): these general principles are incorporated in the Austrian law on non-profit housing sector, the *Wohnungsgemeinnützigkeitsgesetz* (1979). In spite of these strong ties with the public sector, as a tool for welfare strategies, non-profit associations represent a 'third way' and can thus compete with private developers, by influencing them to lower their rents. According to Kemeny, Kersloot, and Thalmann (2005), this trend is characteristic of an integrated rental market, in which non-profit is competitive compared to the conventional private market.

Because of the variety of national housing contexts and of alternative forms of housing, the non-profit housing sector is often defined by what it is not, or by generic terms as third housing sector but it is still influenced by these different sectors so that hybridity is a key concept to characterise the non-profit housing sector (Czischke, Gruis, and Mullins 2012) between State and market (Matznetter 1991), between public and private, between innovation and banality. This hybridity can be seen as a specific adaptability competence of this sector to address various local housing contexts and especially to adapt their discourse to stakeholders in order to ensure access to resources (Czischke, Gruis, and Mullins 2012) but also to foster links between different types of stakeholders (Blessing 2012).

The importance of non-profit within the national housing stock is also a tool to differentiate Western from Eastern Europe: this model is historically well embedded in some Western states whereas former socialist countries still face the challenge to give enough administrative and financial autonomy to non-profit housing associations in providing affordable housing, instead of municipalities which are still responsible for this task (Hegedüs et al. 2014). In spite of a European context characterised by residualisation of social housing with the progression of 'very social' housing instead of generalist social housing (Scanlon and Whitehead 2008; Whitehead 2012), Austria remains the symbol of a conservative corporate welfare state (Matznetter 2002a; Matznetter and Mundt 2012) determining the profile of non-profit housing. Even if social housing is not clearly defined, it 'generally refers to housing operated by the non-profit or limited-profit sector, including public bodies, and the related system of subsides and rent regulations' (Reinprecht 2014, 61–62). This highly fragmented (*Länder* have the competence to provide subsidies to non-profit developers), corporatist, familial and immobile sector (Matznetter 2002a), however, has been facing trends towards commodification since 2000, with the entry of private investors on the subsidised market and the possibility for non-profit developers to sell part of their stock (Novy, Redak, and Jäger 2001). Nevertheless, they still have a stabilising role regarding rent prices, especially in Vienna, and contribute to alleviate the impact of the financial crisis of 2008 upon the housing market (Lang and Novy 2011).

2.2. *Spatial issues of non-profit housing: its role in metropolitan spaces*

The existing literature often analyses the link between housing and metropolisation through the prism of segregation (Filippi 2011; Madoré 2004). The pressure on the housing market is such that inequalities between different land-use types are exacerbated in the metropolises (Coudroy de Lille 2008), since in the context of globalisation, the pressure on housing, especially in urban areas, depends on competition for access to land and increased instability within institutional stakeholders (Bourne 1981). However, cross-border metropolises also increase the degree of integration of metropolises, especially in the case of twin-city regions. These spaces support the emergence of diverse residential environments in order to attract a creative and high-skilled workforce (Meijers, Hoogerbrugge, and Hollander 2014).

The concept of 'metropolitan cohesion' is quite rarely defined with the exception of planning documents at the EU level since the EU fosters social, economic and territorial cohesion. However, this EU driven conception is too restrictive to examine the potential role of non-profit housing as a tool for spatial balance. This cohesion policy is linked with regional policy in order to reduce disparities between regions (Grasland and Hamez 2005). Different forms of cohesion (spatial, territorial, regional and urban) were defined by Miciukiewicz et al. (2012), following criteria of inclusion and exclusion mechanisms, but the authors warned of the withdrawal of welfare and the subsequent unbalance in political, social and economic bonds. Here we define 'metropolitan cohesion' as the production of coherent metropolitan spaces (in the sense of the etymology of the German word '*Zusammenhalt*', holding together different sub-spaces within the metropolitan region) through the rationales of various social stakeholders. Metropolitan cohesion includes cohesion between spaces of the metropolitan region by reducing disparities but also cohesion through spaces by insuring a fair access to services and possibilities for each sub-space of the region (Baudelle 2006). Following Lefebvre's theory upon the production of space (Lefebvre 1974), we assume that space is a social product and thus, that 'metropolitan cohesion' encompasses also 'social cohesion' applied to the metropolitan scale. We still have to be cautious by using 'social cohesion' as it is considered as a 'quasi-concept' with undefined borders (Bernard 1999). Indeed, it is directly derived from politics and needs to be deconstructed to further reduce inequalities, for instance by integrating spaces. Nevertheless, we will consider here the spatial effects of housing as a social product (initiated from welfare policies) and of non-profit housing developers as social stakeholders within the Vienna–Bratislava metropolitan area. According to Kemeny (2006), the organisation of the non-profit sector is crucial in this respect, in order to reach long-term efficiency by creating a sufficient housing stock, fairly distributed amongst different neighbourhoods.

The existing literature often follows an approach inspired by political science but these contributions are spatially disembodied or focus on national and local scales. But how does non-profit housing interact with existing spatial structures at the regional level?

3. The case of the Vienna–Bratislava region

3.1. *A growing region...*

Since transitioning from socialism, joining the European Union and the opening of borders, the Vienna–Bratislava region is often described as a growing region with a high potential that could have been a fully integrated agglomeration already, had Cold War not separated them (Altzinger, Maier, and Fidrmuc 1998).

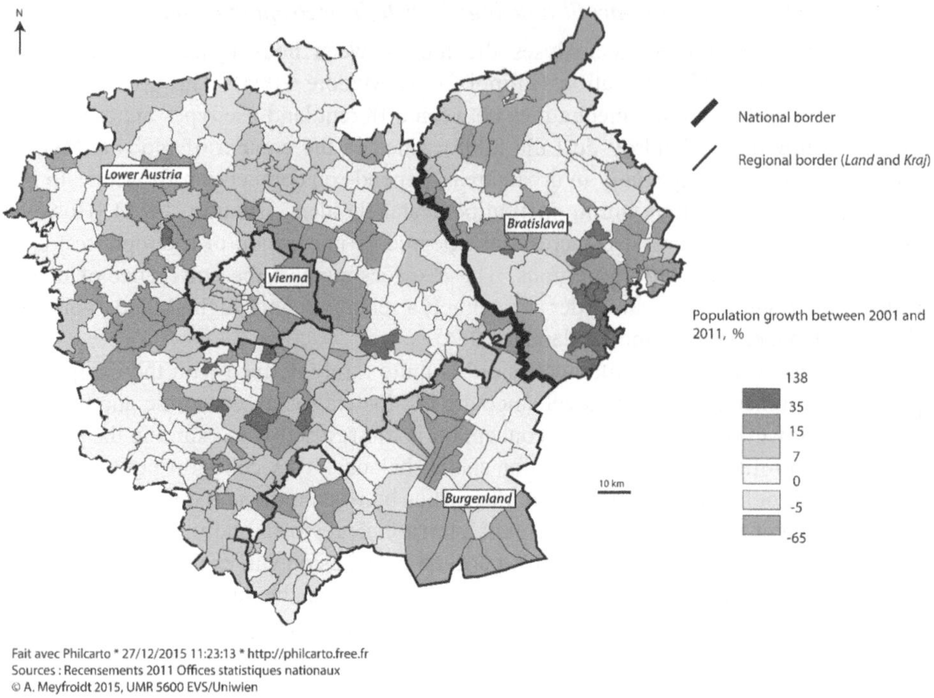

Figure 1. Population growth: A convergence of Austro-Slovak population dynamics through suburbanisation.

But still this growth hides a lot of disparities. When observing demographic evolution between 2001 and 2011 in the region (Figure 1), the disparity between Vienna and Bratislava is striking: Vienna is growing ever faster and should reach two million inhabitants by 2029, whereas Bratislava appears as a shrinking city. However, the two capital cities are addressing converging dynamics, such as suburbanisation, and one should note that these two metropolises are facing suburban developments rather late compared with other European metropolises (Matznetter, Nisch, and Wisbauer 2004).

Our research field is located in the Vienna–Bratislava region and is more specifically defined by the perimeter of the *Stadtregion Ost*, to which was added the Bratislava region. Several different perimeters were used to define this cross-border region, from that of the *Planungsgemeinschaft Ost* joining the three *Länder* of Vienna, Burgenland and Lower Austria, until cross-border polycentric metropolitan regions in ESPON studies where functional urban units build the core of the region (ESPON 2010). This perimeter encompasses Vienna, the eastern part of Lower Austria and the northern part of Burgenland, an area that is to reach the three million inhabitants threshold by 2031 and for which regional planning should be developed to address various issues while ensuring a high quality of life (Fassmann, Görgl, and Helbich 2008). Housing is one of these issues and the selected perimeter allows one to observe the effects of daily mobilities across different regions. The Vienna metropolitan region is covered by daily commuting flows: the Austrian capital city shows a high concentration of these mobilities even if other regional cores such as Schwechat (due to the international airport) or

Wiener Neustadt and Eisenstadt remain important (without, however, counterbalancing Vienna's dynamic). This indicator reveals one of the characteristics of the agglomeration, its polycentricity, often put at the top of the political agenda (Giffinger and Suitner 2014) and which is also reflected by housing developments.

New construction in the non-profit housing sector is concentrated in this region on the Austrian side. While 30% of new construction is made by non-profit developers in Austria as a whole, this share reaches almost 60% in Vienna, 41.5% in Lower Austria and 50% in Burgenland (Statistik Austria). These differences are to be explained by the particular heritage of social housing in Vienna but mostly because housing policy falls under the competence of NUTS 2 regions in Austria. Therefore, conditions are quite different between the three regions, even if the challenges they face are similar. For instance, since non-profit developers should ensure a service of public interest, they cannot build on excessively expensive land, which is however always more difficult because of metropolitan pressure. To address this, the *Land* of Vienna has an organisation, the *Wohnfonds*, dealing with setting some plots of lands aside for non-profit developers. Housing policies regulating the non-profit sector also reflect local contexts: that is why single family dwellings are subsidised in Lower Austria and private developers cannot be eligible for subsidies outside Vienna. This fragmentation into different local welfare regimes is made even more complex by a lack of integration.

3.2. ... facing a lack of institutional and functional integration

Institutional and functional integration are fundamental parts of metropolitan integration and especially in the context of cross-border agglomerations; they are visible through an intensification of interactions and through converging developments from both parts of the border (Decoville et al. 2013).

The Vienna–Bratislava region deals with asymmetries that can be addressed by strengthening relations between both neighbouring countries. Institutional cooperation between Austria and Slovakia began even before concrete cross-border developments, as part of a political agenda to reunite Western and Eastern parts of Europe. This metropolitan region in the making is interlinked by various cooperation agreements, from the CENTROPE region, which brings together the cross-border regions of the Czech Republic, Hungary, Slovakia and Austria, to the Jordes+ project in the context of the INTERREG programme 2007–2013. Nevertheless, these cooperation tools are not legally binding and are linked with time-limited programmes, which does not provide satisfying conditions for creating a common planning instrument (Sohn and Giffinger 2015; Tatzberger 2006; Giffinger and Hamedinger 2013), all the more so as housing remains less visible in these strategies.

The weakness of these cross-border policies is reflected by the rather weak cross-border mobilities (1000 commuters) in comparison with other cross-border regions such as the Greater Region in Luxemburg, with 127,000 commuters living and working in the region in 2006 (ESPON 2010). This is to be explained by strict conditions to enter the market that were loosened only in 2011. Moreover, when observing the share of commuters working abroad,[1] it appears that the border differential remains unequal since very few Austrian commuters work abroad whereas more than 8% of daily commuters living in the city of Bratislava work abroad and one can assume that they work on the Austrian side.

3.3. Two national housing policies creating an unusual border differential

Even if the functional and institutional integration of the Vienna–Bratislava region are not pushed further, the Austrian and the Slovak stakeholders have to address the same challenges, such as growth in their suburban areas, which question the role of the non-profit sector.

Housing remains strongly embedded into national contexts because of its dependency towards public policies even if they affect also local territories and are influenced by exogenous dynamics such as metropolisation. Before focusing upon the specific patterns of non-profit housing in the Vienna–Bratislava region, one has to precise national housing policies at stake in both countries.

Housing policy in Austria appears to be very protective and enables a stable supply of affordable rental housing for middle and low-income households within the State budget (Lawson 2010). Even if recent contributions (Verlic 2013; Kadi 2015) pointed out underlying liberal tendencies beneath the apparently immobile conservative welfare housing regime (Matznetter and Mundt 2012), against the dominant academic discourse about stability in Austrian and especially Viennese housing policies, social rental housing remains a dominant housing type considering both housing stock and construction. For instance, in 2014, 60% of the housing stock belongs to the non-profit housing sector. In Vienna, social housing is equally distributed in the city, especially when observing the repartition of municipal housing. Recent social rental housing built by non-profit developers are rather located in paracentral and peripheral spaces because of land prices but it is still linked with an efficient access to transport infrastructures according to development priorities set by the Viennese Master plan. This ensures a spatial cohesion at the scale of the municipality, as well as a social one because of large financial eligibility criteria that would encompass 80% of the population. However, when considering the whole Vienna metropolitan region, three different regional policies are concerned (Vienna, Lower Austria and Burgenland), which questions the adaptability of non-profit developers facing various spatial contexts.

As for Slovakia, during the communist period, it had a cooperative housing system, considered here solely as a legal status (without any participative approach) which was quite similar to the Austrian system because of a life lease and a feeling of quasi ownership (Balchin and Sykora 1996; Lichtenberger 1995). However, post-socialist transformations have led to the retreat of State from financing housing construction, to support to private markets and to privatisation of almost all housing stock even if privatisation of the cooperative housing stock was slower than the one of State housing (Zapletalova, Antalikova, and Smatanova 2003). Nevertheless Slovakia became than a 'super ownership state' (Lux 2003) since cooperative housing which represented 22% of the total Slovak housing stock in 1991 dropped to 14.9% in 2001 and 3.5% in 2011 (Statistiscky urad slovenskej republiky). Given the high pressure upon land because of the rapid suburbanisation process and the fact that municipalities sold their land to private developers, there are very few possibilities to develop further affordable housing even if the demand is there. Indeed, young households face difficulties to find their own flat (Smith and Rochovska 2007) and even for middle-class households, the housing market in Bratislava becomes quite tight. Therefore, since 2003 and even more since 2007, one can note the development of a cross-border suburbanisation driven by Slovak households who live in municipalities in Lower Austria or Burgenland close to the border but continue working in Bratislava (Hitz and Wohlschlägl 2009).

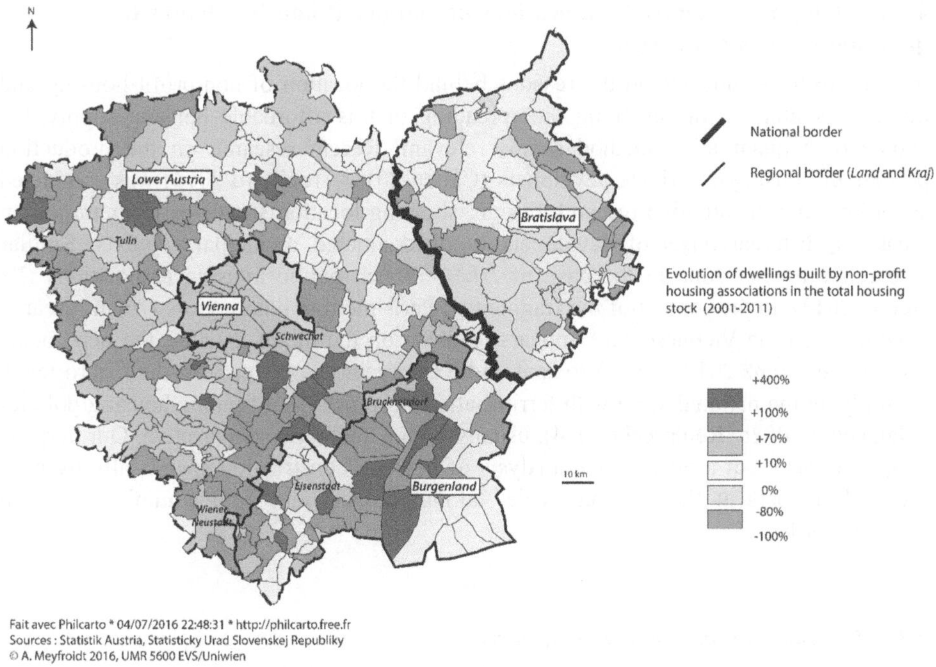

Figure 2. Evolution of the share of non-profit housing between 2001 and 2011.

Thus, these national housing contexts, even though they seem very different, are interrelated because of common heritages and because of the push/pull factor represented by the coexistence of a neoliberal housing regime on the one side and of a still affordable one on the other side.

The evolution of the share of non-profit housing sector between 2001 and 2011 (Figure 2) reveals disparities between Austria and Slovakia, especially because of the post-socialist transformation of the latter. This map reflects a strong border differential between diverging housing dynamics and especially the striking effects of the privatisation of the housing stock and the transformation of housing cooperatives into condominiums or associations of private landlords on the Slovak side. On the Austrian side, non-profit housing is increasing mainly in suburban areas and around local cores in Burgenland that are concentrating population increase as shown on the first map. Therefore, the two diverging housing models, a generalist affordable one on the Austrian side, and a neoliberal one on the Slovak side, are facing each other. This tends to create another border differential regarding housing opportunities, with a flow of Slovak households seeking more affordable subsidised housing in Austria, pushed away by a neoliberal environment, with increasing prices. In this framework, few original socialist housing cooperatives and very few new forms of cooperatives are built because of the monopolistic situation of private property and a lack of appropriate legal status for potential new non-profit associations.

Therefore, even if we will mainly focus on the Austrian side, we still need to understand the socio-spatial context on the Slovak side to understand the role of non-profit housing as a tool for the socio-economic cohesion of the built environment and of the whole metropolitan region.

4. Studying the territorial implications of non-profit housing thanks to a quantitative research design

In order to better understand the reasons behind the location of non-profit housing and the socio-spatial factors enabling the spreading of this affordable housing supply, the choice of a quantitative method seems relevant. Recent research on the production process of housing by private developers (Callen 2011; Trouillard 2014) was conducted according to a quantitative research design, showing location strategies in metropolitan areas for different types of developers in differentiated municipal contexts. Similar research was also done in the case of *HLM*, French public housing associations (Le Hervet 2013), in the context of the fragmented Paris metropolitan region. Urban research conducted on the Viennese case appears to focus on the micro level, at the neighbourhood scale (Franz 2013; Lévy Vroelant and Reinprecht 2014), but also the macro level, by studying the national scale with territorialisation processes of public housing policies (Matznetter 2002b; Reinprecht 2014), usually with a qualitative perspective. Our purpose here is to carry out a quantitative analysis of housing construction specifically by non-profit developers at the regional scale, taking into account both administrative and national borders.

4.1. Determining local housing contexts

We adopted this design thanks to two databases, the first dealing with the determination of 'local housing contexts' and the second dedicated to residential housing projects built by non-profit housing associations, no matter which legal status. In order to understand what kind of regional development is created by the construction of non-profit housing, the conditions of production need to be analysed and especially the socio-spatial profile of municipalities. Hence, the aim here is to outline potential local housing markets which are created by the association of national dynamics and the socio-spatial profile of local spaces (Driant 1995). However, local housing markets seem less and less local in a context of metropolisation, for instance with the standardisation of housing products and also in the context of Europeanisation, with emerging cross-border housing markets.

Using demographic and socio-economic data collected in the 2011 census at the municipal level, we first applied a principal component analysis to choose the most relevant variables in order to determine profiles with a hierarchical cluster analysis. A total of 8 variables were analysed for 372 municipalities. The choice of socio-economic and demographic variables was influenced by patterns regarding the evolution of residential cycles and access to housing, based on the hypothesis that the non-profit housing sector would be more adapted to lower and middle classes. Five types of municipalities were identified through this method (Figure 3):

(1) Type 1 ($N = 53$): The first suburban extension of Vienna, mainly characterised by high rates of academics (21%, it is only 11.8% for the region), high land prices (255 EUR/m^2, 120 EUR/m^2 for the region) and low unemployment rates (2.1%, 2.3% for the region). Privileged residential location in the West of Vienna (*Wienerwald*, Viennese forest). Development of affordable housing built by non-profit developers seems limited because land prices are too high.

(2) Type 2 ($N = 5$): Bratislava, a metropolis that is catching-up.[2] High rates of academics (29.9%, compared with 11.8% for the region) and unemployment (8.3%, against 2.3% for the region), low housing stock (72 dwellings per 1000

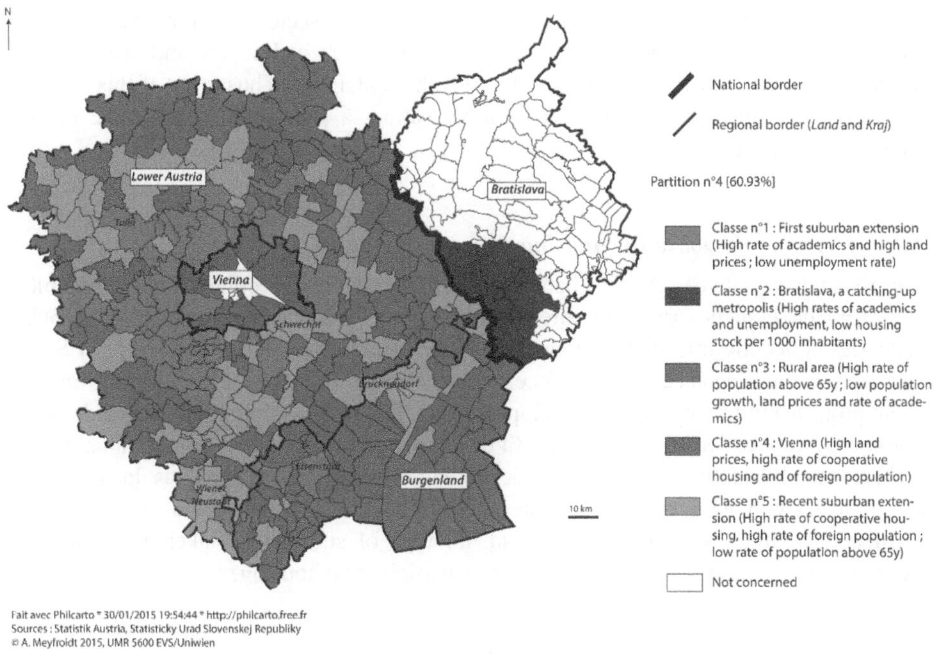

Figure 3. Five spatial contexts for the development of non-profit housing markets.

inhabitants, against 500 per 1000 inhabitants at the regional level). Structural housing shortage in Bratislava due to the wide spread of privatisation of the housing stock and a lack of construction of affordable housing.

(3) Type 3 (N = 137): Austrian rural area. High rate of population above 65 years (19.5% compared to 18.3% at the regional scale), low population growth (+3.7%, 8.3% for the region) and share of academics (9.4% against 11.8%). Potential suburban area in the making. However this casts doubt on the relevance of this local context (is there any demand for affordable housing in a context where land prices are quite low?)

(4) Type 4 (N = 11): Vienna, a growing metropolis.[3] High land prices (590 EUR/m^2 against 121 EUR/m^2), high share of cooperative housing in the total housing stock (10.4%, against 2.1% at the regional level), high share of foreign population (20.1% against 7.7%). Non-profit housing developers as successors to the Municipality of Vienna (as social landlord) for the supply of affordable housing.

(5) Type 5 (N = 83): The second suburban extension. Low rate of population above 65 years of age (16% against 18.4% for the region), high population growth (12.1% against 8.3%) and rapid growth of cooperative housing in the housing stock (3.4% against 2.1%). Strong demand for affordable housing.

These five different local contexts for the development of housing supply by non-profit housing associations reveal specific features of the Vienna–Bratislava region. First, the two capital cities belong to two strictly different classes whose profiles are diverging: whereas Vienna appears as a growing metropolis, Bratislava is shrinking. Regarding housing, although the non-profit housing sector is present in both capital cities because of an existing stock inherited from the end of the nineteenth century, Vienna remains an example of a generalist form of social housing thanks to this particular sector but Bratislava is characterised by the effects of post-socialist privatisation which had severe and lasting consequences upon the housing situation in the Slovak capital city. Thus, even if this region is addressing both metropolisation and suburbanisation, a substantial rural fringe remains mainly in Burgenland.

4.2. A specific database for housing operations

A cross-analysis between this first database and a second one collecting 480 projects built by non-profit developers forms the core of our analysis. Since we had no access to public databases collecting information about real estate operations (such as the BIEN or Sitadel databases in the French case for instance), we created our own database collecting variables about projects built by non-profit developers from 2007 to 2014 within the area under study. These data were collected from non-profit developers themselves and from regional entities dedicated to allocating these dwellings, depending on four types of variables: localisation of the project (with geolocation by address), morphological criteria (housing type, area), financing variables (housing price per sq. m, type of subsidies), stakeholder's network (when coconstruction with another developer, participative housing).

5. Location factors revealing socio-spatial profiles

This section will focus on two main variables (with 319 out of 480 proved valid): the location of housing projects and also the type of financing, analysed using concentration indicators and location quotients (Pumain and Saint-Julien 2001).

5.1. Non-profit housing as a suburban type of housing

When analysing this map showing the location of these projects (Figure 4), non-profit housing construction is concentrated in the city of Vienna, which can be explained by inherited social housing stock and the strong involvement of the City Council to ensure an adequate supply of affordable housing thanks to support for non-profit developers. This development of non-profit housing is reflected in the allocation of plots of land (sale but also long-term lease) through a call for projects and political support from the Austrian Socialist Party which governs in the municipal coalition. Then, it also appears that even new construction of non-profit housing confirms the role of the national border between Austria and Slovakia: while Austria follows the model of conservative welfare (Matznetter and Mundt 2012) with a generalist conception of social housing, Slovakia is a post-socialist neo-liberal state whose handing of social housing reflects a residual conception and comes quite late compared to other post-socialist countries (Smith and Rochovska 2007). Indeed, even if the newly approved State Housing Policy for 2020 recognises the role of non-profit housing, for instance in the form of public-private partnerships linked with public subsidies, housing cooperatives are mainly considered as housing management associations and legal obstacles for the 're-creation' of a third housing sector, which remains as yet unfinished (Ministerstvo Vystavba a rozvoj regiony 2015).

All five types of municipalities are covered by this non-profit housing supply, but this housing production is particularly visible in one type. Indeed, the fifth class, corresponding to the second phase of suburbanisation in the Vienna agglomeration, is one of the main receivers of the non-profit housing supply. This housing construction is concentrated in the south of

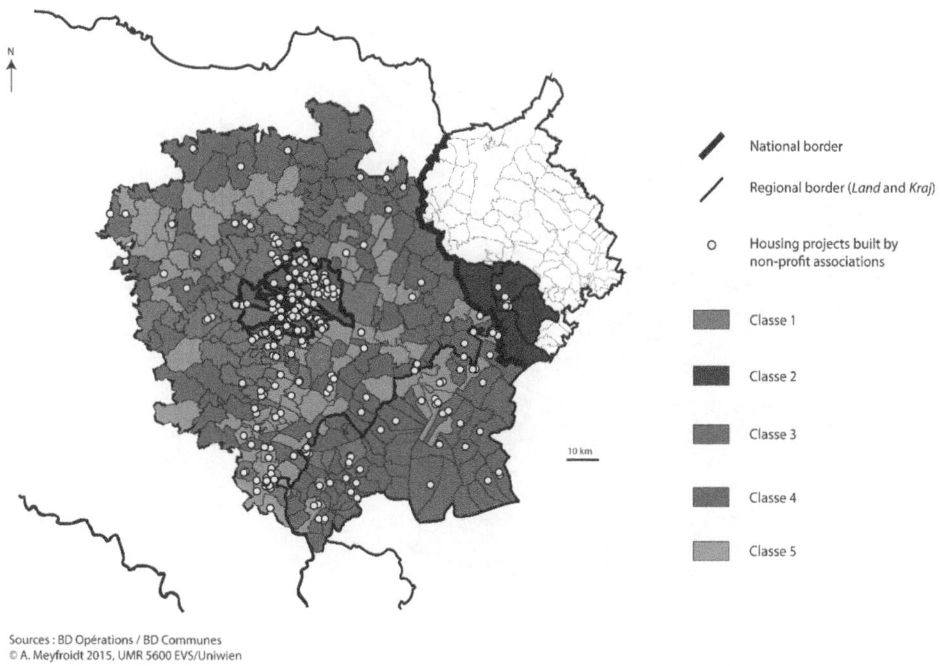

Figure 4. Distribution of housing projects built by non-profit developers.

Vienna, between the Austrian capital city and the regional core of Wiener Neustadt, and also in Burgenland, near the border with Slovakia and Lower Austria, in the area of Parndorf. These spaces gather growing municipalities with a demographic increase of 10% between 2001 and 2011, and contribute to the creation of a double suburbanisation, both for the Vienna and the Bratislava agglomerations. This cross-border suburbanisation is pushed by the global trend of suburbanisation in Bratislava, which began mainly to the north and north-east of the capital city around the 1990s (Sveda 2011) before an extension towards the 'fourth quadrant' on the Austrian side since the opening of the border within the Schengen Area in 2007. The first households, mainly upper-middle classes, were looking for a better local environment and high-quality services but close enough to continue working in Bratislava, invested in single-family dwellings. A second type of Slovak households, rather middle and low-middle classes, exploited the border differential: the existence of a strong subsidised non-profit housing sector open to EU citizens combined with the proximity to Bratislava is the main factor explaining the second flow of Slovak households around 2010. Moreover, local non-profit housing associations decided to tap into that emerging cross-border housing market by building blocks of flats and openly targeting this exogenous clientele. Although housing production in suburban areas often seems carried out by private developers in a rather standardised manner (Callen 2011; Le Goix 2006; Rougé 2005), here non-profit housing developers are at the core of this double suburbanisation process.

5.2. An unusual concentration of non-profit housing construction

However, when aggregating these housing constructions at the municipality level and relating it to the population (Figure 5), the results are slightly different and reveal the relevance of this housing supply according to demographic dynamics.

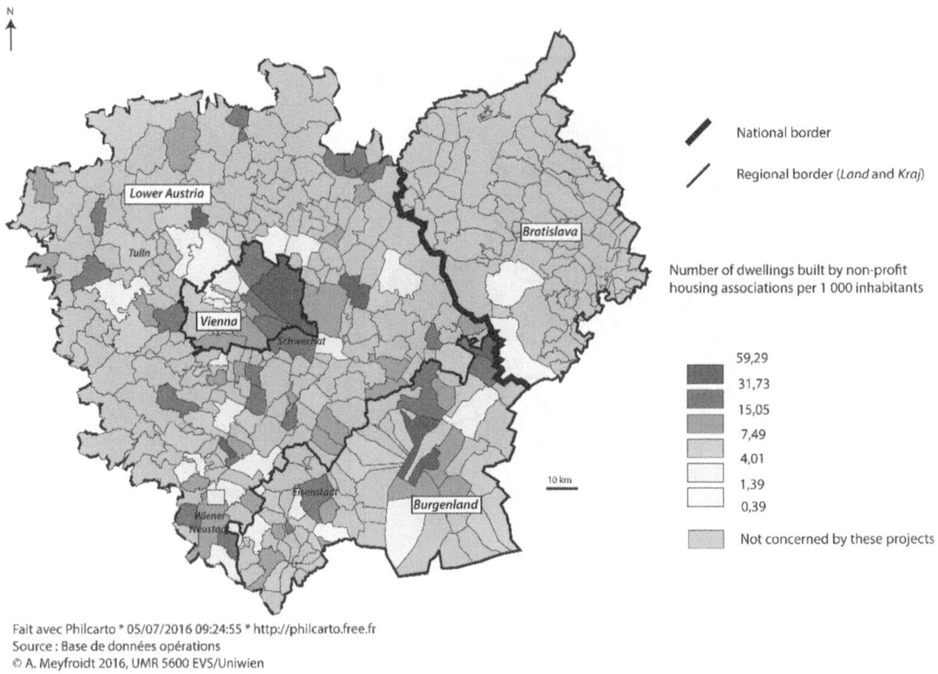

Figure 5. Distribution of non-profit housing projects per municipality.

When observing the number of dwellings per 1000 inhabitants built by non-profit housing developers in this metropolitan region, one can first note that the production volume is concentrated in the peripheral districts of Vienna, then in south-eastern suburban municipalities but also near the national border. This result could seem striking since it does not affect an area where the housing market is particularly under pressure and where there should be a structural demand just as in urban spaces. Actually, it reveals the deadweight effect of the border differential enabling the creation of a local cross-border market mainly targeting Slovak households.

A second result from this map consists in the types of municipalities where housing production is concentrated: if the second suburban extension remains a preferential space for the construction of non-profit housing, rural areas also appear as key spaces. This can be explained by the rather low prices of land but is questionable regarding the actual demand for these spaces where the population is ageing. All types of spaces within the metropolitan region are covered but the concentration in rural areas pleads for a form of territorial solidarity across local contexts.

Finally, Burgenland is, amongst the four administrative regions within the Vienna–Bratislava region, the one where this type of housing production is the most concentrated. This can be attributed to the specific welfare regime of this *Land* which was governed by socialists until May 2015 and was an Objective 1 region for regional European development until 2013, because of the lack of economic development in this very rural region depending on agriculture (especially in the south of Burgenland which is not in our sample).

5.3. A housing production matching with socio-economic local contexts

Non-profit developers, no matter their legal status, can build with or without subsidies, relying on their own capital or bank loans. Nevertheless, they still have to build a majority of subsidised housing due to their nature as housing associations of public interest, set up by a specific law on the Austrian side, the *Wohnungsgemeinnützigkeitsgesetz*. The conditions for receiving subsidies for the construction of affordable housing differ from region to region, some appearing more accessible than others: traditionally, Burgenland allocates quite generous subsidies whereas Lower Austria tends to give subsidies also for the construction of single-family houses to be purchased and not rented. However, non-profit developers within this region, and particularly those whose seat is in Vienna and Lower Austria, tend to build without subsidies. According to our database, in 2007, 11% of housing projects were built without public subsidies but this share increased to 25% in 2014, concentrating mainly in Vienna. Two major factors explain this evolution: first of all the land is less and less affordable, especially in Vienna because of its scarcity,[4] and the development of private property is quite remarkable in the privileged areas in the west and south-west of Vienna.

We will focus on the type of financing of these housing operations according to their localisation. Indeed, we assume that housing production without subsidies will be concentrated in municipalities with a privileged social profile, as shown in our typology of local market contexts. To verify this hypothesis, a chi-square analysis was conducted to find out if there is a significant relationship between the profile of the municipalities and the fact that housing construction is subsidised. With a residual risk of 0.05, our observed chi-square (=9.9) is higher than the theoretical chi-square (=7.8), so we have to reject the null hypothesis: there is a significant relation between the socio-economic profile of the municipality and the type of financing. Therefore, a quantification of this phenomenon could enable us to analyse the concentration of subsidised housing construction and more generally to identify which municipalities appear as local housing markets that seem locked because of the prevalence of non-subsidised housing production. A location quotient according to the share of subsidised projects at the scale of each municipality was then calculated, as shown on the following map (Figure 6). If the location quotient is greater than 1, then the area has proportionally more subsidised projects than the larger study area.

According to this figure, a large majority of municipalities of the metropolitan region show a location quotient greater than 1 and are therefore areas where there is an overrepresentation of subsidised housing. The border effect between Austria and Slovakia is once again reflected by this variable: while a large majority of Austrian municipalities show a high concentration of subsidised housing projects, the projects built in Bratislava were all financed without any public subsidies. This can be explained by a legal vacuum: only municipalities are eligible for housing subsidies for the construction of social housing, with loans and subsidies from the State housing development fund (up to 80% of the total costs), even if there is an attempt to allow private companies to be eligible for these this type of funding if they build dwellings for rent (Ministry Vystavba a rozvoj regiony 2015). One should also mention that Austrian developers, who have the status of non-profit developers under the Austrian *Wohnungsgemeinnützigkeitsgesetz*, cannot transfer this legal status to Slovakia where they are considered as normal private developers. Therefore, these developers build without subsidies, all the more so as a majority of projects are flats for sale.

Thus, this variable reveals two types of suburban developments. When observing municipalities with an underrepresentation of subsidised housing proportionally

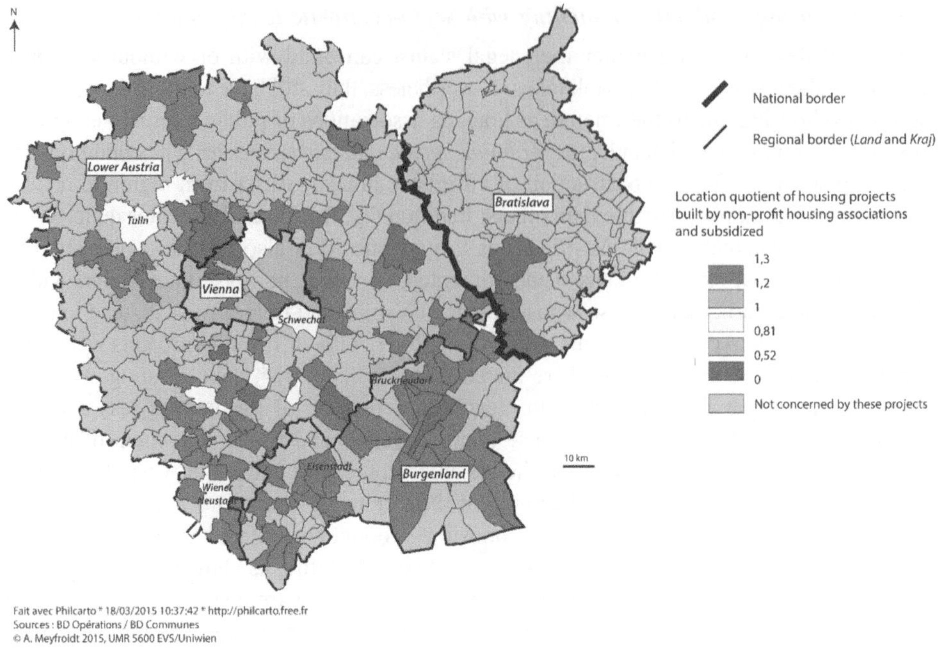

Figure 6. A concentration of subsidised non-profit housing in suburban and rural areas.

compared to the whole area under study, the specificity of suburban zones in the western part of Vienna remains. As shown on this map, the privileged locations of north-western districts within the Austrian capital city and of Klosterneuburg, archetype of the typical suburban municipality for white collars (+4.1% of demographic growth between 2001 and 2011, 32.8% are academics) appear as a closed market for the supply of affordable rental housing. On the contrary, the suburban extensions at the eastern and southern parts of the Viennese agglomeration are those where the concentration of subsidised non-profit housing is the more significant. Here, two main developments need to be pointed out: first, the confirmation of a polycentric development and second, cross-border suburbanisation. If suburbanisation is occurring in the Vienna–Bratislava metropolitan region, the development on the Austrian side reveals a polycentric suburban pattern. Thanks to the high construction of affordable housing by the municipality and then non-profit developers, Vienna did not face a housing crisis which would have caused a rapid suburbanisation process (Matznetter, Nisch, and Wisbauer 2004). When observing the figure, subsidised housing production in suburban areas is concentrated around both regional centres of Wiener Neustadt and Eisenstadt. Then, if cross-border suburbanisation occurs, one should note that non-profit housing being highly subsidised in Burgenland is a pull factor for residential migration for middle-class Slovak populations. The non-profit housing sector acts not only as a compensatory measure for Burgenland, but also indirectly for Bratislava by attracting these populations whose housing needs could not be addressed in the Slovak part. Finally, the specificity of Burgenland with almost 100% of non-profit housing projects that are publicly subsidised is here again stressed.

6. Challenging the centre–periphery model with a fair housing supply?

Metropolisation tends to foster central spaces to better fit into the competition between cities and metropolises at the global scale. This creates then spatial differentiation and fragmentation by building 'winning' and 'losing' spaces. Metropolitan cohesion includes ensuring accessibility to basic infrastructures as housing wherever populations are located, should it be in the core of metropolises or on the fringes of metropolitan regions. Thus, non-profit housing will be here confronted to the structural centre–periphery model, assuming that the expected cohesion effect would alleviate this model.

6.1. The relation between housing prices and the centre–periphery model: a theoretical approach

If non-profit housing seems to fit with socio-spatial contexts, enabling a form of vertical cohesion, horizontal cohesion between spaces thanks to non-profit housing production still needs to be verified. We will question the centre–periphery model and see whether housing prices in this specific housing production can test the validity of this model in the context of publicly subsidised construction.

The centre–periphery model appears as a classic scheme to understand housing price dynamics in urban areas, according to the theory of economic rent developed by Von Thünen and adapted by Alonso-Muth for urban contexts (Derycke 1979). This pricing gradient reflects the desirability of the centre by showing its socio-economic selectivity (Callen 2011). However, the structure of real estate prices within urban contexts can be analysed thanks to two different paradigms: a classic centre–periphery model following the concepts of the Chicago School or a mosaic structure of highly contrasted values increased by some address effects (Le Goix and Guérois 2009). Here, we will rather follow the first approach that seems better adapted for an analysis at the regional scale.

As non-profit housing strongly depends on public authorities and is linked with the aim to ensure a service of public interest, we assume that the role of conventional market dynamics could be lessened so that prices for housing built by non-profit developers should show spatial equity by proportionally low differences. Therefore, we forecast that there should be no link or a weak link between prices and distance in the third housing sector.

6.2. Housing prices in the non-profit housing sector: how valid is the centre–periphery model?

In order to address this issue, the distance between all housing projects (which had been geolocated at the address level) and the city centre of Vienna (St Stephen cathedral) was calculated thanks to a distance matrix, and only projects where information about the price per sq. m[5] was available, were selected. We also chose to focus on the rental segment (with and without subsidies), which explains why Bratislava does not belong to this sample; neither does the Slovak part, which would have included too many distortions. In order to keep the local socio-spatial variables, we also indicated to which type of municipality each observation belongs.

These conditions having been set, a linear regression analysis combined with a chi-square analysis was conducted (Figure 7). If there is a significant relation between housing prices and distance (significance threshold of 0.015), it is nevertheless quite

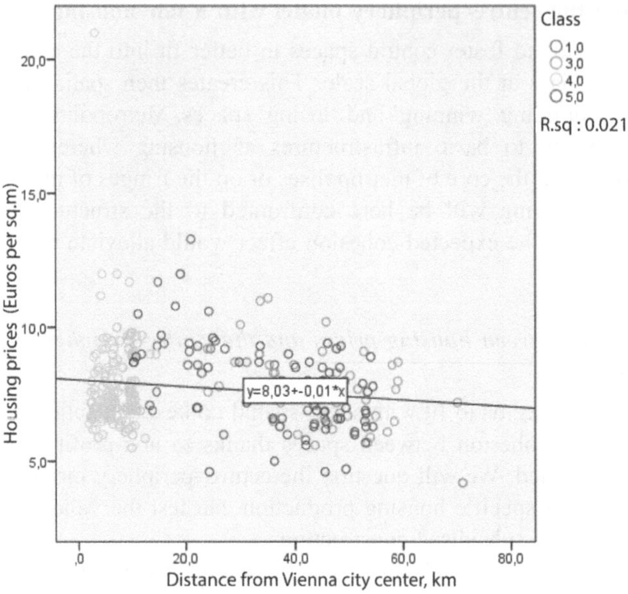

Figure 7. Linear regression between distance to Vienna and housing price.

low, with a chi-square value of −0.021. The shape of the curve shows only a slightly descending slope, so that one may have the impression that no matter the distance, the price does not vary, suggesting that this specific housing sector brings about spatial equity. This trend can be explained by the fact that housing projects located in the fourth class, in Vienna, tend to settle down the slope, all the more so as they are very densely localised on the regression line. This trend shows, first, that the concentration of non-profit housing projects in Vienna can cause distortions when observing spatial rationales at the regional scale. Furthermore, the localisation of the dots reveals that the price spectrum of non-profit construction in Vienna is quite large, which is due to its metropolitan character which covers both diverse types of populations and also some top-segment projects (often without subsidies). Finally, public intervention in the non-profit housing sector is particularly intense in Vienna (this was inherited from the Red Vienna period). It is also due to specific tools such as land being made available by the *Wohnfonds*, in charge of organising calls for housing projects, to ensure this local housing welfare.

Thus, a second analysis excluding projects built in Vienna was conducted, in order to verify if the trend of the slope is modified or not, and to what extent (Figure 8). The relation between distance and price is still significant, to 0.000, but here a sharp increase of the chi-square value is to be observed (−0.218), with a steeper slope. This result would suggest a more conventional relation between price and distance, similar to those of projects built by private developers. This is to be explained by a higher diversity of local contexts, including within each type of municipality, and by a different type of public intervention. Indeed, the *Länder* of Lower Austria and Burgenland do not have tools to make land available for non-profit developers on a large scale. Therefore, negotiations for the land occur on a case-by-case basis, between non-profit developers and each mayor. Nevertheless, if the relation between distance and price can be verified and is more visible compared to the previous sample, it stays quite limited in scope since only

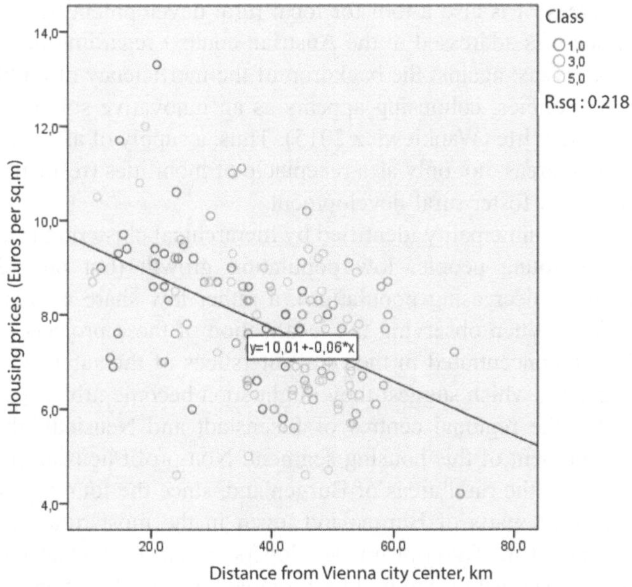

Figure 8. Linear regression between distance to the centre and housing prices, excluding Vienna.

one half of the variation was explained. All this indicates that the classic centre–periphery model remains only partly true when predicting housing prices in the non-profit housing sector, and that this hypothesis of spatial equity could be relevant, even if other factors at the very local scale can also influence price formation.

6.3. Investing in peripheries at all costs? The case of non-profit housing production in rural areas

Amongst the 480 projects analysed, 59 belong to municipalities located in rural areas. These areas are concentrated on the outskirts of the area we study, with only a few within the suburban extension, such as emerging suburban municipalities, and mainly in Burgenland. If these projects represent only 12% of the considered construction sample, they still reveal some trends of the non-profit sector in Austria as a way of promoting territorial solidarity. As Meijers, Hoogerbrugge and Hollander (2014), we also consider metropolisation as the process by which a core city connects different types of networks, including links between cities in rural areas, enabling the supply of services of public interest for these peripheral spaces.

Few contributions focus on social or affordable housing forms in rural areas as they are not seen as areas where there could be pressure upon the housing market. Even if public policies dedicated to housing have been set up in urban areas and in cities, the recent demographic and economic developments are blurring borders between urban and rural areas, so that social housing becomes also an issue for rural areas. The supply of subsidised housing remains low in these areas but they are faced with factors advocating in favour of the development of this segment, such as pressure upon urban real estate markets, increasing number of households or the attractiveness of rurality (Sencébé 2007). But the argument that disadvantaged social groups are relegated further and further away is not the only one to explain the need to develop a supply of affordable housing in rural areas; it is also a tool for local rural development by maintaining daily services. This issue was addressed in the Austrian context regarding the potentialities of co-housing in such areas: against the backdrop of the inefficiency of traditional planning tools and housing policies, cohousing appears as an innovative solution to adapt infrastructures for everyday life (Wankiewicz 2015). Thus, a supply of affordable housing still makes sense in rural areas, not only as a receptacle of mobilities (residential countryside) but also as a means to foster rural development.

The third type of municipality identified by hierarchical clustering is characterised by small numbers of young people, low population growth (but only 30 of the 137 municipalities have a decreasing population), a rather low share of non-profit housing and low land prices. When observing the localisation of these projects in the rural area (Figure 9), they are concentrated in the rural interstices of the suburban sprawl of both Vienna and Bratislava, which suggest they might soon become urban spaces, but also in Burgenland around the regional centres of Eisenstadt and Neusiedl, showing a rather endogenous development of this housing segment. Non-profit housing production is not a new phenomenon in the rural areas of Burgenland, since the four registered non-profit developers build in all parts of Burgenland, even in the most rural one, in the south (outside our sample). But if non-profit developers, in closer contact with local authorities, have a social responsibility to build affordable housing also in less urbanised areas, one may question the viability of such projects. There is still strong political pressure from the mayors who want to keep their citizens and local services as well as maintain employment of the whole construction sector.

But the mean price of projects built in rural areas is almost equal to the mean value of the whole region, which means that the low prices of land are compensated by other characteristics of the projects. Very often, non-profit housing projects in these spaces are

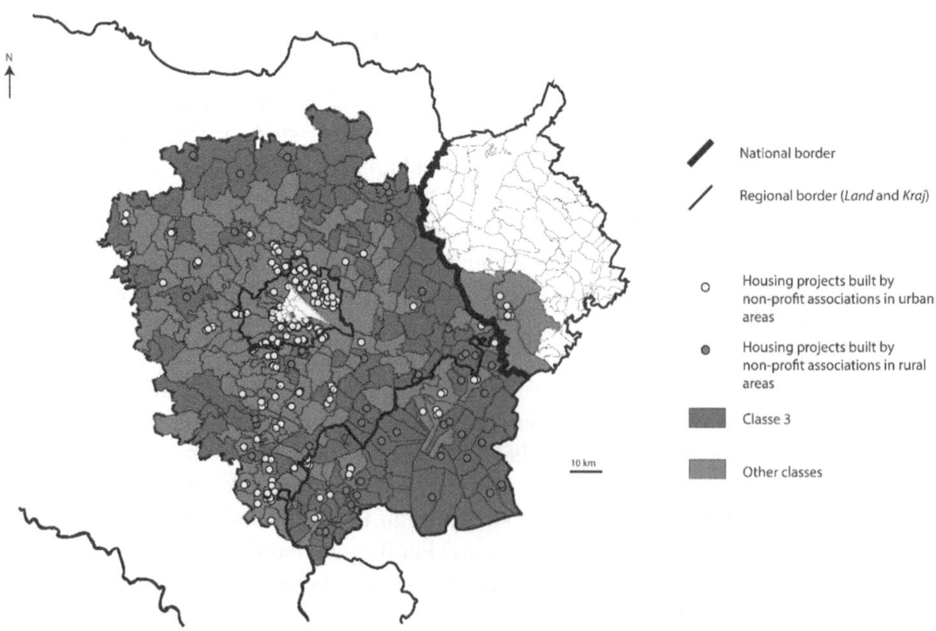

Figure 9. Non-profit housing in rural areas.

'niche' projects with a specialisation on a specific need, especially the development of *betreutes Wohnen*, specific housing types for elderly people. Furthermore, regarding the type of dwellings, 41 of the 59 housing projects are blocks of flats, which could seem surprising in rural areas. This can be explained by the fact that this densification reduces land mobilisation and by the fact that these municipalities are residential rural areas.

7. Conclusion

Thus, the specific contributions of this article have been to prove that non-profit housing could partially contribute to metropolitan cohesion beyond the sole area of the Austrian capital city. Non-profit housing is not only an urban housing type but its localisation in suburban and rural spaces, in the south and south-eastern part of the region, convey cohesion by insuring an affordable subsidised housing supply, especially when supported by public policies and pushed by public stakeholders at every scale. As long as the non-profit sector remains underestimated on the Slovak side, the development regarding housing will continue to diverge even if this region is facing common challenges, with the exception of this very local cross-border housing market. Characteristics inherited from the past are still present in both parts of the metropolitan cross-border region, whether in the built environment or in the housing policies regulating the third housing sector. But even if there seems to be no link between the Viennese side and the Slovak side of the metropolitan region, when observing housing markets, the impressive differences of nature enable the creation of a push/pull effect for some populations.

As for the Austrian side, even if metropolitan cohesion seems ensured through both vertical (by the adaptation of developers to socio-economic contexts) and horizontal (by alleviating the centre–periphery model) matching of non-profit housing projects with local territories, the actual causes are more complex. Metropolitan cohesion remains partial because the adaptation of this housing production to socio-spatial contexts does not depend on the strategies of non-profit developers but rather on land constraints and regional schemes of housing policy and planning. The availability of affordable land is a key condition for developing non-profit housing but municipalities differ a lot on that matter so that the repartition of non-profit housing does not follow a homogeneous and equal pattern but rather a fair, equitable one, according to local resources as land and political willingness of local authorities. Indeed, local mayors of rural areas tend to use newly built non-profit housing to prevent young households from moving in urban areas.

The case of the Vienna–Bratislava can further indicate tendencies at stake in other growing cross-border but differentiated regions. For instance, the Grand Geneva region encompasses three different sub-regions (Nyon, Geneva and the French Savoie department) with different housing policies. But residential mobilities towards the French side are motivated by high housing prices in Geneva, and this region is also facing land shortage. Building non-profit housing not only on the French side (through social or intermediate housing) but also in Geneva (since housing cooperatives exist in Switzerland) could contribute to redesign housing patterns of this tight regional cross-border housing market, combined with a cross-border land use planning.

Finally this analysis could convey recommendations towards regional and local stakeholders of the Vienna–Bratislava region. Since municipalities still have important competences for housing development and planning, in compliance with regional framework documents, a sub-regional level is missing that could better insure an equitable repartition of non-profit housing according to financial and land resources of each municipality as well as their housing needs. Creating sub-regional cross-border housing clusters gathering housing experts and local authorities, and which would have decision-making powers, could contribute to anchor the institutional cooperation of this region that is still 'a vision on the paper' (Sohn and Giffinger 2015, 1204), and address the potential local fragmentation created by this continuous spill-over from Slovakia towards Austria, as well as fostering a sustainable suburban development around Vienna by increasing intercommunal dialogue.

Acknowledgements

The author wishes to thank the reviewers of this article for their constructive comments and is very grateful to Anne-Kathrin Marquardt for assistance on the English-language checks.

Disclosure statement

No potential conflict of interest was reported by the author.

Notes

1. No data per destination country available: 'Based on the statistics, nor Austrian, nor Hungarian, nor Slovak gives the data on the commuting from the suburban areas of Bratislava located in neighboring countries'(ESPON 2012).
2. Other municipalities of the Bratislava Region were not taken into account in this sample since local mayors are responsible for the construction of non-profit housing, but non-profit housing associations are not.
3. Inner districts of Vienna were not considered in the sample since there is no construction of affordable housing by non-profit developers there, due to very high land prices.
4. In order to obtain a subsidy, non-profit developers have to ensure that the price of the land is lower than 250 EUR per sq. m, which becomes very rare. Therefore, the *Land* of Vienna created a specific incentive called '*Wohnbauinitiative*' which guarantees a preferential loan for financing affordable housing projects for both non-profit and private developers.
5. When renting (normal rent or rent with purchasing option), each person has to pay an 'entry' contribution (about 500 EUR/sq. m, depending on the project), and pays then a more affordable monthly rent. To conduct our analysis, we took into consideration only the monthly rent.

References

Altzinger, W., G. Maier, and J. Fidrmuc. 1998. "Cross-Border Development in the Vienna-Bratislava Region: A Review." In *Sustainable Development for Central and Eastern Europe. Spatial Development in the European Context*, edited by Ulrich Graute, 89–114. Berlin: Springer.

Balchin, P., and L. Sykora. 1996. *Regional Policy and Planning in Europe*. Londres: Routledge.

Baudelle, G. 2006. "La Géographie Sociale et La Cohésion Territoriale: Une Question D'échelle." In *Penser et Faire La Géographie Sociale*, edited by V. Veschambre89–97. Rennes: Presses Universitaires de Rennes.

Bernard, P. 1999. "La Cohésion Sociale: Critique Dialectique D'un Quasi-Concept." *Lien Social et Politiques* 41: 23–33.

Blessing, A. 2012. "Magical or Monstrous? Hybridity in Social Housing Governance." *Housing Studies* 27 (2): 189–207. doi:10.1080/02673037.2012.649469.

Bourne, L. S. 1981. *The Geography of Housing*. Londres: Winston & Sons.

Callen, D. 2011. *La "Fabrique Périurbaine": Système D'acteurs et Production Des Ensembles Pavillonnaires Dans La Grande Couronne Francilienne* (PhD dissertation). Paris I Panthéon Sorbonne.

Coudroy de Lille, L. 2008. "Metropolization and Housing in the Central and Eastern European Countries." In *Regional Disparities in Central Europe*, edited by P. Gajdos, 180–195. Bratislava: UNESCO, NK MOST.
Czischke, D., V. Gruis, and D. Mullins. 2012. "Conceptualising Social Enterprise in Housing Organisations." *Housing Studies* 27 (4): 418–437. doi:10.1080/02673037.2012.677017.
Decoville, A., F. Durand, C. Sohn, and O. Walther. 2013. "Comparing Cross-Border Metropolitan Integration in Europe: Towards a Functional Typology." *Journal of Borderlands Studies* 28 (2): 221–237. doi:10.1080/08865655.2013.854654.
Derycke, P.-H. 1979. *Economie et planification urbaines*. Paris: PUF.
Desjardins, X. 2008. "Le Logement Social Au Temps Du Néolibéralisme." *Métropoles*, no. 2 (4): 14.
Driant, J.-C. 1995. "Les Marchés Locaux Du Logement." Savoir et Comprendre Pour Agir. Paris: Presses de l'Ecole Nationale des Ponts et Chaussées.
ESPON. 2010. "Metroborder." Cross-Border Polycentric Metropolitan Regions.
ESPON. 2012. *Polyce Metropolisation and Polycentric Development in Central Europe*.
Fassmann, H., P. Görgl, and M. Helbich. 2008. *Atlas Des Wachsenden Stadtregion*. Wien: PGO. Accessed 2 April 2016. http://www.pgo. wien.at/download/PGO_Atlas%20der%20wachsenden%20Stadtregion.pdf
Filippi, B. 2011. "Repenser Le Logement Social et La Régulation Des Marchés Locaux de L'habitat." Métropolitiques. Accessed 2 April 2016. http://www.metropolitiques.eu/Repenser-le-logement-social-et-la.html
Franz, Y. 2013. "Between Urban Decay and Rejuvenation." Deliberate Employment of Genrification in Neighbourhood Development: Case Studies from New York City, Berlin and Vienna (PhD dissertation). Universität Wien.
Giffinger, R., and A. Hamedinger. 2013. "Borders in Metropolitan Development: The Case of Vienna." *Journal of Borderlands Studies* 28: 205–219. doi:10.1080/08865655.2013.854655.
Giffinger, R., and J. Suitner. 2014. "Polycentric Metropolitan Development: From Structural Assessment to Processual Dimensions." *European Planning Studies 23* (6): 1169-1186.
Grasland, C., and G. Hamez. 2005. "Vers La Construction D'un Indicateur de Cohésion Territoriale Européen?" *L'espace Géographique* 2 (34): 94.
Halbert, L. 2009. *L'avantage Métropolitain*. Paris: PUF.
Halbert, L. 2013. "Les Acteurs Des Marchés Financiers Font-Ils La Ville?" Vers Un Agenda de Recherche. EspacesTemps/net. Accessed 2 April 2016. http://www.espacestemps.net/articles/les-acteurs-des-marches-financiers-font-ils-la-ville-vers-un-agenda-de-recherche/
Harloe, M. 1995. *The People's Home? Social Rented Housing in Europe and America*. Cambridge: Blackwell.
Hegedüs, J., M. Lux, P. Sunega, and N. Teller. 2014. "Social Housing in Post-Socialist Countries." In *Social Housing in Europe*, edited by C. Whitehead, 239–253. Oxford: Wiley.
Hitz, H., and H. Wohlschlägl, eds. 2009. "Das östliche Österreich Und Benachbarte Regionen." *Ein Geographischer Exkursionsführer*. Wien: Böhlau.
Kadi, J. 2015. "Recommodifying Housing in Formerly "Red" Vienna?" *Housing, Theory and Society* 32 (3): 247–265. doi:10.1080/14036096.2015.1024885.
Kemeny, J. 2006. "Corporatism and Housing Regimes." *Housing, Theory and Society* 23 (1): 1–18. doi:10.1080/14036090500375423.
Kemeny, J., J. Kersloot, and P. Thalmann. 2005. "Non-profit Housing Influencing, Leading and Dominating the Unitary Rental Market: Three Case Studies." *Housing Studies* 20 (6): 855–872. doi:10.1080/02673030500290985.
Lacour, C., and S. Puissant. 1999. *La Métropolisation. Croissance, Diversité, Fractures*. Paris: Anthropos.
Lang, R., and A. Novy. 2011. "Housing Cooperatives and Social Capital: The Case of Vienna." *SRE - Discussion Papers WU Vienna University*, no. 2: 46.
Lang, R., and D. Roessl. 2013. "The Governance of Co-Operative Housing: Current Challenges and Future Perspectives." *International Journal of Cooperative Management* 6 (2): 8–12.
Lawson, J. 2010. "Path Dependency and Emergent Relations: Explaining the Different Role of Limtied Profit Housing in the Dynamic Urban Regimes of Vienna and Zürich." *Housing, Theory and Society* 27 (3): 204–220.
Le Goix, R. 2006. "Les « Gated Communities » Aux Etats-Unis et En France: Une Innovation Dans Le Développement Périurbain?" *Hérodote* 122 (122): 107–136. doi:10.3917/her.122.0107.

Le Goix, R., and M. Guérois. 2009. "La Dynamique Spatio-Temporelle Des Prix Immobiliers à Différentes échelles: Le Cas Des Appartements Anciens à Paris (1990-2003)." *Cybergéo*, no. 470.

Le Hervet, M. 2013. *Les Politiques de L'habitat à L'épreuve de La Fragmentation Métropolitaine: Le Cas de l'Île de France* (Phd dissertation). Université Paris Est.

Lefebvre, H. 1974. *La Production de L'espace*. Paris: Anthropos.

Lévy Vroelant, C. 2011. "Le Welfare vu Du Logement: Logement Social et Etat-Providence En Question." In *Loger l'Europe. Le Logement Social Dans Tous Ses états*, edited by N. Houard, 207–231. Paris: La documentation Française.

Lévy Vroelant, C., and C. Reinprecht. 2014. "Housing the Poor in Paris and Vienna: The Changing Understanding of the "Social"." In *Social Housing in Europe*, edited by K. Scanlon, 297–313. Oxford: Wiley.

Lichtenberger, E. 1995. "Der Immobilienmarkt Im Politischen Systemvergleich." In *Märkte in Bewegung. Metropolen Und Regionen in Ostmitteleuropa*, edited by H. Fassmann, 47–57. Böhlau.

Lux, M. 2003. *Housing Policy: An End or a New Beginning?* Budapest: Local Government and Public Service Reform Initiative/Open Society Institute.

Madoré, F. 2004. *Ségrégation Sociale et Habitat*. Rennes: Presses Universitaires de Rennes.

Matznetter, W. 1991. *Wohnbauträger Zwischen Staat Und Markt*. Frankfurt: Campus Forschung.

Matznetter, W. 2002a. "Social Housing Policy in a Conservative Welfare State: Austria as an Example." *Urban Studies* 39 (2): 265–282. doi:10.1080/00420980120102966.

Matznetter, W. 2002b. "Wohnungmarkt Und Wohnungspolitik in Österreich - Ein Überblick. Geographische Wohnungsmarktforschung." Die Wohnungsmärkte Deutschlands, Österreichs Und Der Schweiz Im Überblick Und Aktuelle Forschungsberichte 32, 55–70. Zürich: Wirtschaftsgeographie Und Raumplanung.

Matznetter, W., and A. Mundt. 2012. "Housing and Welfare Regimes." In *The SAGE Handbook of Housing Studies*, edited by D. Clapham, 274–294. London: SAGE.

Matznetter, W., D. Nisch, and A. Wisbauer. 2004. "Stadtregionen Im Systemvergleich. Räumliche Bevölkerungsentwicklung in Und Um Wien Und Bratislava 1950/1951 Bis 2001." *Geographischer Jahresbericht Aus Österreich. Forschungsberichte – Geographie Wien LX.* Wien: Universität Wien.

Meijers, E., M. Hoogerbrugge, and K. Hollander. 2014. "Twin Cities in the Process of Metropolisation." *Urban Research & Practice* 7 (1): 35–55. doi:10.1080/17535069.2013.827906.

Miciukiewicz, C., F. Moulaert, A. Novy, S. Musterd, and J. Hillier. 2012. "Introduction: Problematising Urban Social Cohesion: A Transdisciplinary Endeavour." *Urban Studies* 49 (9): 1855–1872. doi:10.1177/0042098012444877.

Ministerstvo Vystavba a rozvoj regiony. 2015. *Koncepcia Statnej Bytovej Politiky Do Roku 2020.* Bratislava.

Montabone, B. 2011. *La Cohésion Territoriale En Périphérie de l'Union Européenne: Les Enjeux Du Développment Régional En Turquie*, 2 (PhD dissertation). Université Rennes.

Novy, A., V. Redak, and J. Jäger. 2001. "The End of Red Vienna. Recent Ruptures and Continuities in Urban Governance." *European Urban and Regional Studies* 8 (2): 131–144. doi:10.1177/096977640100800204.

Pumain, D., and T. Saint-Julien. 2001. *Les Interactions Spatiales*. Paris: Armand Colin.

Reinprecht, C. 2014. "Social Housing in Austria." In *Social Housing in Europe*, edited by K. Scanlon, 61–74. Oxford: Wiley.

Renard, V. 2008. "La Ville Saisie Par La Finance." *Le Débat* 148 (148): 106–117. doi:10.3917/deba.148.0106.

Rougé, L. 2005. "Accession à La Propriété et Modes de Vie En Maison Individuelle Des Familles Modestes Installées En Périurbain Lointain Toulousain. Les « Captifs » Du Périurbain?" (PhD dissertation). Université Toulouse II Le Mirail.

Scanlon, K. J., and C. Whitehead, eds. 2008. *Social Housing in Europe II. A Review of Policies and Outcomes*. London: LSE Press.

Sencébé, Y. 2007. "Le Logement Social Dans Un Pays Rural Sous Influence Urbaine: Une Forme Hybride Du Périurbain." *Norois* 205 (4): 11–22. doi:10.4000/norois.1226.

Smith, A., and A. Rochovska. 2007. "Domesticating Neo-Liberalism: Everyday Lives and the Geographies of Post-Socialist Transformations." *Geoforum* 38 (6): 1163–1178. doi:10.1016/j.geoforum.2007.03.003.

Sohn, C., and R. Giffinger. 2015. "A Policy Network Approach to Cross-Border Metropolitan Governance: The Cases of Vienna and Bratislava." *European Planning Studies* 23 (6): 1187–1208. doi:10.1080/09654313.2014.994089.

Statisticky urad Slovenskej Republiky. Accessed 2 April 2016. http://www.statistics.sk/

Statistik Austria. Accessed 2 April 2016. http://www.statistik-austria.at/

Sveda, M. 2011. "Bytova Vystavba a Zazemi Bratislavy (Housing construction and suburbanization in Bratislava)." *Surburbanizace* 18.

Tatzberger, G. 2006. *A Global Economic Integration Zone in Central Europe? Vienna–Bratislava-Györ as a Laboratory for EU Territorial Cohesion Policy* (PhD dissertation). TU Delft.

Tewdwr-Jones, M. 2011. "Cohesion and Competitiveness: The Evolving Context for European Territorial Development." In *Territorial Development, Cohesion and Spatial Planning. Knowledge and Policy Development in an Enlarged EU*, edited by N. Adams, 69–83. Londres: Routledge.

Trouillard, E. 2014. *La Production de Logements Neufs Par La Promotion Privée En Île de France (1980-2012): Marchés Immobiliers et Stratégies de Localisation* (PhD dissertation). Université Paris VII.

Verlic, M. 2013. "Housing Neo-Liberalization and Displacement? Emerging Rent Gaps in Vienna's Highly Regulated Housing Market." Paper presented at Resourceful Cities, Berlin, August 29-31. http://www.rc21.org/conferences/berlin2013/RC21-Berlin-Papers-4/08-1-RT-Verlic_HousingNeoliberalizationVienna.pdf

Wankiewicz, H. 2015. "The Potential of Cohousing for Rural Austria." *Urban Research & Practice* 8 (1): 46–63. doi:10.1080/17535069.2015.1011426.

Whitehead, C. 2012. "The Neo-Liberal Legacy to Housing Research." In *The SAGE Handbook of Housing Studies*, edited by D. Clapham, 113–130. London: SAGE.

Zapletalova, J., M. Antalikova, and E. Smatanova. 2003. "Homeownership Model. The Role of Self-Government in Housing Development in Slovakia." In *Housing Policy: An End or a New Beginning?* edited by M. Lux, 295–351. Budapest: Open Society Institute.

Moving towards age-inclusive public housing in Singapore

Belinda Yuen

Like many countries around the world, Singapore is ageing rapidly. Its age-65-and-older population is expected to double to 1 in 4 persons by 2030, propelling Singapore towards a super-aged society. Where will they live? Notwithstanding the wider debate about high-rise living suitability, Singapore has started to retool its high-rise public housing where 80% of its resident population reside, for an ageing society. This paper discusses Singapore's public housing development to meet the changing needs of population ageing. It explicates the process of physical transformation and key strategies towards ageing in place as well as older residents' satisfaction with public housing.

1. Introduction

Singapore's public housing experience, from slums and squatter settlements to modern apartment living with cradle-to-grave amenities within one generation, is a subject of wide scholarly interest. Public housing is the common living space in Singapore. More than 80% of Singapore's 3.9 million resident population live and grow old in public housing, predominantly in a high-rise, high-density built environment. The tallest public housing is 50-storey. Understandably, much has been written about Singapore's public housing policy, housing access and affordability (see, e.g. Tan 1998; Yuen, Teo, and Ooi 1999; Yuen 2007; Mah 2011; Phang and Helble 2016). Yet, there has been relatively little study of the remake of Singapore's public housing spaces for its ageing population (Yuen and Soh 2017). This paper takes as its departure point the fast ageing population in Singapore and interrogates the emerging public housing options and lived experiences of its older population.

Singapore residents are living longer – 82.4 years in 2013, the 5th highest life expectancy in the world (Ministry of Health, Singapore 2016a). Importantly, older Singaporeans are enjoying more years in good health than global average. Singapore's healthy life expectancy at birth is 70.8 years for men (10.16 years above global average) and 73.4 years for women (9.22 years above global average). The age-65-and-older population is projected to double to 1 in 4 (900,000) residents by 2030. By 2030, 13% (117,000) of older Singaporeans may be semi-/non-ambulant, more than double current numbers.

Instead of putting the concerns of population ageing on the back burner, Singapore has, since the 1980s, identified the scope of issues that require attention and placed them on the agenda for government (Yuen and Soh 2017). An Inter-Ministerial Committee on Ageing Population has been formed to coordinate relevant policies. In particular, the built environment to improve elder-friendly housing, community and environment has come to attention since the late 1990s (Inter-Ministerial Committee on the Ageing Population 1999). In the area of housing, the Committee has recommended ageing in place, a popular preference, as the key principle of an age-inclusive built environment.

A range of strategies has been recommended to support the production of age-friendly homes and places. These covered the review of building codes and standards on elder-friendly homes, awareness-raising and education of the development industry towards developing a safe home environment for older people, and retrofitting and remaking public housing into 'the best place for Singaporeans to grow old in and a model for successful ageing' (*Ageless Online* 2015). The vision to make Singapore an elder-friendly place – the best home for all ages is further enshrined in the Committee on Ageing Issues (2006) and Action Plan for Successful Ageing (Ministry of Health 2016b). The intent is to enable older people to live independently within their homes for as long as possible.

Population ageing is not unique to Singapore. According to the 2015 United Nations population statistics, the world is urbanising rapidly and ageing rapidly at the same time. The number and proportion of older people in the population is increasing in nearly all countries due to trends in increased longevity, falls in fertility and maturing of the baby boomer generation. The global share of age-60-and-older population has risen from 9.2% in 1990 to 12.3% (901 million people) in 2015 and is projected to increase by 56% to 21.1% (2.1 billion people) by 2050 (United Nations 2015).

Drawing on historical and empirical data, this paper seeks to discuss the key policies and strategies in the physical transformation of Singapore's public housing, in particular, its recent remaking of the built environment to support aging in place. More than urban planners and architects' production of housing form, life in public housing will be explored through residents' satisfaction with high-rise living. Residential satisfaction is widely used as an indicator of the extent to which the housing environment meet a person's needs, aspirations and quality of life (Galster and Hesser 1981; Kahana et al. 2003; Braubach 2007).

The remainder of this paper is organised as follows. The next section, Section 2, introduces the theoretical and conceptual considerations about age-inclusive housing while Section 3 examines how Singapore is future-proofing the ubiquitous public housing to promote an age-friendly built environment, explicating the approach and key strategies. Section 4 moves the analytical lens to consider the older residents' response and environmental preferences for public housing. Section 5 concludes the discussion.

2. Age-inclusive housing

The role of the built environment, in particular, the home and neighbourhood as the major physical-spatial location to support late life, has been variously discussed (see, e.g. Sixsmith and Sixsmith 1991; Lawton 1999; Oswald and Wahl 2005; World Health Organisation 2007; AARP Livable Communities 2016). The World Health Organisation (2007) in promoting the idea and principles of active ageing where older people are enabled to continue participating in all aspects of life has acknowledged the importance of physical infrastructure – housing, outdoor spaces and buildings, transportation as well as the inter-related social and cultural infrastructures required to start age-friendly environments.

The review of the existing literature and studies on environmental psychology and gerontology highlighted two fundamental theories that are helpful to understanding the interconnected ways that people have with their built environments. The first is Bronfenbrenner's theory of human ecology, which suggests that there is a mutual relationship and reciprocity between individuals and their environments, interacting at multiple levels, from micro- to macro-systems in their everyday lives (Bronfenbrenner 1994; Turchin 2001; Rosa and Tudge 2013). As Barker (2003, 136) observed, the ecological perspective 'emphasizes understanding people and their environment and the nature of their transactions'.

Also of relevance is the 'person-environment fit' approach, which highlights that the individual's interaction and behaviour in the built environment is continually modified and changed – control what can be modified and adapt to conditions that cannot be changed (Lawton and Nahemow 1973; Lawton 1990; Germain and Gitterman 1995). As Germain and Gitterman (1995, 816) reminded, this approach examines the degree to which environmental characteristics would match 'an individual's or a collective group's needs, rights, goals and capacities'.

Even though the person-environment fit has been discussed in the scientific literature for decades, the field has yet to reach consensus on how to conceptualise and operationalise the concept, especially of older adults' adaptation to person-environment fit challenges (Baltes and Baltes 1990; Wahl, Iwarsson, and Oswald 2012; Lien, Steggell, and Iwarsson 2015). Crucially, as Clarke and Nieuwenhuijsen (2009) reviewed, the majority of studies on individuals and the environments in which they live do not focus on older adult populations even though they are especially vulnerable to barriers in their local environments. In this regard, Goldsmith (1997) has highlighted architectural disability – how the physical design of buildings and places can invoke disablement or barriers for people – as an environmental discrimination, eroding older people's self-esteem of maintaining a full and independent life in their own homes.

Goldsmith went on to argue that the needs of everyone should be variously considered and offered two concepts: 'treat-as-normal' (no one is excluded) and 'treat-as-different' (those with special needs) as starting points in any built environment design (Goldsmith 1997, 19). This perspective is perhaps best embodied in universal design and design for all, which are increasingly being adopted in many countries, e.g. Europe as they seek a more user-friendly society (Steinfeld and Maisel 2012; European Commission n.d.). Universal design posits that there are generic needs and special needs, and that a design that satisfies generic needs will also be appropriate for most people.

Since 2006, universal design has been assiduously promoted in Singapore. All housing units built after 2007 must provide for easy retrofitting to meet the needs of occupants who may need wheelchair accessibility. The public housing authority has adopted universal design in all new housing design and begun to retrofit the existing public housing. The retrofitting works happen at several scales, from the micro level of the flat to the block, precinct and wider neighbourhood and town. Examples include the installation of ramps and handrails within flats; lift improvement to high-rise blocks that do not have lift access at every floor; accessible footpaths in precincts. A key aspect of the housing modification is to ensure barrier-free accessibility within the home and neighbourhood. Even so, the National Survey of Senior Citizens in Singapore 2011 concluded, 'Within public housing, a large proportion of flats with elderly-friendly features tended to be the one- and two-room flats compared to the other flat types. Overall, 26 per cent of all dwelling types did contain elderly-friendly fixtures. There remains room for improvement to enable the elderly population to live independently within the community'. (Institute of Policy Studies 2013, iii)

While inspired by the British new town planning, Singapore has developed its own model of public housing new towns since the 1960s. When compared to the majority of Western new town development, Singapore's public housing town is relatively dense with a gross density at 92-114 dwelling units per hectare. At the town level, each new town with an anticipated population of 200,000 to 300,000 is a planned spatial organisation of mixed use – housing, employment, education and recreational facilities (Table 1).

At the individual dwelling level, the guiding principle is to provide a range of flat types to meet different family needs and affordability – people of different income, age and household size. A typical 4-room flat with a net floor area of about 90 square metres would have 3 bedrooms, 1 living/dining room and a kitchen, that is, about 27 square metres per person (mean household size is 3.3 persons). The dwelling units are each provided with modern sanitation, water, energy and refuse collection, among others.

3. Responding to the challenge and opportunity

In Singapore, about 70% of older people are community dwelling. To meet the changing needs of a rapidly ageing population, the city has in recent decades begun to future-proof its ubiquitous public housing stock. Evidence review suggests that priorities have included the provision of special housing design, home care and community service, and safety and convenience equipment to improve the match between environmental characteristics and the individual's functional capacity as one ages. The suitability of housing stock is important as unsuitable housing can constrain and have a damaging effect on individual wellbeing (World Health Organisation 2007).

Table 1. Singapore public housing town land use.

	Prototype new town Toa Payoh (1960s) 60,000 dwelling units		Prototype new town Punggol (2000s) 96,000 dwelling units	
Land use	Land area (hectare)	%	Land area (hectare)	%
Residential[1]	347	53.4	432	51.2
Commercial[2] (town centre and neighbourhood centre)	30	4.6	13	1.5
Industry[3]	44	6.8	-	-
Schools and institutions	77	11.8	83	9.8
Open space	26	4.0	107	12.7
Sports complex	7	1.1	20	2.4
Major roads	89	13.7	134	15.9
Utilities and others	30	4.6	55	6.5
Total	650	100.0	844	100.0
Gross town density	92 dwelling units/ hectare		114 dwelling units/ hectare	

Note: [1]Includes private housing within the town boundary; [2] Includes civic, cultural, recreational uses and incidental developments in the town and neighbourhood centres; [3] Non-polluting industries only. Source: Housing and Development Board 2000 [2011].

As early as 1987, the public housing authority, namely, the Housing and Development Board has built specialised accommodation for older residents. Taking the form of multi-generation-granny flat, this housing comprises a 4- or 5-room flat with an adjoining granny flat (a studio apartment of about 40 square metres) that has its own kitchen and entrance. Around 367 units of these granny flats were built in several towns around Singapore (e.g. Bishan, Tampines and Yishun). But, demand was somewhat lacking and their construction was soon ceased.

In more recent time (since 2009), the idea of granny flat has re-emerged as dual key condominium in private housing. This housing typology received wide interest, especially among dual-income young couples who are looking to their parents for child care support or collecting rental income from letting the adjoining sub-unit (Tan 2014). In public housing, elderly studio apartments (35–45 square metres) have been constructed since 1997 as a customised housing option for older residents. They are outfitted in a ready-to-move-in condition with elder-friendly fixtures like lever taps, non-slip tiles, support hand bars, emergency pull cords and heat detectors that activate alarms. Their applicants, however, must be Singaporean, at least of age 55 at time of flat application and subject to the household income eligibility condition. Spouse must be included in the application and where the older person is unmarried, divorced or widowed, he/she may apply for this apartment on his/her own.

The latest edition of the elderly studio apartment (2014) provides not just dwelling but seeks to integrate housing with a range of social and healthcare facilities as a one-stop development to support active ageing. The first project is Kampung Admiralty, a 9000 square metres site located atop the Admiralty mass rapid transit station. Partially opened to the public in September 2017, it is Singapore's first multi-agency project involving the public housing authority (project initiator and developer) and various land development (environment, transport and parks), social, family and health agencies as well as local hospital and the private sector. Rather than working in silos, the project testifies to the cross-agency collaboration needed to ensure a coherent response to the housing, health and social needs of older adults.

The development, designed by a local private architectural firm, features elderly housing (two 11-storey residential blocks of 104 studio apartments) with healthcare, eldercare, childcare and commercial/social communal facilities (two 8-storey commercial/medical centre/community institution use building with two basement car parks). Three layers of activities are envisaged – a ground space of retail shops and community plaza; a mid-tier of hawker centre[1] and medical centre; and upper levels of elderly studio apartments, roof gardens (including space for community gardening), function hall (for social and recreational activities), eldercare facilities (e.g. day care services) and childcare centre.

This development represents a paradigm shift, addressing not just housing but also developing medical and wellbeing environments to maintain health and wellbeing of individuals as they age. It reflects an evolving wider national effort to develop a network of community and eldercare facilities in public housing towns to expand at-home and community-based health-social care and provide joined-up primary and person-centric care facilities so people can age in place over their life course and maintain independent lives (Ministry of Health, Singapore 2016c). Older residents can look forward to 10 active ageing hubs (one-stop day care/rehabilitation centres for older adults) in future public housing developments by 2020.

The needs of older people living in the existing public housing are not overlooked. The Housing and Development Board has introduced the Enhancement for Active Seniors

Programme (EASE) under its Home Improvement Programme to maximise the possibility of older residents remaining in their homes as their needs change. Implemented since July 2012, this programme offers elder-friendly modifications like slip-resistant treatment to the existing floor tiles in toilets, grab bars within flats and ramps to make the flat wheelchair accessible.

Residents have the flexibility to choose and customise from this range of elder-friendly improvements to address their needs. To ensure affordability, the government provides up to 95% subsidy, depending on flat type (Table 2). For rental flats, the EASE improvement items are fully funded by the government. A toll-free hotline, information brochures and video are available to help residents understand the programme and its procedures.

The policy is to actively engage residents in public housing management. Listening and engaging the residents is central to Singapore's strategy of delivering public housing that works for them; it provides a better understanding of residents' experiences and views about their towns. Residents are asked to decide on estate upgrading (e.g. lift upgrading); a 75% vote in favour is needed for the upgrading to proceed. The approach is not provider-focused but rather user-centric and increasingly towards the co-creation of public housing with residents and other agencies.

Housing design and facilities aside, another important strategy is to help older residents who may be asset/equity-rich but cash-poor, to right-size to another, usually smaller dwelling unit near their existing flat. Several support schemes, e.g. subletting of rooms, lease buyback, housing bonus, shorter lease terms, are implemented to help older residents monetise their housing equity and fund retirement. About 11% of age-55–64 public housing residents and 11.8% of age-65-and-older residents have reported taking up at least one monetisation option after turning 50 years old in 2013, the most popular being subletting of rooms and right-sizing to a smaller flat (HDB 2014). It has been reported that those who moved into smaller flats (elderly studio apartments) after selling their larger flats could realise net sale proceeds of about S$200,000 each, after paying fully for the new studio unit and any outstanding housing loans (TODAY Online 2014). Even so, many older people express a reluctance to move in their interview with *The Straits Times* (major local English-language daily newspaper),

Table 2. Public housing EASE improvement cost.

Flat type	1-, 2-, 3-room	4-room	5-room	Executive
Estimated cost for having all three EASE improvement work per flat S$		2500		
Government pays S$	2375 (95%)	2312.50 (92.5%)	2250 (90%)	2187.50 (87.5%)
Singapore citizen household pays* S$	125 (5%)	187.50 (7.5%)	250 (10%)	312.50 (12.5%)

Note: *subject to prevailing goods and services tax. Source: HDB Enhancement for Active Seniors, Housing and Development Board (HDB) website http://www.hdb.gov.sg/cs/infoweb/residential/living-in-an-hdb-flat/for-our-seniors/ease. Accessed 12 December 2017.

> ...the $20,000 bonus being offered as incentive for them to exchange their current flats for smaller ones is not attractive enough for them to consider doing so...The respondents who were not keen to downgrade gave reasons such as reluctance to leave a familiar neighbourhood, desire to be close to their children, inconvenience of relocating and not being in need of the money at the moment (AsiaOne 2012)

4. Older residents' satisfaction

International evidence suggests that residential satisfaction is an important determinant of older residents' wellbeing and successful ageing (Kahana et al. 2003; Reynolds and Beamish 2003; Phillips et al. 2004; Hui et al. 2014). As Grzeskowiak, Sirgy, and Widgery (2003) observed, housing and its neighbourhood are the residents' most proximal and psychological representation of their community. A review of the HDB sample household survey reports reveals that residential satisfaction with public housing has remained consistently high (over 90%) through the decades. These are large-scale national surveys conducted by the Housing and Development Board (HDB) in-house social research once every five years since 1968 to understand how public housing residents adapt to and assess their physical living environment. The latest survey in 2013 covered 7800 households living in all 23 public housing towns and included the age-65-and older residents' satisfaction (Housing and Development Board 2014).

Statistics from the early period of public housing indicate an improvement in living space. Residents appear to enjoy more floor area per person after moving to public housing from overcrowded low-rise shophouse and squatter settlements. The average number of persons per room has declined from 4.8 in 1957 to 2.5 by 1970 while living space per person doubled from under 3 square metres before 1960 to 6 square metres per person after 1960 and further to an average of 20–25 square metres per person by 1990 (Yeh and Lee 1968; Urban Redevelopment Authority 1991).

Yet, a review of the extant literature on high-rise public housing shows that this modern dwelling form is often criticised for its negative impacts on community in the new estates like higher incidence of depression, phobias, isolation, crime and vandalism (see, e.g. Cappon 1977; Church and Gale 2000; Green, Gilberson, and Grimsley 2002; Gifford 2007; Loomans 2014). Cappon (1977) argues that high-rises tend to encourage the older person to stay at home and watch TV because of the extra effort it takes to go outside, suggesting negative impact on health and even shorten lives. More recently, Drennan et al. (2016) reported lower survival rate of cardiac arrest for patients, especially older age, living on higher floors in high-rise buildings in Toronto, Canada.

Notwithstanding, other studies have reported neutral or even positive results. In particular, high-rise living is valued for its spectacular views, sensation of height and air quality (Haber 1977; Benson et al. 1998), privacy and quietness (Conway and Adams 1977), efficient land use and potential for sustainable energy options (Park, Girardet, and Cox 2002; Weiβ 2004), wellbeing, sense of community and social capital (Allain 2013; Hagan 2013; Panczak et al. 2013; Sowden and White 2014). Others have contended that many of the 'failures' of high-rise are mistakes 'more to do with bad management, low quality construction, lack of maintenance and lack of choice'. (BBC News 2003)

As Church and Gale (2000) asserted, high-rise living works when you get people who want to live there and 'it is...wrong to identify tower blocks as "vertical slums" and insist that they should all be flattened. Many are clearly acceptable places to live for their residents'. This seems to point to the need for a greater understanding of the person-environment fit. Newman (1975), among others, has suggested that older people are well suited to high-rise living; they no longer do/are interested in mowing huge garden lawns or clean large interiors and may feel safer within an apartment building than living alone in a single-family dwelling. That is, apartment living may be easier to manage than landed houses, generally cost less to rent/buy and operate, readily lend itself to social living and has non-senior demographics as well.

In Singapore, the majority of older residents (age 65 and older) appear to have adjusted to and optimised the person-environment fit in their high-rise public housing environments. If the latest HDB sample household survey 2013 is any indication, the majority of them expressed no intention to move within the next 5 years; 80% are keen to age in the same flat (Housing and Development Board 2014). Over 95% of older residents reported a sense of belonging to their public housing towns and satisfaction with their flat and neighbourhood.

As a whole, older residents are proportionately more satisfied than younger residents. The key reasons include a combination of place (the flat is spacious, comfortable, in good condition, convenient location, there is good provision of facilities and care about maintenance of their block, lift is reliable), economic value (the flat is value for money) and people (neighbours are friendly, being able to get help from neighbours when in need). The findings show strong familial support between parents and their younger married children – 90.3% visiting one another at least once a month, week or daily in 2013 (Housing and Development Board 2014). Another indication of social connectivity is that three-quarters of them (74.9%) would meet and interact with neighbours within the block along common corridors, lift lobby/within lift and void deck or at markets and parks in the neighbourhood. These findings on sense of satisfaction among older residents lend support to the wider literature on the contribution of 3 key aspects: functional aspects (services and facilities), space aspects (architecture and urbanism) and human aspects (social connectivity and relationships) in residential satisfaction (Canter 1997).

Examining residents' space perceptions further reveals that the three most-liked features about life in public housing are the conveniences afforded – location (close to estate facilities and transportation), transportation network (convenient to travel to most places) and provision of estate facilities (sufficient in general) (Housing and Development Board 2014). Many (9 in 10) older respondents have found the lifts reliable and are satisfied with the provision of elder-friendly facilities built to facilitate ageing in place such as support handbars in lifts/along corridors, fitness station for elderly, lift landing on every level, senior citizens' corner/centre. These findings further underscore the possible importance of person-environment fit among residents.

Most (7 in 10 respondents) have expressed an awareness of eldercare-social support services like senior activity centres and day care/rehabilitation centres even though the majority have not used these services (Housing and Development Board 2014). It should, however, be noted that the majority of respondents are ambulant and do not require such services at present time. Notwithstanding, the general consensus (9 in 10 respondents) is that these services would be essential to facilitate ageing in place. Among those who have used the senior activity centres, 95% indicated satisfaction with the services and activities of those centres (National Council of Social Service 2013).

Even though they liked many aspects of public housing living, public housing is not without detractions. Two-thirds of the respondents (65%) expressed various dislikes about their public housing even as one-third (35%) opined no dislike about living in public housing (Housing and Development Board 2014). The three most-disliked areas of public housing living are related to the condition of their neighbourhood like cleanliness and maintenance (irregular cleaning schedule, prevalence of littering/disposal of bulky items by inconsiderate neighbours), noise (from nearby facilities, neighbours and traffic) and protection from weather (given Singapore's hot and humid weather throughout the year). These findings reveal some of the everyday realities associated with high-rise high-density public housing living.

While useful in providing a pulse on residents' spatial satisfaction and preferences, the Housing and Development Board household sample surveys were more inclined towards macro aspects of housing. To better understand the older residents' micro-environmental preferences, an independent survey of some 2400 age-55-and-older public housing residents was conducted in 2015 to identify their lived experiences and perceptions about their housing and neighbourhood spaces. Approved by the university institutional review board, the study design involved the use of personal interview with the help of a questionnaire (see Yuen, Chathura, and Nair 2016). Among others, respondents were asked to rate a list of 13 housing attributes (physical, home ownership and social capital variables) in terms of their level of satisfaction and importance based on their needs and aspirations. About 7 in 10 respondents expressed satisfaction with their public housing environments (Table 3).

Of the housing attributes considered, the aspects of housing location, ease of access to key services and the sense that this is my house registered the highest satisfaction ratings (over 80% satisfied/most satisfied) and the least ambivalent responses. These attributes are rated important/most important by almost all respondents (more than 9 in 10). Respondents' least satisfied space aspects are with the provision of elder-friendly features, adaptability and flexibility of their dwelling for ageing needs. Interestingly, eight in ten respondents rated the provision of elder-friendly features in my house important/most important though the comparable importance scores for housing adaptability and flexibility were slightly lower, around 69%, perhaps hinting at their somewhat lack of control over these design elements.

When asked about the one new desired facility they would like to have in their neighbourhoods to help ageing well, many singularly selected health facilities within their neighbourhood. It is, perhaps not surprising, that the older respondents appeared especially concerned about access to healthcare and safety and security as they age. About one in four respondents chose a health and wellness centre or a public park as their one desired new facility to have in their neighbourhood. Their key reason is very much associated with personal wellbeing and the need to maintain independence, and included the motivation to keep fit and healthy, they can go there by themselves at any time, and to be close to nature.

Access to healthcare was repeated when asked about their preferred cluster of 3 desired facilities within the neighbourhood to support personal wellbeing as they age. Most respondents identified a combination of health, transport and cooked food facilities as their preferred cluster of desired facilities Almost half (44.4%) of oldest-old (age 85+) respondents voted health facilities as their number one priority while the emerging old (age 55–64) placed transport facilities (44.3%) and cooked food facilities (37.9%) as their topmost choice. Between the genders, more male respondents would select health and cooked food facilities while more female respondents ranked transport facilities as their first choices. These choices seem to hint at the role and importance of healthcare, meals and mobility in the older person's life space.

These choices are perhaps understandable when viewed against individual preference to continue to dwell in place. Most (7 in 10 respondents) would like to continue living at home if they or their spouse became dependent on others and needed assistance (Table 4). Less than 10% would opt to move to a residential aged care facility while 13% would

Table 3. Older respondents' public housing satisfaction and importance.

Housing aspects	Satisfaction			Importance		
	Least/less satisfied	Neither satisfied/ dissatisfied	Satisfied/most satisfied	Least/less importance	Neither important/ unimportant	Important/ most important
Number of rooms in my house	105 (4.4%)	372 (15.5%)	1923 (80.1%)	260 (10.8%)	452 (18.8%)	1696 (70.4%)
Size of rooms in my house	131 (5.5%)	546 (22.8%)	1717 (71.7%)	251 (10.5%)	459 (19.1%)	1690 (70.4%)
Layout of the house	125 (5.2%)	605 (25.2%)	1667 (69.6%)	156 (6.5%)	435 (18.1%)	1815 (75.4%)
Provision of elder friendly features in my house	420 (17.5%)	819 (34.2%)	1157 (48.3%)	124 (5.1%)	276 (11.5%)	2008 (83.4%)
Degree of flexibility of my house for ageing needs	268 (11.1%)	895 (37.4%)	1234 (51.5%)	192 (8.0%)	533 (22.2%)	1679 (69.8%)
Degree of adaptability of my house for ageing needs	246 (10.3%)	1026 (42.8%)	1125 (46.9%)	182 (7.6%)	567 (23.6%)	1656 (68.8%)
Ease of maintenance within the home	155 (6.4%)	712 (29.8%)	1527 (63.8%)	78 (3.2%)	418 (17.4%)	1909 (79.4%)
Location of my house	101 (4.3%)	308 (13.0%)	1962 (82.7%)	39 (1.6%)	134 (5.6%)	2210 (92.8%)
Ease of access to key services	145 (6.1%)	343 (14.3%)	1907 (79.6%)	32 (1.3%)	123 (5.1%)	2250 (93.6%)
Having close ties with community	245 (10.2%)	752 (31.4%)	1395 (58.4%)	133 (5.5%)	588 (24.5%)	1680 (70.0%)
Interaction with my neighbours	157 (6.6%)	599 (25.0%)	1635 (68.4%)	109 (4.5%)	439 (18.3%)	1852 (77.2%)
Proximity to family and friends	257 (10.7%)	655 (27.3%)	1484 (62.0%)	120 (5.0%)	400 (16.6%)	1888 (78.4%)
The sense that this is my home	65 (2.7%)	240 (10.0%)	2092 (87.3%)	32 (1.3%)	139 (5.8%)	2235 (92.9%)

Table 4. Respondents' housing preferences.

Housing option	*N* (%)
Continue living in house with outside help	880 (36.6)
Have adult children at home	458 (19.1)
Hire a live-in domestic helper	349 (14.5)
Rent a part of the house	65 (2.7)
Move to a retirement village	312 (13.0)
Move to a residential aged care facility	231 (9.6)
Move to age-specific boarding houses	48 (2.0)
Others e.g. move to live with children	60 (2.5)

think of moving to a retirement community. These findings while underscoring individual preference to age in place have implications for future research, policy and practice, especially in terms of the older person's ability to access supportive neighbourhoods for a positive experience of ageing.

5. Conclusion

Like many other countries, Singapore is promoting ageing in place to optimise the housing situation of its ageing population. Singapore's action plan to achieve ageing in place comprises many constituents including retooling housing and urban infrastructure. The multiplicity of constituents attests to the large and wide range of aspects that need to be taken into account when attempting ageing in place.

In its public housing development, multiple actions have been initiated to remake housing and neighbourhoods into inclusive spaces. Two key spatial thrusts can be identified. They involve integrating housing, transportation, healthcare and social care (e.g. Kampung Admiralty project) while investing the built environment with elder-friendly features. These range from specialised housing designs for older residents (provide more housing choices) to the installation of safety and convenience equipment (enable independent living) and the provision of home care and community services (improve health and social connections). Slowly but surely, Singapore is moving towards mitigating environmental barriers and improving the person-environment fit to support ageing in place.

Increasingly, the effort is directed towards a people-centric approach that recognises the need to integrate the ageing population into the community through services and processes to support shareable places and elderly care. Singapore's development *albeit* work in progress highlights the need for greater coordination and partnership between agencies and across sectors in the provision of affordable, age-appropriate housing and community services. Resident satisfaction survey has shown that many are especially keen on having health facilities in their neighbourhoods, especially among the oldest-old. Aside from health facilities, transport and cooked food facilities are the other topmost preferred community facilities in their everyday milieu, *albeit* the Singaporean living context. These hint at the role and importance of healthcare, meals and mobility in the life space of older people and bear closer investigation in future housing development.

While most were generally satisfied with the physical features and service provision within public housing environments, the findings show that a majority of the respondents are least satisfied with the provision of elder-friendly features, adaptability and flexibility of their dwelling for ageing needs. These are potential features of the environment that could cause problems and become barriers for persons with functional limitations and thus, constitute an important area for further investigation. The physical features with the highest levels of satisfaction relate to the sense that this is my home, followed by location of my house and the number of rooms in my house. Also, appreciated are the opportunities for social connectivity. The findings share an example of how high-rise public housing, when imbued with physical, functional and social aspects can offer a satisficing home to older adults.

Crucially, Singapore's public housing retooling testifies to the importance of reviewing housing as a process (not just a product), a process that seeks to build homes and neighbourhoods that support the needs and expectations (generic and special) of residents, leaving no one behind and yet attending to the particular needs of older people. The resultant levels of satisfaction with public housing living remind the multiplicity of factors that are often considered important in such assessment. It is as much about individual dwelling characteristics and pride of home ownership as about the wider environmental factors of good neighbours, good location and convenience to key services. Although many of these dimensions may not be new, their consideration (and proper provision), however, speaks to the residents' living needs and concerns, and bears bethinking in the planning and design of high-rise public housing development, as the population is getting older.

Acknowledgements

This material is based on work supported by the Lee Li Ming Programme in Ageing Urbanism, Lee Kuan Yew Centre for Innovative Cities. I thank my colleagues, Dr Chathura Withanage and Parvathi Nair for assistance with the 2015 survey data analysis although all interpretations and conclusions are my own.

Disclosure statement

No potential conflict of interest was reported by the author.

Funding

This work was supported by the Lee Li Ming Programme in Ageing Urbanism, Lee Kuan Yew Centre for Innovative Cities, Singapore University of Technology and Design.

Note

1. This is a cooked food centre comprising many different food stalls selling relatively inexpensive food. Its establishment has totally eliminated street hawking in Singapore.

References

AARP Livable Communities. 2016. "Better Together: Age-Friendly and Dementia Friendly Communities." Accessed December 10 2017. https://www.aarp.org/livable-communities/network-age-friendly-communities/info-2016/dementia-friendly-communities.html

Ageless Online. 2015. "New National Plan to Age Successfully." September 1. Accessed 26 August 2016. http://www.agelessonline.net/6461/new-national-plan-to-age-successfully/

Allain, J. M. 2013. "The Demolition of Public Housing in American Cities." *Neoamericanist* 6 (2): 1–13.

AsiaOne. 2012. "Elderly Not Ready to Leave Flats for Silver Housing Bonus." February 20. Accessed 1 September 2016. http://news.asiaone.com/News/Latest+News/Singapore/Story/A1Story20120220-329015.html

Baltes, P. B., and M. M. Baltes. 1990. "Psychological Perspectives on Successful Aging: The Model of Selective Optimization with Compensation." In *Successful Aging: Perspectives from the Behavioral Sciences*, edited by P. B. Baltes and M. M. Baltes, 1–34. Cambridge: Cambridge University Press.

Barker, R. 2003. *The Social Work Dictionary.* Washington, DC: NASW Press.

BBC News. 2003. *High-Rise Living to Solve Housing Crisis*, February 10. London, UK.

Benson, E. D., J. L. Hansen, J. A. L. Schwartz, and G. T. Smersh. 1998. "Pricing Residential Amenities: The Value of a View." *Journal of Real Estate Finance and Economics* 16 (1): 55–74. doi:10.1023/A:1007785315925.

Braubach, M. 2007. "Residential Conditions and Their Impact on Residential Environment Satisfaction and Health: Results of the WHO Large Analysis and Review of European Housing and Health Status (LARES) Study." *International Journal of Environment and Pollution* 30 (3/4): 384–403. doi:10.1504/IJEP.2007.014817.

Bronfenbrenner, U. 1994. "Ecological Models of Human Development." T Husen & T N Postlethaite (Eds) In *International Encyclopedia of Education*. Vol 3, 1643-1647. Oxford, UK: Elsevier.

Canter, D. V. 1997. *The Psychology of Place*. London: Architectural Press.

Cappon, D. 1977. "Mental Health in the High-Rise." *Canadian Journal of Public Health* 62 (5): 426–431.

Church, C., and T. Gale. 2000. *Streets in the Sky, First Report of the National Sustainable Tower Blocks Initiative (NSTBI)*. London: NSTBI.

Clarke, P., and E. R. Nieuwenhuijsen. 2009. "Environments for Healthy Ageing: A Critical Review." *Maturitas* 64 (1): 14–19. doi:10.1016/j.maturitas.2009.07.011.

Committee on Ageing Issues. 2006. *Report on the Ageing Population, Singapore*: Ministry of Community Development, Youth and Sports.

Conway, J., and B. Adams. 1977. "The Social Effects of Living off the Ground." *Habitat International* 2 (5–6): 595–614. doi:10.1016/0197-3975(77)90032-7.

Drennan, I., R. P. Strum, A. Byers, J. E. Buick, S. Lin, S. Cheskes, S. Hu, and L. J. Morrison. 2016. "Out-of-Hospital Cardiac Arrest in High-Rise Buildings: Delays to Patient Care and Effect on Survival." *CMAJ Online*, January 18. Accessed 28 August 2016. doi:10.1503/cmaj.150544.

European Commission, n.d. *Design for All.* Accessed December 10 2017. https://www.cencenelec.eu/standards/Sectors/Accessibility/DesignForAll/Pages/default.aspx

Galster, G., and G. Hesser. 1981. "Residential Satisfaction: Conceptual and Contextual Correlates." *Environment and Behavior* 13 (6): 735–758. doi:10.1177/0013916581136006.

Germain, C. B., and A. Gitterman. 1995. "Ecological Perspective." In *The Encyclopedia of Social Work*, edited by R. L. Edwards, 816–824. Silver Spring, MD: National Association of Social Workers.

Gifford, R. 2007. "The Consequences of Living in High-Rise Buildings." *Architectural Science Review* 50 (1): 1–16. doi:10.3763/asre.2007.5002.

Goldsmith, S. 1997. *Designing for the Disabled: The New Paradigm*. London: Architectural Press.

Green, G., J. Gilberson, and M. Grimsley. 2002. "Fear of Crime and Health in Residential Tower Blocks: A Case Study in Liverpool, UK." *European Journal of Public Health* 12: 10–15. doi:10.1093/eurpub/12.1.10.

Grzeskowiak, S., M. Sirgy, and R. Widgery. 2003. "Residents' Satisfaction with Community Services: Predictors and Outcomes." *The Journal of Regional Analysis and Policy* 33 (2): 1–36.

Haber, G. M. 1977. "The Impact of Tall Buildings on Users and Neighbors." In *Human Response to Tall Buildings*, edited by D. J. Conway. Stroudsburg: Dowden, Hutchinson and Ross .

Hagan, P. 2013. "The secret to a long and healthy life?" *MailOnline*, May 21. Accessed 25 August 2016. http://www.dailymail.co.uk/health/article-2328400/The-secret-long-healthy-life-A-HIGH-rise-flat-People-live-eighth-floor-22-likely-die-early.html

Housing and Development Board (HDB). 2014. "Public Housing in Singapore: Social Wellbeing of HDB Communities." HDB Sample Household Survey 2013. Singapore: HDB.

Housing and Development Board (HDB). 2000 [2011]. *Facts on Public Housing in Singapore.* Singapore: HDB.

Hui, E. C. M., F. K. W. Wong, K. W. Chung, and K. Y. Lau. 2014. "Housing Affordability, Preferences and Expectations of Elderly with Government Intervention." *Habitat International* 43: 11–21. doi:10.1016/j.habitatint.2014.01.010.

Institute of Policy Studies. 2013. *National Survey of Senior Citizens in Singapore 2011 Report*. Singapore: Institute of Policy Studies.
Inter-Ministerial Committee on the Ageing Population. 1999. *Report on the Ageing Population*. Singapore: Ministry of Community Development.
Kahana, E., L. Lovegreen, B. Kahana, and M. Kahana. 2003. "Person, Environment and Person-Environment Fit as Influences on Residential Satisfaction of Elders." *Environment and Behavior* 35 (3): 434–453. doi:10.1177/0013916503035003007.
Lawton, M. P. 1990. "Residential Environment and Self-Directedness among Older People." *American Psychologist* 45 (5): 638–640. doi:10.1037/0003-066X.45.5.638.
Lawton, J. H. 1999. *Are there general laws in ecology?* Oikos 84 (2): 177–192.
Lawton, M. P., and L. Nahemow. 1973. "Ecology and the Ageing Process." In *The Psychology of Adult Development and Aging*, edited by C. Eisdorfer and M. P. Lawton, 619–674. Washington, DC: American Psychological Association.
Lien, L. L., C. D. Steggell, and S. Iwarsson. 2015. "Adaptive Strategies and Person-Environment Fit among Functionally Limited Older Adults Aging in Place: A Mixed Methods Approach." *International Journal of Environmental Research and Public Health* 12: 11954–11974. doi:10.3390/ijerph120911954.
Loomans, T. 2014. "7 Reasons Why High-Rises Kill Livability." *SustainableCitiesCollective*. Accessed April 25 2015. http://sustainablecitiescollective.com/bloomingrock/561536/7-reasons-why-high-rises-kill-livability
Mah, B. T. 2011. *Reflections on Housing A Nation: A Collection of Commentaries*. Singapore: Ministry of National Development.
Ministry of Health, Singapore. 2016a. *Life Expectancy in Singapore*. Singapore: Ministry of Health.
Ministry of Health. 2016b. *I Feel Young in My Singapore! Action Plan for Successful Ageing*. Singapore: Ministry of Health.
Ministry of Health, Singapore. 2016c. *Better Health, Better Care, Better Life*. Singapore: Ministry of Health.
National Council of Social Service (NCSS), Singapore. 2013. *Impact Report for Senior Activity Centres*, Singapore: NCSS.
Newman, O. 1975. "Reactions to the 'Defensible Space' Study and Some Further Findings." *International Journal of Mental Health* 4 (3): 48–70. doi:10.1080/00207411.1975.11448692.
Oswald, F., and H. W. Wahl. 2005. "Dimensions of the Meaning of Home in Later Life." In *Home and Identity in Late Life: International Perspectives*, edited by G. D. Rowles and H. Chuadhury, 21–45. New York: Springer.
Panczak, R., B. Galobardes, A. Spoerri, M. Zwahlen, and M. Egger. 2013. "High Life in the Sky? Mortality by Floor of Residence in Switzerland." *European Journal of Epidemiology* 28 (6): 453–462. doi:10.1007/s10654-013-9809-8.
Park, W., H. Girardet, and G. Cox. 2002. *Tall Buildings and Sustainability*. London: Corporation of London.
Phang, S. Y., and M. Helble. 2016. "Housing Policies in Singapore." ADBI Working Paper 559. Tokyo: Asian Development Bank Institute.
Phillips, D. R., O.-L. Siu, A. G. O. Yeh, and K. H. C. Cheng. 2004. "Factors Influencing Older Persons' Residential Satisfaction in Big and Densely Populated Cities in Asia: A Case Study in Hong Kong." *Ageing International* 29: 46–70. doi:10.1007/s12126-004-1009-0.
Reynolds, S. G., and J. O. Beamish. 2003. "Residential Satisfaction of Older Adults in Age-Segregated Facilities." *Housing and Society* 30: 33–49. doi:10.1080/08882746.2003.11430481.
Rosa, E. M., and J. Tudge. 2013. "Urie Bronfenbrenner's Theory of Human Development: Its Evolution from Ecology to Bioecology." *Journal of Family Theory and Review* 5 (4): 243–258. doi:10.1111/jftr.12022.
Sixsmith, A., and J. Sixsmith. 1991. "Transitions in Home Experience in Later Life." *Journal of Architectural and Planning Research* 8: 181–191.
Sowden, S., and M. White. 2014. "High-Rise Health: A Qualitative Study of the Effect of Social Housing Improvements on the Health and Wellbeing of Residents in High-Rise Flats." *The Lancet* 384: S76. doi:10.1016/S0140-6736(14)62202-9.
Steinfeld, E., and J. Maisel. 2012. *Universal Design: Creating Inclusive Environments*. Hoboken, NJ: John Wiley & Sons.
Tan, M. 2014. "Developers 'Still Keen' on Dual-Key Units." *The Straits Times*, May 20.

Tan, S. Y. 1998. *Private Ownership of Public Housing in Singapore*. Singapore: Times Academic Press.
TODAY Online. 2014. *Studio Apartment Scheme Supports Seniors' Retirement Needs, Says Khaw*, May 8.
Turchin, P. 2001. "Does Population Ecology Have General Laws?" *Oikos* 94: 17–26. doi:10.1034/j.1600-0706.2001.11310.x.
United Nations. 2015. *World Population Prospects: The 2015 Revision*. New York: United Nations.
Urban Redevelopment Authority, Singapore (URA). 1991. *Living the Next Lap: Towards a Tropical City of Excellence*. Singapore: URA.
Wahl, H.-W., S. Iwarsson, and F. Oswald. 2012. "Aging Well and the Environment: Toward an Integrative Model and Research Agenda for the Future." *The Gerontologist* 52: 306–316. doi:10.1093/geront/gnr154.
Weiβ, K. 2004. "From Isolation in the Peripherie to the Highrise of Homes in the City." In *High-Density Housing: Concepts, Planning, Construction*, edited by C. Schittich. Munchen: Birkhäuser.
World Health Organisation. 2007. *Global Age-Friendly Cities: A Guide*. Geneva: World Health Organisation.
Yeh, S. H. K., and Y. S. Lee. 1968. "Housing Conditions in Singapore." *Malayan Economic Review* 8 (1): 11–38.
Yuen, B. 2007. "Squatters No More: Singapore Social Housing." *Global Urban Development Magazine* 3 (1). Accessed August 26 2016. http://www.globalurban.org/GUDMag07Vol3Iss1/Yuen.htm
Yuen, B., W. Chathura, and P. Nair. 2016. "Understanding the Changing Needs of Singapore' Older Population: National Survey Report." Unpublished report. Singapore: Lee Kuan Yew Centre for Innovative Cities, Singapore University of Technology and Design.
Yuen, B., and E. Soh. 2017. *Housing for Older Population in Singapore: An Annotated Bibliography*. Cham: Springer.
Yuen, B., H. P. Teo, and G. L. Ooi. 1999. *Singapore Housing: An Annotated Bibliography*. Singapore: National University of Singapore.

Transformative change: energy-efficiency and social housing retrofits in Canadian cities

Sasha Tsenkova

The article provides the first comparative assessment of the energy-efficiency retrofit programs in social housing of the largest cities in Ontario, British Columbia and Alberta, focusing on program efficiency and effectiveness. The analytical framework explores key policy instruments – regulatory, fiscal and institutional – in relation to major results achieved. In terms of efficiency, the grant programs were highly relevant, timely and successful in meeting their objectives generating improvements in two-thirds of the social housing in Toronto, Vancouver and Calgary. The effectiveness was moderate, with targeted approaches to retrofits, integrating both mechanical and building envelope measures with high potential for energy savings. One of the greatest challenges was the high cost of the program, the lack of sustainability in funding and and the cost recovery of comprehensive retrofits..

Rationale and objectives

The Canadian government has responded to global and local imperatives for reducing energy consumption and use of non-renewable resources through programs for housing retrofits. Housing accounts for 17% of secondary energy use and 16% of greenhouse gases (GHG) emissions in Canada, with over 80% of residential energy use related to space and hot water heating (Natural Resources Canada 2006). Within this context, support for transformation of existing housing and energy retrofits is gaining popularity across Canada (Fuller 2009). The federal government has announced its renewed support for energy-efficiency retrofits in social housing in 2017 (Government of Canada 2017). Such strategic policy statements revisit the commitments of *Canada's Economic Action Plan of 2009* and its fiscal support for social housing and green jobs.[1] The social housing sector is targeted as a field of policy intervention, where socially responsible and professional housing providers have the potential to capitalize on government funding to showcase the results of transformative change. This policy article has the following objectives:

- To review the results of energy-efficiency retrofit programs in social housing of the largest cities in Ontario, British Columbia and Alberta, exploring program efficiency and effectiveness;

- To identify program successes and challenges for different social housing providers – public, private non-profit and cooperative.

Analytical framework and methodology

The general hypothesis advanced in this research is that a more supportive policy framework for energy-efficient transformation of social housing will yield better results. Furthermore, the institutional culture, market share and commitment to sustainability of social housing providers will put them in a better position to implement innovative strategies for energy-efficiency retrofits in their portfolio (Niebor et al. 2012). The analytical framework draws on network theory and presents the investment strategies of social housing providers as contextually dependent on the policy environment in which they operate (see Van Bortel and Mullins 2009). The policy environment is deconstructed through analysis of key policy instruments – regulatory and fiscal – to determine the main factors affecting the types of retrofits implemented and investment priorities (Gruis, Tsenkova, and Nieboer 2009).

The article draws on the first comprehensive assessment of program results and is based on literature review, content analysis of policy documents, policy briefs, consulting reports and field visits. The geographic focus is limited to large cities in three provinces with the highest concentration of social housing, where federal programs such as Social Housing Renovation and Retrofit program (SHRRP) have leveraged substantial provincial funding, complemented by other smaller scale initiatives. The primary research draws on analysis of 18 case studies[2] and over 45 key informant interviews carried out in the three cities in 2012 (see Tsenkova 2013 for a detailed overview). The analytical model employed in the research project centres on links between policy objectives, policy instruments – regulatory, fiscal and institutional – and implementation by social housing providers. The primary research explores investment decisions at the project level by different types of social housing organizations – public, private non-profit and cooperative – to capture important differences in their institutional model and results achieved.

At the project level, attention is paid to the types of energy retrofits, building envelope improvements, costs, energy savings and cost recovery (see Beerepoot 2007; Fuller 2009; Mlecnik, Visscher, and van Hal 2010). The profiling of these project-based outcomes is integrated in a broad comparative evaluation of *Canada Economic Action Plan (CEAP) Social Housing Renovation and Retrofit* program results focused on efficiency and effectiveness. Given the lack of any program monitoring and evaluation criteria, the efficiency of results is reviewed with reference to relevance of objectives, institutional arrangements and the quality of program design and implementation. The efficiency is particularly important as it concerns the achievement of objectives with optimal use of resources and the overall impact over the social housing sector (see Tsenkova 2011, 2016). The effectiveness of the CEAP program is reviewed with reference to project achievements, quality of the retrofits and energy savings (European Commission 2008).

Energy-efficiency programs in the social housing sector

Canada's Economic Action Plan provided $850 million for the renovation and retrofit of existing social housing over 2 years, plus a further $475 million to build new rental housing for low-income seniors and persons with disabilities.[3] *The SHRRP* was implemented through federal–provincial agreements requiring matching funds from the

Table 1. Canada's Economic Action Plan renovation and retrofit of existing social housing – provincially/territorially administered.[1]

Province/territory	Fund (federal $M)	Project	Fund (provincial $M)
Ontario	$352.16	5817	$352.16
British Columbia	$88.82	105	$88.82
Alberta	$45.38	1105	$45.38
All Provinces	**$850.00**	**11,355**	**$850.00**

[1]Program details are available at http://cmhc.ca/en/inpr/afhoce/fias/fias_017.cfm
Source: CMHC, 2012 (Interview Data, Program Manager, Canada Mortgage and Housing Corporation, Ottawa, October, 2012).

provinces. Federal funding allocation to different provinces with a corresponding number of projects is presented in Table 1.

The four main objectives of the *CEAP Social Housing Renovation and Retrofit Program* were to:

- Address the demand for renovations and general improvements;
- Address the need for energy-efficiency upgrades;
- Address the accessibility needs for persons with disabilities;
- Create jobs (CMHC, 2010).

The program did not have specific guidelines and procedures, but delegated the allocation and administration to the provinces. These investments demonstrated a significant departure from previous decades of non-interventionist federal social housing policy. In Ontario, they were complemented by *The Renewable Energy Initiative* (REI), launched in 2009, with $70 million in funding for energy efficiency in existing social housing projects. In British Columbia, *Solar British Columbia (BC)* provided support for the installation of a solar water system. Provincial utilities offered additional opportunities for investing in energy efficiency and reducing energy costs. In addition to these funds, the Canada Mortgage and Housing Corporation (CMHC) – the federal housing agency – administered $150 million in grants to housing providers who manage social housing under CMHC agreements.

Retrofits were required to meet minimum energy standards and projects were 'shovel-ready' with the expectation to be completed by March 2011. While there was a formal extension by the Prime Minister of the CEAP infrastructure stimulus fund until December 2011, the social housing projects were considered 'on-schedule'.

Social housing sector characteristics

The context of social housing provision in Canada is important for the evaluation of program effectiveness and efficiency. Social housing in Canada is less than 6% of the housing stock (approximately 630,000 units). The sector operates in a market-driven environment for the provision, allocation and maintenance of housing, with limited government support. About one-third of the social housing is publicly owned, 12% is cooperative housing and the rest is owned and managed by a wide range of non-profit housing organizations (CMHC 2010). Social housing is a provincial responsibility. The federal government historically has supported the sector through a variety of financial instruments and programs that were largely discontinued in 1993. The devolution of responsibilities for social housing started in the mid-1980s, with provinces gradually moving away from the sector and eventually 'passing the buck' to municipalities and community partnerships, which resulted in a growing housing crisis, particularly in cities.[4]

This prompted a reengagement by the federal government in social housing in 2001 through the *Affordable Housing Initiative*, a multilateral agreement between federal, provincial and municipal governments. This initiative consisted of two phases. The first phase, with a budget of $680 million, was to create new rental housing and to renovate existing social housing, while the second phase, with a budget of $320 million, was to create housing for low-income households, aboriginals, people with disabilities, recent immigrants and seniors, resulting in 27,000 new units across Canada (Leone and Carroll 2010). Eligibility criteria for social housing vary according to the funding regime under which it was developed. Social housing stock developed since 1986 has been targeted to households that meet 'core housing need' requirements, defined by a measure of suitability (overcrowding), adequateness (need for repairs) and affordability (over 30% of gross income) in addition to an income threshold test (Ditch, Lewis, and Wilcox 2001). Social rents are set as fixed proportions of tenants' income rather than being property based. Rents for social housing range from 25% to 30% of household income and increase to 'net cost' or 'low end of the market' for higher income households (Steele 2007).

The downside of expanded provincial government social housing responsibilities is constrained investment in the maintenance and rehabilitation of the aging stock owned by public and non-profit housing providers. Small-scale social housing providers also exist, largely as a result of idiosyncratic subsidy arrangements, changing systems of financial support and specific target groups such as special needs housing. The majority of social housing stock is between 20 and 50 years old and is in need of repairs and modernization. Public housing tends to be older with higher turnover, which contributes to higher operation costs. The allocation predominantly to low-income households also places additional requirements for ongoing social service support and capital to bridge the revenue/expenditure gap. Most cooperatives and non-profit providers have inadequate capital reserves and are not in a financial position to fulfil upkeep, major maintenance costs or essential capital replacements (Pearson 2010). In addition to structural and technical problems related to backlogs in maintenance, repairs and lifecycle replacement of roofs and heating and cooling installations, social housing tends to have high energy intensity, which increases the operation costs.[5]

Program results

Ontario, Toronto

In Ontario, The Ministry of Municipal Affairs and Housing administered *SHRRP* and REI funds. It used notional equity allocation principle to distribute the funds to the 47 consolidated municipal service providers in the province. If the service manager administers 30% of the total social housing units, they received 30% of the funding available. Service managers had full authority on how they distributed funds to social housing providers (Interview data, Provincial Program manager, August 2012). In Toronto, which is the largest service provider, program funds were managed by the Shelter, Support and Housing Administration division of the City of Toronto. An Agreement between the city and the province specified the principles, requirements and procedures guiding reporting and payments. City staff was responsible for site visits and verification of invoices and financial statements submitted by housing providers.

Table 2. SHRRP and REI funding allocations and impact.

	SHRRP		REI	
Proportion of SHRRP and REI funding allocated				
TCHC	$150,688,073	58%	$21,396,674	70%
Non-profits (other than TCHC)	$79,841,232	31%	$5,797,272	19%
Cooperatives	$28,505,246	11%	$3,478,297	11%
Total	**$259,034,551**	**100%**	**$30,672,243**	**100%**
Proportion of units impacted by SHRRP and REI				
TCHC	32,419	55%	7645	70%
Non-profits (other than TCHC)	19,924	34%	2200	20%
Cooperatives	6610	11%	1152	10%
Total	**58,953**	**100%**	**10,997**	100%

Source: Interview Data, Program Manager, City of Toronto, September 2012.

The total SHRRP allocation of $259 million had a significant impact on the social housing portfolio in Toronto (see Table 2). The Toronto Community Housing Corporation (TCHC) received the largest share (58%), followed by the non-profit housing providers (31%). In terms of the impact measured by the number of units affected, the TCHC improved over half of its portfolio with SHRRP funds, while units impacted in the non-profit and cooperative sector accounted for 34% and 11% of the total. However, a comparison of these statistics against the number of units managed by non-profits and cooperatives in the city reveals that every non-profit and cooperative housing provider received funding and support to upgrade over 90% of the units in their portfolios.

REI included $70 million in federal and provincial funding in social housing retrofits. As a one-time funding opportunity, it supported investment in: (i) solar photovoltaic (roof top systems), (ii) solar water heating, (iii) solar air heating, (iv) geothermal, and (v) mid-sized wind technologies. The allocation model used to distribute funding was based on submissions from each social housing provider. The data indicate that TCHC projects accounted for 70% of the funds, perhaps due to its institutional capacity and previous experience with renewable energy retrofits since 2006 (Table 2).

British Columbia, Vancouver

In British Columbia, SHRRP funding of $164 million was implemented through *British Columbia Housing Renovation Partnership*. The program accounted for improvements in one-third of the social housing in the BC housing portfolio (the provincial social housing agency), which manages about 27,000 units. The decision was strategic, not necessarily very equitable, but resulted in comprehensive improvements of housing quality and energy efficiency in the provincial housing portfolio. Most of the funds were directed toward repairs at 84 social housing developments with 8338 units (managed by BC Housing) and 38 projects by the non-profit housing sector (with over 2000 units). Half of the social housing developments are located in Vancouver. Interview data indicate that energy and costs savings were realized, and feedback from tenants was positive. Overall, housing providers believe that the goals of the programs were realized, but it remains to be seen how much actual energy is saved across the entire portfolio (Tsenkova 2013). BC Housing used a business model where they partner capital projects with sustainability initiatives from other provincial programs, such as *Public Sector Energy Conservation Agreement* (see Box 1) and *BC LiveSmart.*[6]

Program implementation was managed in two ways: through an intermediary third party or through a self-managed process. BC Housing used third-party contract services in 62% of

Box 1. Greenbrook sustainability project, Vancouver.

Built in 1974, Greenbrook is a public housing development owned and operated by BC Housing, consisting of 127 units in 28 townhouses with 380 residents. The Greenbrook sustainability project combined both building envelope replacement and energy upgrades to achieve significant energy savings and physical improvements. The use of high-efficiency heating and electrical systems reduced the GHG emissions by 86%. The project boasts the largest residential solar panel installation in Western Canada, resulting in a housing complex that is very close to being carbon neutral.

Source: Tsenkova and Youssef 2012.

the projects (52 out 84). Two energy service companies (ESCOs) were selected through competitive bidding processes and tasked with the responsibility to carry out energy-efficiency audits, management of the construction and renovation process and the monitoring energy savings . The retrofit program for each development was assessed by the BC Housing Portfolio Management Team using a set of criteria including lifecycle assessment, costs and energy savings (Interview data, BC Housing Senior Asset Manager, February 2012).

Alberta, Calgary

The institutional framework for SHRRP management in Alberta was centralized with the Ministry of Housing and Municipal Affairs responsible for assessment, approval and disbursement of project funds. The Ministry did not have specific guidelines or priorities to complement the federal guidelines; it considered requests for building envelope improvements, measures addressing safety and accessibility, replacement of heating and ventilation systems and other specific energy-efficiency retrofits (Interview data, Director, November 2012). All of the projects were self-managed by housing providers with general monitoring and control exercised by the Ministry. Contractors were chosen based on a tendering process, following standard procurement guidelines for public works. The disbursement of funds was done on the basis of invoices for completed retrofits in the project approval document (Interview data, Senior Program Administrators, November, 2012).

Interview data provide essential metrics of performance and program results for the province of Alberta. Provincially administered program funds were allocated to 747 projects and impacted over 20,827 units, out of a total of 26,000 units in the social housing portfolio (see Table 3). Two-thirds of these units were in Edmonton and Calgary, with the largest share of funding allocated to the two largest social housing providers in the province.

Table 3. CEAP social housing retrofit program results in Alberta.

Province/city	Fund allocated (federal $M)	Fund allocated (provincial $M)	Total funding (provincial and federal $M)	Project (not necessarily the number of Housing Management Bodies)	Unit
Alberta	$42.43	$42.43	$84.86	747	20,827
Edmonton	$13.78	$13.78	$27.56	169	7774
Calgary	$16.48	$16.48	$32.96	164	7005
Rest of Alberta	$12.17	$12.17	$24.34	414	6048

Source: Interview data, Senior Program Administrators, November, 2012.

Program successes

SHRRP has provided a major opportunity for the implementation of a comprehensive package of retrofits and improvements in the social housing sector. The program – managed by the provinces – provided $972[7] million of public funding in Ontario, British Columbia and Alberta from 2009 to 2012. In terms of efficiency, the investment was critical in addressing the lack of resources to fund capital repairs and system upgrades in the aging social housing stock. The programs were highly relevant, timely and successful in meeting their broad objectives, and account for improvements in about 20–50% of the social housing in British Columbia, Ontario and Alberta. The SHRRP provided grant funds for a variety of mechanical, structural and building envelope retrofits affecting two-thirds of the social housing in Toronto, Calgary and Vancouver. The impact, in terms of units upgraded, was particularly significant for the non-profit and cooperative housing providers, which saw on average over 60% of their portfolio affected by program measures (see Tables 2 and 3).

Part of the success is attributed to the efficient management of the programs by existing federal, provincial and municipal housing institutions. The institutional framework for rapid deployment of program funds (centralized in British Columbia vs. decentralized in Ontario) left the service providers sufficient autonomy to address priority needs. Large social housing providers in Vancouver, Toronto and Calgary, due to their institutional capacity, were able to address in a more comprehensive manner both energy efficiency and capital improvement needs in their social housing portfolio (Tsenkova 2013, 2016). A more robust policy framework for energy-efficiency retrofits in Ontario and British Columbia – incorporating a range of regulatory, fiscal and institutional policy instruments – positively influenced portfolio investment strategies. In Alberta, less emphasis was placed on energy-efficiency retrofits for the benefit of general renovations of the social housing stock, safety improvements and enhanced accessibility for persons with disabilities. By contrast, BC Housing developed a business model where energy efficiency was systematically pursued through partnering of SHRRP capital projects with provincial sustainability initiatives, while in Ontario housing providers leveraged funding from REI and other utility managed programs to maximize the reduction in energy use and GHG emissions (see Box 2).

The effectiveness of SHRRP is difficult to evaluate in the absence of a systematic monitoring and post-retrofit evaluation system (Kaufman and Palmer 2011; Kikuchi, Bristow, and Kennedy 2009). Nevertheless, evidence from 18 case study projects demonstrates substantial improvements in the quality of social housing, targeted approaches to retrofits, integrating both mechanical and building envelope measures and high potential for energy savings (20–45%). Notwithstanding the emphasis on 'best practices' in the analysis, it

Box 2. Wilmar Court non-profit seniors residence, Toronto.

Built in 1974, Wilmar Court is a joint venture between Wilmar Heights United Church Non-Profit Homes Inc. and the City of Toronto Shelter, Support & Housing. It has 72 units of RGI and market mix housing for seniors. The residence is managed through an integrated approach including a three-step process. Step one introduces education programs to residents (marketing brochures, information packages and orientation training) to alter behaviour and assist in the implementation. Step two ensures maintenance and quality control of existing equipment. Step three introduces new technologies to support energy-efficient performance. This includes the installation of solar thermal technology for a supplemental domestic hot water and boiler system.

The results indicate savings of natural gas for water heating of 40%, a 15% reduction in gas consumption (70,000 m^3) and a reduction of 20.4 tons of CO_2 emission per year. Solar thermal collectors with evacuated tube technology have high capital costs, but a 50% subsidy ensures a return on investment of 11.5% and an average payback period of 9.7 years. Half of the subsidies are provided through a federal 'ecoENERGY for Renewable Heat' program, matched by the Ontario government.

Source: Tsenkova 2016.

is evident that the programs have prompted a more strategic approach to asset management and energy retrofits by major public, non-profit and cooperative housing providers. Another critical success factor was institutional innovation in BC using ESCOs (Tsenkova 2013). While the ESCO model was more expensive than the project manager/contract services model, there were value-added components including economies of scale, 'one-stop shop' approach and enhanced accountability for planning, financing and monitoring of projects.

Program challenges

Program challenges were associated with tight timelines and difficulties in coordinating and planning strategic retrofits. Although the projects supported through SHRRP were deemed 'shovel-ready', housing providers and building managers had to operate within a 2-year timeframe. Unexpected building envelope problems were frequently reported, resulting in cost overruns, project delays and potential loss of funding, if projects were not implemented on time.

The tight deadlines for program management and administration, which given the sometimes unpredictable nature of construction work, have led to program extensions and reallocation of funds for other types of measures. Unofficial prolongation of the 2-year period of the program is mainly due to the time needed for tendering and contracting retrofit work, as the delays result from permit applications and building inspection processes. Some of the smaller social housing organizations reportedly faced capacity constraints and difficulties in the management of construction work, contracts and even qualifying for program funds due to complex guidelines and procedures.

One of the greatest challenges was the high cost of the program and the lack of sustainability in funding. In a more comprehensive improvement and energy-efficiency projects, such as those in the case studies, simple payback periods are anywhere between 39 and 67 years. Even though the financial viability and cost benefit of these programs were not the main objectives, they highlight future economic challenges, if programs need to be operated on a cost recovery principle. *Limited market penetration of energy efficiency in social housing is constrained by lack of access to capital, high risk and split incentives* (Schüle 2009; Stephenson et al. 2010). Small housing providers face significant challenges accessing standard loans and mortgages based on cash flow and general rent revenue, making investments in energy-efficient components much more challenging, given their high upfront costs, lengthy payback period and uncertainty in energy pricing. Rents in the social housing sector are often set as a percentage of household income, inclusive of utilities, so tenants do not have a direct incentive to reduce their energy consumption. While social housing providers are interested in investing in energy-efficient mechanical systems, tenants often object to such measures as they create temporary inconvenience during the implementation period. Such split incentives, in addition to general behavioural failures and reluctance on behalf of consumers to adopt an energy responsible behaviour, hinder the adoption of energy-efficiency measures (Moezzi 2009).

Furthermore, for a number of social housing providers, particularly in Alberta, energy efficiency was a low priority relative to other portfolio considerations. This is also true for a number of small community-based social housing organizations (non-profits and cooperatives) in British Columbia and Ontario which lack the institutional capacity to comprehensively plan for energy-efficient retrofits due to limited, asymmetric information and other structural barriers (Leone and Carroll 2010). The physical condition of the social housing portfolio and the lack of adequate reserves to address capital needs significantly affected the implementation of the programs. *The trade-off between energy-efficient retrofits and the replacement of deteriorated mechanical and building envelope components was a major challenge of the programs.* Sometimes, there was not enough funding to do both (Tsenkova 2016).

The specific retrofit measures in the case studies are diverse and illustrate the significant challenges of such programs in economic terms. If the simple payback of energy-efficiency measures is used as an overall consideration for return on investment, it will be difficult to make the case for green retrofits in the social housing sector. Feasibility studies, however, point to significant environmental benefits resulting from reduced energy and water consumption and reduced GHG emissions (Brophy et al, 2010). Some of these metrics of performance, as well as the social impact measured in tenant satisfaction and improved health and well-being, are difficult to quantify, and there has been a very limited attempt to introduce a system of monitoring and evaluation of results achieved, even on a pilot basis.

While the greening of social housing has many benefits, the installation of green technologies is a strain on capital reserves. CEAP and REI have provided an important financial boost to experimentation with sustainable design and green technologies such as solar walls/roofs and green roofs, but there are significant market barriers for effective implementation.

Concluding comments

This article provided a concise summary of key findings from the first evaluation of SHRRP and REI initiatives that targeted improvements and energy-efficiency retrofits in social housing. Its conclusions are particularly important in the context of the *2017 Housing Strategy* of the Canadian government. They demonstrate that both federal and provincial governments need to secure sustainable funding with well-defined program targets that link general quality improvements in the social housing sector to energy-efficiency retrofits. It is important to continue to address the funding gap in the sector, as well as to provide a more structured policy framework for energy efficiency in order to avoid the negative effect of 'start-and-stop' programs (Tsenkova 2016).

The analytical model employed in the research centred on links between policy objectives, policy instruments – regulatory, fiscal and institutional – and implementation by social housing providers. SHRRP and REI provided a major opportunity for the implementation of a comprehensive package of retrofits and improvements in the social housing sector. In terms of efficiency, the grants addressed the lack of resources to fund capital repairs and system upgrades in the aging social housing stock. The programs were highly relevant, timely and successful in meeting their broad objectives, and account for improvements in two-thirds of the social housing in Toronto, Calgary and Vancouver. The impact, in terms of units upgraded, was particularly significant for the non-profit and cooperative housing providers, which saw on average over 60% of their portfolio affected by program measures.

The effectiveness of SHRRP is moderate, with targeted approaches to retrofits, integrating both mechanical and building envelope measures, and high potential for energy savings (20–45%). *One of the greatest challenges was the high cost of the program and the lack of sustainability in funding*. In more comprehensive improvement and energy-efficiency projects, simple payback periods are from 39 to 67 years, which is challenging for cost recovery. Federal and provincial government agencies need to commit to monitoring and evaluation of social housing programs. The issues are particularly critical for small social housing providers in the non-profit and cooperative sector that do not have the capacity to raise funds for critical upgrades, nor the institutional expertise to deal with complex retrofit programming and budgeting operations. Monitoring and evaluation would be beneficial for more strategic approaches in the execution of social housing retrofit programs in the future.

Disclosure statement

No potential conflict of interest was reported by the author.

Funding

The research was supported through a grant by the Canadian School of Energy and the Environment, Canada.

Notes

1. *Canada's Economic Action Plan* provided $850 million for the renovation and retrofit of existing social housing over 2 years, with another $2 billion for new and existing social housing.
2. The case study projects were selected on the basis of recommendations from program managers with the purpose of demonstrating innovative practices in energy-efficiency upgrades and some of the more comprehensive measures implemented, including building envelope, technical system upgrades and installation of renewable energy sources. Data on investment strategies and policy responses by social housing providers were collected through primary research and site visits.
3. Overall, CEAP included $2 billion for new and existing social housing, plus up to $2 billion in loans to municipalities for housing-related infrastructure. It supported Government of Canada's commitment in 2008 to invest $1.9 billion over 5 years to help the homeless and improve and build new affordable housing.
4. The annual supply of new social housing declined by over 65% and reached levels of output lower than 5000 per year. Meanwhile, estimates indicate that there are 1.7 million Canadians with core housing needs, unable to afford adequate housing in the marketplace.
5. For example, the average energy intensity for an apartment building in BC is 0.86 GJ/m^2 (239 kWh/m^2) compared to 1.36 GJ/m^2 (377 kWh/m^2) in the non-profit housing sector. Apartment buildings also have the highest heating and gas use and the largest percentage of hydroelectricity use in the sector, and they produce the most CO^2 (City Green Solutions 2010).
6. The program has more modest targets, but the subsidy of $2000 per unit provides an incentive to introduce measures with quick returns.
7. Includes federal and provincial matching funds.

References

Beerepoot, M. 2007. *Energy Policy Instruments and Technical Change in the Residential Building Sector*. Amsterdam: IOS Press.

Brophy, H., H. Jamasb, L. Platchkov, and M. Pollitt. 2010. "Demand-Side Management Strategies and the Residential Sector: Lessons from International Experience." *EPRG Working Paper 1034; Cambridge Working Paper in Economics 1060: Electricity Policy Research Group*. Cambridge: University of Cambridge.

Canada Mortgage and Housing Corporation (CMHC). 2010. *CHS - Public Funds and National Housing Act (Social Housing) 2009*. Ottawa: Canada Mortgage and Housing Corporation.

Canada Mortgage and Housing Corporation (CMHC). 2012. *CEAP- Renovation and Retrofit Projects*. Ottawa: Canada Mortgage and Housing Corporation. Accessed 12 November 2012 http://www.cmhc.ca/housingactionplan/reresoho/lipr.cfm.

Ditch, J., A. Lewis, and S. Wilcox. 2001. *Social Housing, Tenure and Housing Allowance: An International Review*. New York: Department of Works and Pensions.

European Commission. 2008. *EVALSED; the Resource for Evaluation of Socio-Economic Development*. Luxembourg: European Commission.

Fuller, M. 2009. *Enabling Investments in Energy Efficiency; a Study of Energy Efficiency Programs that Reduce First-Cost Barriers in the Residential Sector*. Berkeley: University of California, California Institute for Energy and Environment.

Government of Canada. 2017. "National Housing Strategy." Place to Call Home. Accessed 12 January 2018. https://www.placetocallhome.ca/

Gruis, V., S. Tsenkova, and N. Nieboer, eds. 2009. *Management of Privatised Housing: International Perspectives*. Chichester: Wiley-Blackwell.

Kaufman, N., and K. Palmer. 2011. "Energy Efficiency Program Evaluations: Opportunities for Learning and Inputs to Incentive Mechanisms.." *Energy Efficiency* 1–26.

Kikuchi, E., D. Bristow, and C. Kennedy. 2009. "Evaluation of Region-Specific Residential Energy Systems for GHG Reductions: Case Studies in Canadian Cities." *Energy Policy* 37 (4): 1257–1266. doi:10.1016/j.enpol.2008.11.004.

Leone, R., and B. W. Carroll. 2010. "Decentralisation and Devolution in Canadian Social Housing Policy." *Environment and Planning C: Government and Policy* 28: 389–404. doi:10.1068/c09153.

Mlecnik, E., H. Visscher, and A. van Hal. 2010. "Barriers and Opportunities for Labels for Highly Energy-Efficient Houses." *Energy Policy* 38 (8): 4592–4603. doi:10.1016/j.enpol.2010.04.015.

Moezzi, M. 2009. *Behavioral Assumptions in Energy Efficiency Potential Studies*. California: California Institute for Energy and Environment CIEE.

Natural Resources Canada. 2006. *The State of Energy Efficiency in Canada*. Ottawa: Natural Resources Canada.

Niebor, N., S. Tsenkova, V. Gruis, and H. van, eds. 2012. *Energy Efficiency in Housing Management*. London: Routledge.

Pearson, S. N. 2010. *Financing Capital Improvements and Renovation of Social Housing in Ontario*. Ontario: Social Housing Services Corporation.

Schüle, R. 2009. *Energy Efficiency Watch; Final Report on the Evaluation of National Energy Efficiency Action Plans*. Berlin: Wuppertal Institute.

Steele, M. 2007. "Canadian Housing Allowances." In *Housing Allowances in Comparative Perspective*, edited by P. A. Kemp. Bristol: Policy Press, University of Bristol.

Stephenson, J., B. Barton, G. Carrington, D. Gnoth, R. Lawson, and P. Thorsnes. 2010. "Energy Cultures: A Framework for Understanding Energy Behaviours." *Energy Policy* 38 (10): 6120–6129. doi:10.1016/j.enpol.2010.05.069.

Tsenkova, S. 2011. *Investing in Social Housing: Lessons from Ex Post Evaluations of CEB Programmes*. Paris: Council of Europe Development Bank.

Tsenkova, S. 2013. *Retrofits for the Future. Renovation and Energy Efficiency Programs in Canada*. Calgary: University of Calgary. Cities, Policy & Planning Research series, January.

Tsenkova, S. 2016. "Energy Efficiency Retrofits and Planning Solutions for Sustainable Housing in Canada." In *Planning Canada: A Case Study Approach*, edited by R. Thomas, 196–208. Toronto: Oxford University Press Canada.

Tsenkova, S., and K. Youssef. 2012. "Canada: Energy Efficiency Retrofits – Policy Solutions for Sustainable Social Housing." In *Energy Efficiency in Housing Management*, edited by N. Nieber, S. Tsenkova, V. Gruis, and A. van Hal, 209–231. London: Routledge.

Van Bortel, G., and D. Mullins. 2009. "Critical Perspectives on Network Governance in Urban Regeneration, Community Involvement and Integration." *Journal of Housing and the Built Environment* 24 (2): 203–219. doi:10.1007/s10901-009-9140-6.

Index

Page numbers in italics and bold refer to figures and tables, respectively. Page numbers with 'n' denote notes.

For Product Safety Concerns and Information please contact our EU representative GPSR@taylorandfrancis.com Taylor & Francis Verlag GmbH, Kaufingerstraße 24, 80331 München, Germany